D0507049

CEH™
Certified Ethical
Hacker Practice Exams

Matt Walker, an IT Security and Education professional for over 20 years, has served as the Director of the Network Training Center and the Curriculum Lead/Senior Instructor for the local Cisco Networking Academy on Ramstein AB, Germany. After leaving the U.S. Air Force, Matt served as a Network Engineer for NASA's Secure Network Systems (NSS), designing and maintaining secured data, voice, and video networking for the Agency. Soon thereafter, Matt took a position as Instructor Supervisor and Sr. Instructor at Dynetics, Inc., in Huntsville, Alabama, providing onsite certification awarding classes for ISC2, Cisco, and CompTIA, and after two years came right back to NASA as the IT Security Manager for UNITeS, SAIC, at Marshall Space Flight Center. He has written and contributed to numerous technical training books for NASA, Air Education and Training Command, the U.S. Air Force, as well as commercially, and he continues to train and write certification and college-level IT and IA Security courses. Matt holds numerous commercial certifications, including CEHv7, CPTS, CNDA, CCNA, and MCSE. Matt is currently an IT Security Engineer for Hewlett-Packard at Kennedy Space Center.

About the Technical Editor

Brad Horton currently works as an Information Security Specialist with the U.S. Department of Defense. Brad has worked as a security engineer, commercial security consultant, penetration tester, and information systems researcher in both the private and public sectors.

This has included work with several defense contractors, including General Dynamics C4S, SAIC, and Dynetics, Inc. Brad currently holds the Certified Information Systems Security Professional (CISSP), Certified Ethical Hacker (CEH), Certified Information Systems Auditor (CISA) and a recently expired Cisco Certified Network Associate (CCNA) trade certifications. Brad holds a bachelor's degree in Commerce and Business Administration from the University of Alabama, a master's degree in Management of Information Systems from the University of Alabama in Huntsville (UAH), and a graduate certificate in Information Assurance from UAH. When not hacking, Brad can be found at home with his family or on a local golf course.

CEH™
Certified Ethical Hacker Practice Exams

Matt Walker

New York • Chicago • San Francisco • Lisbon
London • Madrid • Mexico City • Milan • New Delhi
San Juan • Seoul • Singapore • Sydney • Toronto

McGraw-Hill Education books are available at special quantity discounts to use as premiums and sales promotions, or for use in corporate training programs. To contact a representative, please e-mail us at bulksales@mcgraw-hill.com.

CEH™ Certified Ethical Hacker Practice Exams

1 2 3 4 5 6 7 8 9 0   QFR QFR   1 0 9 8 7 6 5 4 3

ISBN: Book p/n 978-0-07-181023-4 and CD p/n 978-0-07-181024-1
of set 978-0-07-181026-5

MHID: Book p/n 0-07-181023-4 and CD p/n 0-07-181024-2
of set 0-07-181026-9

Sponsoring Editor	Technical Editor	Indexer
Tim Green	Brad Horton	Jack Lewis
Editorial Supervisor	**Copy Editor**	**Composition**
Jody McKenzie	Bart Reed	Cenveo Publisher Services
Project Manager	**Proofreader**	**Illustration**
Harleen Chopra, Cenveo® Publisher Services	Carol Shields	Cenveo Publisher Services
Acquisitions Coordinator	**Production Supervisor**	**Art Director, Cover**
Stephanie Evans	James Kussow	Jeff Weeks

The book is dedicated to my lovely
and talented wife, Angela Walker.

CONTENTS

ACKNOWLEDGMENTS

I, like most of you, hardly ever read the acknowledgments portion of a book. In the past, when I bought a book, I just wanted to get to the meat of the thing and see what I could drag out of it—either intellectually or entertainment-wise—and didn't care about what the author thought about those who helped put it all together. Then, of all things, I *wrote* a book.

Now, I read the acknowledgment of *every* book I purchase. Why? Because having gone through the trials and tribulations of writing, editing, arguing, planning, research-ing, rewriting, screaming at a monitor, and restarting the whole thing all over again, I understand why they're so important. I know what it means when the writer says he or she "couldn't have done it without *fill-in-the-blank*." Trust me, if it's written there, then the author truly means he or she *couldn't have done it without them*. My "fill-in-the-blanks" deserve more than just a mention in an Acknowledgments section because they really did make the book possible, and I most assuredly couldn't have written it without them, but this will have to do for now.

First off, I've got to tip the hat to Tim Green and Stephanie Evans at McGraw-Hill Education. Once again, they provided me the chance to do something I dearly love: talking/teaching about something I have a real passion for. Tim's incessant desire to drag me into more and more writing projects brought this one to light, and I can't thank him enough. Hopefully, he can bug others into another project or two, and he's really going to have to: We still haven't enjoyed a cold adult beverage together yet.

Although Stephanie didn't need to beat me as much this go-around (which I know she was looking forward to when I agreed to this project and probably deeply regretted once we started it), she still provided the guidance and governing presence any project of this size needs. If you've read the opening to the companion *All-in-One CEH* book, then you know how much regard I have for her. She's one in a million, and I will always be grateful for the opportunity I've had to work with her, laugh a little, and call her friend.

Lastly, I can't thank our technical editor, Brad Horton, enough. Brad makes a diffi-cult process—technically scrubbing everything to make sure it's all in good order—not only bearable, but downright fun. His edits were spot on, and were always designed to make this project the absolute best it could be. But he did it in such a way that I couldn't wait to read the criticism. I've never been the target of biting sarcasm expressed in a SQL query before, and I loved every minute of it. From the bottom of my heart, thank you my friend—you are, without a doubt, the best.

INTRODUCTION

Welcome back, dear reader! If you're standing there in your local bookstore, or reviewing these pages on your computer at an online retailer, then I think I'm safe in assuming you fall into one of a few different categories. Some of you may be curious about what a "hacking" study guide book looks like, or are thinking about attempting a new certification or career choice. Some of you may have already taken that decisive leap, started down the path, and are now looking for the next resource to help you along the journey. And some of you reading this may even be simply looking for some credentials for your career—most of this group are true professionals who already know how to do this job, and are just finally ready to get the certification knocked out, whereas a small few are simply looking for a resume bullet (one more certification you can put on your e-mail signature line to impress others).

Regardless of where you stand in your career or desires for this certification, I need to clear the air about a couple things right up front, before you commit to purchasing and reading this book. First and foremost (before I get to the bad stuff), I firmly believe this book will assist you in attaining your CEH certification. The entire team involved in this effort has put a lot of time, energy, thought, research, and bourbon into producing what we feel is the best companion resource guide on the market. I'm proud of it, and proud to have been associated with the professionals who helped put it together.

That said, if you're looking for a silver bullet—a virtual copy of the exam that you can simply memorize, go take the test, and then forget everything—please stop reading now and go take your chances elsewhere.

Part of the ethics of attaining, and maintaining, a CEH credential is the non-disclosure agreement all candidates sign before attempting the exam. I, and everyone else involved in this project, have taken great pains to provide you with examples of questions designed to test your knowledge of the subject at hand, not to provide you questions to memorize. Those who are looking for that, and use that method to attain the certification, belittle and cheapen the hard work the rest of the community puts into this, and I would be sickened to know of any of them using this work for that purpose.

If you want to pass this exam and have the respect and benefits that come along with holding the certification, you better damn well know how to do the job. The memorization/test-taking junkies out there may get an interview or two with this cert on their resume, but trust me, they'll be discovered as frauds before they ever get to round 2. This community knows the difference between a contender and a pretender, so don't try to take shortcuts. Learn the material. Become an expert in it. Then go take the exam. If you're not willing to put in the effort, maybe you should pick up another line of study, such as online gaming or housecleaning. To quote a really bad 80's testosterone movie, "There's always barber college."

With all that out of the way—and now that I'm talking to the *real* CEH candidates—I firmly believe this book will help you in your attempt to attain the certification. As always, however, I must caution the rest of you: Relying on a single book—any single book—to pass this exam is a recipe for disaster. Yes, this is a great resource, and you should definitely buy it (right now—don't wait!). However, you simply will not pass this exam without the time and benefit that can only come from experience. As a matter of fact, EC Council now requires candidates sitting for the exam to have at least two years of IT Security–related experience. Bolster your study in this book with practice, practice, and more practice. You'll thank me for it later.

Lastly, keep in mind this certification isn't a walk in the park. Certified Ethical Hacker (CEH) didn't gain the reputation and value it has by being easy to attain. It's worth has elevated: It is one of the top certifications a technician can attain, and is now a part of DoD 8570's call for certification on DoD networks. In short, this certification *actually means something* to employers, because they know the effort it takes to attain it.

The exam itself—now on version 8—is a four-hour, 125-question grueling marathon that will leave you exhausted when you click the Finish button. EC Council has provided a handbook on the certification and exam (as of this writing, located at https://cert .eccouncil.org/wp-contents/uploads/CEH-Candidate-Handbook-v1.6-31012012.pdf) that provides all you'll need to know about qualifications, content, and other information about the exam and certification. I've included some highlights from this handbook here, detailing the exam and what you'll need.

To begin, the exam is proctored (that is, you take it in person at an authorized testing facility). As I stated earlier, it's four hours long and is composed of 125 questions. It's computer based, and allows you to skip and mark questions to revisit at the end. Your exam score is tabulated immediately after completion, so be sure to review everything before clicking Finish. A passing score is 70%, which means you need to answer at least 88 questions correctly. You can find authorized Prometric or VUE test facilities at their respective websites (www.prometric.com/ec-council and www.vue.com/eccouncil, respectively). Here are more details you'll need to know:

- **Test content:** Version 8 of the CEH exam, per EC Council, is designed to test six different tasks and seven different knowledge categories. Tasks listed for the exam include "System Development & Management, System Analysis & Audits, Security Testing/Vulnerabilities, Reporting, Mitigation, and Ethics." Knowledge categories tested on the exam include "Background, Analysis/Assessment, Security, Tools/Systems/Programs, Procedures/Methodology, Regulation/Policy, and Ethics."

- **Eligibility:** Per EC Council, you must either attend their official training—an official CEH instructor-led training (ILT), computer-based training (CBT), or online live training—or submit an Exam Eligibility Form (along with a $100 nonrefundable fee) proving you've been in the Security field for at least two years. In either case, once you're approved to sit for the exam, EC Council will forward you a code that must be presented at the Authorized Prometric or VUE Testing Center on the date of the exam.

- **Forms:** Before sitting for the exam, you'll be required to sign non-disclosure forms and candidate agreement forms (indicating you promise to be ethical in your hacking). If you're taking the exam without attending any training, you'll also need to submit the CEH Eligibility Form to certmanager@eccouncil.org. The eligibility form requires the signatures of your colleagues and boss(es), and you'll need to include a copy of valid government-approved identification. EC Council will contact your boss(es) for a follow-up interview to complete the process and verify your eligibility. All forms and submission instructions (fax numbers and e-mail addresses) are available within the handbook itself.

- **Test-retake policy:** If you fail the first attempt, there is no waiting period—you can immediately retake the test if you wish. On the second, third, and fourth failures, you must wait 14 days before a reattempt. The only other restriction is that you are not allowed to attempt the exam five times within a 12-month period.

- **Getting your certification:** Per the handbook, "Upon successful attainment of a minimum score, you will be issued your CEHv8 credential and will receive your CEHv8 welcome kit within 4–8 weeks. The CEH credential is valid for 3 year periods, but can be renewed each period by successfully earning EC-Council Continued Education (ECE) credits. All EC-Council-related correspondence will be sent to the email address provided during exam registration. If your email address changes, it is your responsibility to notify certadmin@eccouncil.org; failing which you will not be able to receive critical updates from EC-Council."

Best of luck to you, dear reader. I sincerely hope your exam goes well for you, and your career is filled with great experiences.

Ethical Hacking Basics

This domain includes questions from the following topics:
- Identifying basic elements of information security
- Understanding security, functionality, and ease of use
- Defining and profiling an ethical hacker
- Defining classifications of hackers and terms associated with hacking
- Understanding the five stages of ethical hacking
- Defining the types of system attacks
- Understanding U.S. Federal laws related to cyber crime
- Understanding various international laws related to cyber crime

In one of my earliest memories, I'm sitting at the table on Thanksgiving, staring lovingly at a hot apple pie being sliced into pieces and doled out onto plates. I remember watching an ice cream bowl chase the pie slices around the table, and each person scooping out delicious vanilla goodness for the top of their pie. And I remember looking at that flaky crust and the sugary, syrupy insides and thinking how great it was going to be when I got mine. But then I remember my mom looking right at me and saying, "Looks good, doesn't it? All you've got to do is finish your vegetables and you can have some."

I dearly love apple pie a la mode. It's my favorite dessert on the planet—my ambrosia, if you will. I love it so much that aggressively displacing toddlers out of my way to get to dessert nirvana isn't out of the question (okay, maybe just sternly threatening them, but you get the idea). But I absolutely *despised* most of the veggies I was forced to eat as a kid. Greens, peas, carrots, asparagus? Might as well have been kryptonite for Superman. Why not just ask me to stab my eyes out with a fork—or, worse yet, ask me to wear Auburn colors, Mom?

But when push came to shove, I ate the vegetables. Not because I liked them or because I wanted to, but because I had to in order to get what I *really* wanted.

Welcome to your veggie plate, dear reader. No, it's not the exciting dessert you're drooling over—all those sexy hacking questions come later—but this is stuff you just have to get out of the way first. The good news with this part of your exam is that this is the easy stuff. It's almost pure memorization and definitions—with no wacky formulas

1

or script nuances to figure out. And don't worry, it's not nearly as bad as you think it's going to be. At least I'm not making you put on blue and orange.

When it comes to studying this chapter, where mostly definitions and rote memorization are all that is required for the exam, repetition is the key. Tables with words on one side and corresponding definitions on the other can be pretty effective—and don't discount the old-school flash cards either. When studying, try to find some key words in each definition you can associate with the term. That way, when you're looking at a weird test question on the exam, a key word will pop out and help provide the answer for you.

For example, the most confusing questions for you in this section will probably come from the CIA triad and the methodology steps. Be careful with *confidentiality* versus *integrity* (watch out for that pesky *authentication* word as well), and know the methodology like the back of your hand. Concentrate on key words for each, and you should be fine.

Additionally, at the risk of generating derision from the "Thank you, Captain Obvious" crowd, here's another piece of advice I have for you: Spend your time on the things you don't already know (trust me, I'm on to something here). Many exam prospects and students spend way too much valuable time repeating portions they already know, instead of concentrating on the things they don't. If you understand the definitions regarding white hat and black hat, don't bother reviewing them over and over. Instead, spend your time concentrating on areas that aren't so "common sense" to you.

And, finally, keep in mind that this certification is provided by an international organization. Therefore, you will sometimes see some fairly atrocious grammar on test questions here and there, especially in this section. Don't worry about it—just keep focused on the main point of the question and look for your key words.

 STUDY TIPS   When it comes to studying this chapter, where mostly definitions and rote memorization is all that is required for the exam, repetition is the key.

1. A Certified Ethical Hacker follows a specific methodology for testing a system. Which step comes after footprinting in the CEH methodology?

   A. Scanning

   B. Enumeration

   C. Reconnaissance

   D. Application attack

2. You've been hired as part of a pen test team. During the in brief, you learn the client wants the pen test attack to simulate a normal user who finds ways to elevate privileges and create attacks. Which test type does the client want?

   A. White box

   B. Gray box

   C. Black box

   D. Hybrid

3. Which of the following is true regarding an ethical hacker?

   A. The ethical hacker points out vulnerabilities, but does not exploit them.

   B. The ethical hacker has authorization to proceed from the target owner.

   C. The ethical hacker does not use the same tools and techniques as unauthorized attackers in the wild.

   D. The ethical hacker provides reports on vulnerabilities publicly.

4. You begin your first pen-test assignment by checking out IP address ranges owned by the target as well as details of their domain name registration. Additionally, you visit job boards and financial websites to gather any technical information online. What activity are you performing?

   A. Security assessment

   B. Vulnerability assessment

   C. Active footprinting

   D. Passive footprinting

5. You send a message across a network and are primarily concerned that it is not altered during transit. Which security element ensures a message arrives at its destination with no alteration?

   A. Confidentiality

   B. Authentication

   C. Integrity

   D. Availability

6. An ethical hacker is given no prior knowledge of the network and has a specific framework in which to work. The agreement specifies boundaries, nondisclosure agreements, and a completion date definition. Which of the following statements are true?

   A. A white hat is attempting a black box test.

   B. A white hat is attempting a white box test.

   C. A black hat is attempting a black box test.

   D. A black hat is attempting a gray box test.

7. Which of the following attacks is considered an integrity attack, where the attacker is not concerned with deciphering the entirety of a plaintext message?

   A. Social engineering

   B. Denial of service

   C. Shrink wrap

   D. Bit flipping

   E. Spoofing

8. As part of a pen test on a U.S. Government system, you discover files containing social security numbers and other PII (Personally Identifiable Information) sensitive information. You are asked about controls placed on dissemination of this information. Which of the following acts should you check?

   A. FISMA

   B. Privacy Act

   C. PATRIOT Act

   D. Freedom of Information Act

9. Joe has spent a large amount of time learning hacking tools and techniques, and has even passed certification exams to promote himself in the ethical hacking field. Joe uses his talents during the election season to deface websites and launch denial of service attacks against opponents of his candidate. Which answer most closely correlates with Joe's actions?

   A. Hactivism

   B. Black box attacks

   C. Black hat hacking

   D. Cracking

10. A hacker is attempting to gain access to a target inside a business. After trying several methods, he gets frustrated and starts a denial of service attack against a server attached to the target. Which security control is the hacker affecting?

    A. Confidentiality

    B. Integrity

    C. Availability

    D. Authentication

11. The security, functionality, and ease of use (SFE) triangle states which of the following as true?

    A. As security increases, ease of use decreases and functionality decreases.

    B. As security increases, ease of use increases and functionality increases.

    C. A decrease of security has no effect on ease of use or functionality.

    D. An increase of security has no effect on ease of use or functionality.

12. In which phase of the ethical hacking methodology would a hacker discover available targets on a network?

    A. Reconnaissance

    B. Scanning and enumeration

    C. Gaining access

    D. Maintaining access

    E. Covering tracks

13. Which of the following are potential drawbacks to a black box test? (Choose all that apply.)

    A. The client does not get a full picture of an external attacker focused on their systems.

    B. The client does not get a full picture of an internal attacker focused on their systems.

    C. This test takes the longest amount of time to complete.

    D. This test takes the shortest amount of time to complete.

14. In which phase of a penetration test would an ethical hacker perform footprinting?

    A. Preparation

    B. Assessment

    C. Conclusion

    D. Reconnaissance

    E. Scanning and enumeration

15. Which of the following would not be considered passive reconnaissance?

    A. Dumpster diving for valuable, discarded information

    B. Thoroughly examining financial sites for clues on target inventory and other useful information

    C. Ping sweeping a range of IP addresses found through a DNS lookup

    D. Using a search engine to discover competitive intelligence on the organization

16. As part of the preparation phase for a pen test that you are participating in, the client relays their intent to discover security flaws and possible remediation. They seem particularly concerned about external threats and do not mention internal threats at all. When defining scope, the threat of internal users is not added as part of the test. Which test is this client ignoring?

    A. Gray box

    B. Black box

    C. White hat

    D. Black hat

17. In which phase of an attack would vulnerability mapping occur?

    A. Assessment

    B. Active reconnaissance

    C. Scanning and enumeration

    D. Fingerprinting

18. While performing a pen test, you find success in exploiting a machine. Your attack vector took advantage of a common mistake—the Windows 7 installer script used to load the machine left the administrative account with a default password. Which attack did you successfully execute?

    A. Application level

    B. Operating system

    C. Shrink wrap

    D. Social engineering

    E. Misconfiguration

19. A machine in your environment uses an open X-server to allow remote access. The X-server access control is disabled, allowing connections from almost anywhere and with little to no authentication measures. Which of the following are true statements regarding this situation? (Choose all that apply.)

    A. An external vulnerability can take advantage of the misconfigured X-server threat.

    B. An external threat can take advantage of the misconfigured X-server vulnerability.

    C. An internal vulnerability can take advantage of the misconfigured X-server threat.

    D. An internal threat can take advantage of the misconfigured X-server vulnerability.

20. You are examining security logs snapshotted during a prior attack against the target. The target's IP address is 135.17.22.15, and the attack originated from 216.88.76.5. Which of the following correctly characterizes this attack?

    A. Inside attack

    B. Outside attack

    C. Black box attack

    D. Spoofing

21. An ethical hacker needs to be aware of a variety of laws. What do Sections 1029 and 1030 of United States Code Title 18 specify?

    A. They criminalize the collection of personal information.

    B. They provide guidance on the right to obtain information from governmental agencies.

    C. They increase the government's ability to monitor communications.

    D. They define most of the U.S. laws concerning hacking and computer crime.

22. Which of the following should a security professional use as a possible means to verify the integrity of a data message from sender to receiver?

    A. Strong password requirements for encryption of the file

    B. Access controls on all network devices

    C. Hash algorithm

    D. Strong password requirements on operating system login

23. Which of the following describes activities taken in the conclusion phase of a penetration test?

    A. Reports are prepared detailing security deficiencies.

    B. Vulnerability assessment is conducted.

    C. Security control audits are performed.

    D. Contract and scope agreement is created.

24. Which of the following best describes an ethical hacker?

    A. An ethical hacker never knowingly or unknowingly exceeds the boundaries of the scope agreement.

    B. An ethical hacker never performs a denial of service attack on a target machine.

    C. An ethical hacker never proceeds with an audit or test without written permission.

    D. An ethical hacker never performs social engineering on unsuspecting members of the target organization.

25. In which phase of the attack would a hacker set up and configure "zombie" machines?

   A. Reconnaissance

   B. Covering tracks

   C. Gaining access

   D. Maintaining access

1. A
2. B
3. B
4. D
5. C
6. A
7. D
8. B
9. A
10. C
11. A
12. B
13. B, C
14. B
15. C
16. A
17. C
18. B
19. B, D
20. B
21. D
22. C
23. A
24. C
25. D

1. A Certified Ethical Hacker follows a specific methodology for testing a system. Which step comes after footprinting in the CEH methodology?

   A. Scanning

   B. Enumeration

   C. Reconnaissance

   D. Application attack

   ☑ **A.** CEH methodology is laid out this way: reconnaissance (footprinting), scanning and enumeration, gaining access, escalating privileges, maintaining access, and covering tracks. While you may be groaning about scanning and enumeration both appearing as answers, they're placed here this way on purpose. This exam is not only testing your rote memorization of the methodology, but how the methodology actually works. Remember, after scoping out the recon on your target, your very next step is to scan it. After all, you have to know what targets are there first before enumerating information about them.

   ☒ **B** is incorrect because, although it is mentioned as part of step 2, it's actually secondary to scanning. Enumerating is used to gather more in-depth information about a target you already discovered by scanning. Things you might discover in scanning are IPs that respond to a ping. In enumerating each "live" IP, you might find open shares, user account information, and other goodies.

   ☒ **C** is incorrect because *reconnaissance* and *footprinting* are interchangeable in CEH parlance. An argument can be made that footprinting is a specific portion of an overall recon effort; however, in all CEH documentation these terms are used interchangeably.

   ☒ **D** is incorrect because it references an attack. As usual, there's almost always one answer you can throw out right away, and this is a prime example. We're talking about step 2 in the methodology, where we're still figuring out what targets are there and what vulnerabilities they may have. Attacking, at this point, is folly.

2. You've been hired as part of a pen test team. During the in-brief, you learn the client wants the pen test attack to simulate a normal user who finds ways to elevate privileges and create attacks. Which test type does the client want?

   A. White box

   B. Gray box

   C. Black box

   D. Hybrid

☑ **B.** A gray box test is designed to replicate an inside attacker. Otherwise, known as the *partial knowledge* attack (don't forget this term), the idea is to simulate a user on the inside who might know a little about the network, directory structure, and other goodies in your enterprise. You'll probably find this one to be the most enlightening attack in out-briefing your clients in the real world—it's amazing what you can get to when you're a trusted, inside user. As an aside, you'll often find in the real world that "gray box" testing can also refer to a test where *any* inside information is given to a pen tester—you don't necessarily need to be a fully knowledgeable inside user. In other words, if you have useable information handed to you about your client, you're gray box testing.

☒ **A** is incorrect because a white box test provides all knowledge to the pen tester up front, and is designed to simulate an admin on your network who, for whatever reason, decides to go on the attack. For most pen testers, this test is really just unfair. It's tantamount to sending him into the Roman Coliseum armed with a .50 Caliber automatic weapon to battle a gladiator who is holding a knife.

☒ **C** is incorrect because black box testing indicates no knowledge at all. And if you think about it, the name is easy to correlate and remember: black = no light. Therefore, you can't "see" anything. This is the test most people think about when it comes to hacking. You know nothing and are (usually) attacking from the outside.

☒ **D** is incorrect because, as far as I can tell from the EC Council's documentation, there is no terminology for a "hybrid box" test. This is a little tricky because the term *hybrid* is used elsewhere—for attacks and other things. If you apply a little common sense here, this answer is easy to throw out. If you know everything about the target, it's white. If you know nothing, it's black. If you're in the middle, it's gray. See?

3. Which of the following is true regarding an ethical hacker?

   A. The ethical hacker points out vulnerabilities, but does not exploit them.

   B. The ethical hacker has authorization to proceed from the target owner.

   C. The ethical hacker does not use the same tools as unauthorized attackers in the wild.

   D. The ethical hacker provides reports on vulnerabilities publicly.

   ☑ **B.** This question will be asked multiple times and in numerous ways to reinforce a simple concept: The main difference between a CEH and a cracker is *permission*. Ethical hackers will take advantage of every tool and technique in the book to break into a target. They'll be just as ruthless and cunning as the people trying to break in illegally. They'll lie, cheat, steal, sneak around, and try to use every opportunity available to get in. The only difference is, they don't do any of it without the owner of the target(s) knowing about and approving everything up front.

☒ **A** is incorrect because an ethical hacker on a pen test team is paid to exploit vulnerabilities—unless, of course, the scope of the test prevents this in the first place. Usually speaking, if a pen tester can find a way in, he'll exploit it all the way up to the line drawn in the scope agreement, to prove security problems exist. Do not fall into the trap that pen testers are nice people during a test. We're not, and we're not paid to be.

☒ **C** is incorrect because pen testers are merciless, cold-blooded mercenaries paid to use every single tool and technique the bad guys have at their disposal. The only thing keeping them at bay is a signed agreement allowing them to go forth and conquer, within and agreed-upon scope. If, as a pen tester, you do not avail yourself of everything the bad guy might be using, you're doing yourself and your client a disservice. The point of an ethical hacker is to show what a bad guy can do so that preventative measures can be put in place, and you can't do that by playing nice.

☒ **D** is incorrect because the statement is blatantly silly. The thought that any business owner would want a group of professional digital ninjas to come into his network and then post everything that's wrong about it on Yahoo! News is preposterous. Yes, the team will out-brief the client to let him know what they found, but trust me, this info won't leave the room for anyone else to know. It is okay, however, for you to post details of how you succeeded in any given attack, so long as the information on who you attacked and when you attacked them as part of the pen test is removed. For example, if you used a tactic against ACME, Inc., and are giving a presentation at a conference, it's okay to mention details of how that attack was successful, so long as no one can tie it to that particular pen test or client.

4. You begin your first pen-test assignment by checking out IP address ranges owned by the target as well as details of their domain name registration. Additionally, you visit job boards and financial websites to gather any technical information online. What activity are you performing?

   A. Security assessments

   B. Vulnerability assessment

   C. Active footprinting

   D. Passive footprinting

   ☑ **D.** This question is another potential stumbling block on the test. The desire is to look at the question and think, "Wow, I'm typing things and using the Internet to gather information, so I'm *actively* working on the target." The key when it comes to *active* versus *passive* recon is to think of your probability of being caught doing it. For example, the activities of checking Internet pages, performing Google searches, and looking up DNS entries aren't going to alert anyone. These are things everyone does everyday anyway. Walking into the offices and checking locked doors, or trying to elicit information from people out in the parking lot probably will get you caught. Two other things on this topic you'll need to keep in mind are social engineering and what you're actually touching during your information gathering.

Social engineering can be tricky, because it can be both passive and active recon. Dumpster diving is considered passive, whereas walking in and talking to users *can* be considered active. Pay attention to the circumstances on these types of questions.

What's more, when it comes to active and passive recon, sometimes a question can be answered based on the target network itself: If you touch it, you're active; if you don't, you're passive. Think of it this way: Imagine the network you're paid to examine is actually a big wire that's electrified with 10,000 volts. If you walk around it, look over the fence, and take pictures, you're passively gathering information. Touch that wire, though, and you become active. *Real* active. Active footprinting involves touching the target network, and it can bleed over into the scanning and enumeration phase.

☒ **A** is incorrect because *security assessments* is a broad term that can indicate actual pen tests or basic security audits. Pen tests are designed to discover, exploit, and report on security vulnerabilities within a target. A security audit doesn't necessarily intentionally exploit any vulnerability—it just finds them and points them out.

☒ **B** is incorrect because it has nothing to do with what is being described in the question. A *vulnerability assessment* lists potential vulnerabilities and considers the potential impact of loss from a successful attack against any of them. In CEH parlance—and on your test—this term is more often than not used as a distractor. If you do see it on an exam, remember it is designed as more of a measurement technique and not an attack vector.

☒ **C** is incorrect because active footprinting indicates you're touching the target network itself. In the question, you (as the attacker) never actually touch the target. You are availing yourself of all that competitive intelligence lying around. Remember, competitive intelligence is freely available for anyone to get, and is often used by competitors seeking an advantage in the marketplace. It's not only legal to pull and analyze this information, it's *expected*, and it does not require any active reconnaissance at all to acquire.

5. You send a message across a network and are primarily concerned that it is not altered during transit. Which security element ensures a message arrives at its destination with no alteration?

   A. Confidentiality

   B. Authentication

C. Integrity

D. Availability

☑ **C.** You have to think about the security triad very carefully for your exam. Remember, *integrity* refers to the methods and actions taken to protect the information from unauthorized alteration or revision—regardless of whether the data is at rest or in transit. The key words in any question on your exam involving integrity will be *alter, change,* and so on. Another thing to look for is the use of a hash for verification, because this is primarily an integrity control method. The good news is, when it comes to the triad, integrity questions are usually pretty easy to discern.

☒ **A** is incorrect because confidentiality keeps the wrong eyes from seeing the data. Confidentiality addresses the secrecy and privacy of information, and refers to the measures taken to prevent disclosure of information or data to unauthorized individuals or systems. Your key words on this are usually *secrecy, privacy,* and *authentication.* Additionally, remember the use of pass-words as an authentication/confidentiality control—authentication is the measure; confidentiality is the control.

☒ **B** is incorrect for a couple of reasons. First, authentication is used as a distractor here because it's not a control listed in the security triad (confidentiality, integrity, and availability). Second, the question does not refer to any method of determining who the sender or recipient is—only that the data is protected from tampering during transit. That's the type of pseudo-critical thinking you'll need for these types of questions. Remember, identifying who the recipient is (authentication) doesn't have anything to do with whether or not the data arrives unaltered.

☒ **D** is incorrect because availability refers to the communications systems and data being ready for use when legitimate users need them, and has nothing to do with the actual data itself. Availability is all about maintaining the access channels to the data, not what state the data is in. For example, I can boastfully proclaim my availability is covered by providing plenty of band-width and an open, unrestricted path to the data share for you; however, if I don't have integrity measures in place, the data sitting there may be useless.

6. An ethical hacker is given no prior knowledge of the network and has a specific framework in which to work. The agreement specifies boundaries, nondisclo-sure agreements, and a completion date definition. Which of the following statements are true?

A. A white hat is attempting a black box test.

B. A white hat is attempting a white box test.

C. A black hat is attempting a black box test.

D. A black hat is attempting a gray box test.

☑ **A.** I love these types of questions. Not only is this a two-for-one question, but it involves identical, but confusing descriptors, causing all sorts of havoc. The answer to attacking such questions—and you *will* see them, by the way—is to take each section one at a time. Start with what kind of hacker he is. He's hired under a specific agreement, with full knowledge and consent of the target, thus making him a white hat. That eliminates C and D right off the bat. Second, to address what kind of test he's performing, simply look at what he knows about the system. In this instance, he has no prior knowledge at all, thus making it a black box test.

☒ **B** is incorrect because although the attacker is one of the good guys (a white hat, proceeding with permission and an agreement in place), he is not provided with full knowledge of the system. In fact, it's quite the opposite—according to the question he knows absolutely nothing about it, making this particular "box" as black as it can be. A white box target indicates one that the attacker already knows everything about. It's lit up and wide open.

☒ **C** is incorrect right off the bat because it references a black hat. Black hat attackers are the bad guys—the ones proceeding without the target's knowledge or permission. They usually don't have inside knowledge of their target, so their attacks often start "black box."

☒ **D** is incorrect for the same reason just listed—this attacker has permission to proceed and is operating under an agreement; therefore, he can't be a black box attacker. Additionally, this answer went the extra mile to convince you it was wrong—and missed on both swings. Not only is this a white hat attacker, but the attack itself is black box. A gray box attack indicates at least some inside knowledge of the target.

7. Which of the following attacks is considered an integrity attack, where the attacker is not concerned with deciphering the entirety of a plaintext message?

  A. Social engineering

  B. Denial of service

  C. Shrink wrap

  D. Bit flipping

  E. Spoofing

☑ **D.** This one is cut and dry, and right out of the book (not just mine, by the way). Integrity attacks are designed to alter or change data at rest or in transit. They're normally not necessarily designed to make *all* the data readable to the attacker (although it's very easy to surmise that in order to change the price of the doodad you ordered from $300 to $3, you'd need to first be able to read the price column, or at least know where it is). Of the choices listed, only bit flipping matches this definition. In bit flipping, the attacker isn't interested in learning the entirety of the plaintext message.

Instead, bits are manipulated in the ciphertext itself to generate a predictable outcome in the plaintext once it is decrypted.

☒ **A** is incorrect because social engineering in and of itself is not considered an integrity attack. Sure, you can affect data as a by-product of a successful social engineering attack, but that's not what it's designed for. Social engineering refers to that joyful portion of nontechnical hacking involving actual human interaction—the art of simply asking people for and getting their security credentials without hardly any effort at all.

☒ **B** is incorrect because any denial of service attack (DoS) is all about affecting availability, not integrity. DoS attacks are designed either to take the resource itself down or to restrict or close all access to it. The integrity of the data isn't the point of these attacks—it's the availability they're out to affect.

☒ **C** is incorrect because shrink-wrap attacks aren't necessarily related to data integrity. A shrink-wrap attack takes advantage of the built-in code and scripts that most off-the-shelf applications come with. These portions of shrink-wrapped scripts and code pieces are designed to make installation and administration easier, but can lead to vulnerabilities if not managed appropriately.

☒ **E** is incorrect because spoofing doesn't refer to data integrity at all. Spoofing is all about pretending to be something you're not. Spoofing a MAC address to get past switch port access controls, for instance, or spoofing an IP to convince other machines *you're* the server doesn't have anything to do with data integrity, but it has lots to do with affecting confidentiality and availability.

8. As part of a pen test on a U.S. Government system, you discover files containing social security numbers and other PII sensitive information. You are asked about controls placed on dissemination of this information. Which of the following acts should you check?

   A. FISMA

   B. Privacy Act

   C. PATRIOT Act

   D. Freedom of Information Act

   ☑ **B.** The Privacy Act protects information of a personal nature, including social security numbers. The Privacy Act defines exactly what "personal information" is, and it states that government agencies cannot disclose any personal information about an individual without that person's consent. It also lists 12 exemptions for the release of this information (for example, information that is part of a law enforcement issue may be released). In other questions you see, keep in mind that the Privacy Act generally will define the information that is *not* available to you in and after a test. Dissemination and storage of privacy information needs to be *very* closely controlled to keep you out of hot water.

☒ **A** is incorrect because FISMA isn't designed to control dissemination of PII or sensitive data. Its primary goal is to ensure the security of government systems by promoting a standardized approach to security controls, implementation, and testing. The act requires government agencies to create a security plan for their systems and to have it "accredited" at least once every three years.

☒ **C** is incorrect because the USA PATRIOT Act is not an effort to control personal information. Its purpose is to aid the United States government in preventing terrorism by increasing the government's ability to monitor, intercept, and maintain records on almost every imaginable form of communication. As a side effect, it has also served to increase observation and prevention of hacking attempts on many systems.

☒ **D** is incorrect because the Freedom of Information Act wasn't designed to tell you what to do with information. Its goal is to define how you can get information—specifically information regarding how your governments work. It doesn't necessarily help you in hacking, but it does provide a cover for a lot of information. Anything you uncover that could have been gathered through FoIA is considered legal, and should be part of your overall test.

9. Joe has spent a large amount of time learning hacking tools and techniques, and has even passed certification exams to promote himself in the ethical hacking field. Joe uses his talents during the election season to deface websites and launch denial of service attacks against opponents of his candidate. Which answer most closely correlates with Joe's actions?

   A. Hactivism

   B. Black box attacks

   C. Black hat hacking

   D. Cracking

☑ **A.** So called "hactivists" are hackers who use their skills and talents to forward a cause or a political agenda. The key in hactivism is that it doesn't really matter if you feel like the political cause or the hacker himself is attempting to do good. If the attacks in question forward a political agenda, it's hactivism.

☒ **B** is incorrect because, although the attacks carried out by Joe may very well have come from black box efforts (that is, Joe knows nothing about his target to start with), his efforts are all due to a political agenda. The key here isn't the methods or what he actually did, it's why he did it.

☒ **C** is incorrect, but just barely so. Without question, what Joe is doing can be categorized as "black hat." He's not operating under any agreed-upon scope, and isn't paid to share security shortcomings with the owners of his targets. He's attacking from the outside, without permission, in an attempt to do harm. However, the reason behind his actions is political in nature and represents a cause or ideology, thus making this a "less correct" response.

☒ **D** is incorrect; however, just like answer C, it's not incorrect by much. Although it is true Joe fits the definition of a cracker (using his skills, tools, and techniques for either personal gain or destructive purposes, or to achieve a goal outside the interest of the system owner), again we have to fall back on the reason *why* he's doing this.

10. A hacker is attempting to gain access to a target inside a business. After trying several methods, he gets frustrated and starts a denial of service attack against a server attached to the target. Which security control is the hacker affecting?

   A. Confidentiality

   B. Integrity

   C. Availability

   D. Authentication

   ☑ **C. Denial of service attacks are always attacks against the availability of the system. Regardless of whatever else the hacker has tried to accomplish against the machine, a successful DoS attack removes the availability of the machine. Remember, availability refers to the communications systems and data being ready for use when legitimate users need them. Many methods are used for availability, depending on whether the discussion is about a system, network resource, or the data itself. However, they all attempt to ensure one thing: When the system or data is needed, it can be accessed by the appropriate personnel. Attacks against availability always fall into the denial of service realm.

   ☒ **A** is incorrect because the attacker is not affecting the machine's ability to discern his true identity. As a matter of fact, it seems the confidentiality controls in place on the machine are working well. Remember, confidentiality addresses the secrecy and privacy of information, and refers to the measures taken to prevent disclosure of information or data to unauthorized individuals or systems.

   ☒ **B** is incorrect because the attacker didn't get frustrated and attempt to change or alter any data—he simply decided to cut off access to it. Remember, integrity refers to the methods and actions taken to protect the information from unauthorized alteration or revision—whether the data is at rest or in transit.

   ☒ **D** is incorrect because the hacker appears to be having problems authenticating at the machine—which boasts well for the security personnel devoted to protecting it. Authentication is a subset of the larger confidentiality factor.

11. The security, functionality, and ease of use (SFE) triangle states which of the following as true?

    A. As security increases, ease of use decreases and functionality decreases.

    B. As security increases, ease of use increases and functionality increases.

    C. A decrease of security has no effect on ease of use or functionality.

    D. An increase of security has no effect on ease of use or functionality.

☑ **A.** The SFE triangle is a simple line chart depicting something that should be common sense for most people: As you apply more security controls, the system gets harder to use and has less functionality. If you've worked in security for any length of time, you know this to be true. Machines and networks that are wide open allow users to do all sorts of productive (and not so productive) things. The drawback is that the system is more open to attack as well. The key is to find a good balance between implementing controls to protect your resources and personnel, and leaving the system usable enough for people to get their jobs done.

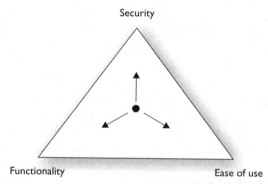

Security

Functionality   Ease of use

☒ **B** is incorrect because increasing security on a system decreases ease of use. Don't believe me? If you have kids, try this at home: Open Tools, Internet Options in Internet Explorer on your Windows machine, and go to Content. Enable the Content Advisor and set a password access control on websites you know your kids go to. A security measure is in place, and your kids will definitely notice IE is not as easy to use now.

☒ **C** is incorrect because decreasing security directly increases the ease of use and functionality of the system. Security, functionality, and ease of use are all connected. Most security practitioners think of these on a line instead of in a triangle—as you move along the line away from security, you move closer to usability.

☒ **D** is incorrect because increasing security directly decreases the ease of use and functionality of the system. As stated previously, security, functionality, and ease of use are all connected. If you move along the line closer to security, you move further away from usability.

12. In which phase of the ethical hacking methodology would a hacker discover available targets on a network?

    A. Reconnaissance

    B. Scanning and enumeration

    C. Gaining access

    D. Maintaining access

    E. Covering tracks

    ☑ **B.** The scanning and enumeration phase is where you'll use things such as ping sweeps to discover available targets on the network. This step occurs *after* reconnaissance. In this step, tools and techniques are actively applied to information gathered during recon to gather more in-depth information on the targets. For example, reconnaissance may show a network subnet to have 500 or so machines connected inside a single building, whereas scanning and enumeration would discover which ones are Windows machines and which ones are running FTP.

    ☒ **A** is incorrect because the reconnaissance phase is nothing more than the steps taken to gather evidence and information on the targets you wish to attack. Activities that occur in this phase include dumpster diving and social engineering. Another valuable tool in recon is the Internet. Look for any of these items as key words in answers on your exam.

    ☒ **C** is incorrect because the gaining access phase is all about attacking the machines themselves. You've already figured out background information on the client and have enumerated the potential vulnerabilities and security flaws on each target. In this phase, you break out the big guns and start firing away. Key words you're looking for here are the attacks themselves: Accessing an open and nonsecured wireless access point, manipulating network devices, writing and delivering a buffer overflow, and performing SQL injection against a web application are all examples.

    ☒ **D** is incorrect because this phase is all about back doors and the steps taken to ensure you have a way back in. For the savvy readers out there who noticed we skipped a step here (escalating privileges), well done. Key words you'll look for on this phase (maintaining access) are back doors, zombies, and rootkits.

    ☒ **E** is incorrect because this phase is all about cleaning up when you're done and making sure no one can see where you've been. Clearing tracks involves steps to conceal success and avoid detection by security professionals. Steps taken here consist of removing or altering log files, hiding files with hidden attributes or directories, and even using tunneling protocols to communicate with the system.

13. Which of the following are potential drawbacks to a black box test? (Choose all that apply.)

   A. The client does not get a focused picture of an external attacker dedicated on their systems.

   B. The client does not get a focused picture of an internal attacker dedicated on their systems.

   C. This test takes the longest amount of time to complete.

   D. This test takes the shortest amount of time to complete.

   ☑ **B and C.** Black box tests are conducted to simulate an outside attacker. The problem with this test, if done solely on its own, is two-fold. First, it concentrates solely on what most people think of as the biggest threat—an outside attacker. You know—some guy in a dark room surrounded by green tinted monitors who has decided to break into the enterprise network. This totally ignores one of the biggest threats to the network in the first place—the disgruntled insider. Additionally, because of its very nature, a black box test takes longer than any other type to complete. If you think about it, this makes sense.

   ☒ **A** is incorrect because the *point* of the black box test is to simulate the external attacker. It's designed to simulate an outside, unknown attacker, takes the most amount of time to complete, and is usually (by far) the most expensive option.

   ☒ **D** is incorrect because black box testing takes the longest amount of time to complete. The reason for this is obvious: With white or gray box testing, you've already got a leg up on your black box brethren, in that you already have some insider information. With black box testing, you need to go through all the phases of the CEH methodology.

14. In which phase of a penetration test would an ethical hacker perform footprinting?

   A. Preparation

   B. Assessment

   C. Conclusion

   D. Reconnaissance

   E. Scanning and enumeration

   ☑ **B.** Oh, I can hear you all the way from down here in Florida, screaming and hollering that footprinting occurs as part of reconnaissance. And I absolutely agree with you—it certainly does. However, this question asked what stage of a *penetration test* it occurs in. In the CEH world, pen tests have three phases—preparation, assessment, and conclusion. Reconnaissance is one of the five stages of an actual attack. Be sure to keep the two separate in your head, or you'll miss this easy question on the test.

☒ **A is incorrect** because the preparation phase of a pen test is where all the agreements are hammered out. The preparation phase defines that time period where you meet with clients and agree upon the actual contract. The scope of the test, the types of attacks allowed, and the individuals assigned to perform the activity are all agreed upon in this phase.

☒ **C is incorrect** because the conclusion phase happens after all the activity and tests are complete. The conclusion phase constitutes the time when final reports are prepared for the customer. These reports detail the findings of the tests (including the types of tests performed) and sometimes even provide recommendations to improve security. This phase is sometimes referred to as the *post-assessment phase*, but you'll probably see it as the *conclusion phase* on the test.

☒ **D is incorrect** because reconnaissance is one of the attack phases. Although it's certainly true that footprinting occurs here, you're going to have to be very careful about understanding what the question is asking you for. Pen tests have three phases, and during the assessment phase are the five steps in the attack.

☒ **E is incorrect** because scanning and enumeration is an attack step, not a phase of the penetration test. Savvy test takers will have picked this out quickly and eliminated it as an answer right off the bat. If, however, you missed the pen-test-versus-attack-phase link, you should note that this answer is also wrong because footprinting doesn't occur in the scanning and enumeration phase. This answer is incorrect on both fronts.

15. Which of the following would not be considered passive reconnaissance?

    A. Dumpster diving for valuable, discarded information

    B. Thoroughly examining financial sites for clues on target inventory and other useful information

    C. Ping sweeping a range of IP addresses found through a DNS lookup

    D. Using a search engine to discover competitive intelligence on the organization

    ☑ **C.** When it comes to active versus passive recon, remember the two golden rules. First rule: If it's something that exposes you to more risk in being caught, the recon is active. Second rule: If you touch the target, the recon is active. For example, walking up to locked doors and checking them or going into the building to attempt social engineering on the user are both active measures. Dumpster diving, "quiet" social engineering, and using Google to find information on the target are all examples of passive reconnaissance (a.k.a., passive footprinting). And lastly, ping sweeping is done in the scanning and enumeration phase, not during reconnaissance, so this answer should have been an easy one for you eliminate.

    ☒ **A is incorrect** because dumpster diving is one of the prime examples of passive recon. It's simple, easy, and doesn't expose you to very much risk of being caught. It also doesn't require you to interact with your target at all.

☒ **B** is incorrect because examining competitive intelligence is free, readily available, and should be gathered as part of your passive reconnaissance. Other avenues for this type of recon include job boards, social networking sites, and the company's own website. Pull a copy down and explore it. You'll be amazed what you can find passively.

☒ **D** is incorrect because this is also a prime example of passive reconnaissance. During passive recon, you are expected to use all avenues of the Internet to find information on your target. In addition to the other avenues mentioned here, don't neglect the blogosphere—that wonderful world of blogging that has sprung up over the past few years. Sometimes people post the strangest stuff on their blogs, and sometimes that posted material is just the ticket you need to successfully complete your task.

16. As part of the preparation phase for a pen test that you are participating in, the client relays their intent to discover security flaws and possible remediation. They seem particularly concerned about external threats and do not mention internal threats at all. When defining scope, the threat of internal users is not added as part of the test. Which test is this client ignoring?

A. Gray box

B. Black box

C. White hat

D. Black hat

☑ **A.** Once again, this is a play on words the exam will throw at you. Note the question is asking about a *test type,* not the attacker. Reviewing CEH documentation, you'll see there are three types of tests—white, black, and gray—with each designed to test a specific threat. White tests the internal threat of a knowledgeable systems administrator or an otherwise elevated privilege level user. Black tests external threats with no knowledge of the target. Gray tests the average internal user threat, to expose potential security problems inside the network.

☒ **B** is incorrect because black box testing is designed to simulate the external threat, which is exactly what this client is asking for. Black box testing takes the most amount of time to complete because it means a thorough romp through the five stages of an attack (and removes any preconceived notions of what to look for) and is usually the most expensive option. Another drawback to this type of test is that it focuses solely on the threat *outside* the organization and does not take into account any trusted users on the inside.

☒ **C** is incorrect because a hat color refers to the attacker himself. True, the client is hiring a white hat in this instance to perform the test; however, the hat does not equate to the test. White hats are the "good guys"—ethical hackers hired by a customer for the specific goal of testing and improving security. White hats don't use their knowledge and skills without prior consent.

⊠ **D** is incorrect because this question refers to the test itself, not the type of attacker. Black hats are the "bad guys" and are otherwise known as *crackers*. They illegally use their skills for either personal gain or for malicious intent, seeking to steal or destroy data, or to deny access to resources and systems. Black hats do *not* ask for permission or consent.

17. In which phase of an attack would vulnerability mapping occur?

   A. Assessment

   B. Active reconnaissance

   C. Scanning and enumeration

   D. Fingerprinting

   ☑ **C.** This is a textbook definition of an activity occurring in the scanning and enumeration phase. Sure, this would also occur in the assessment phase of the pen test, but the question did not reference that: It specifically mentioned the attack phase. Attack phases are reconnaissance, scanning and enumeration, gaining access, elevating privileges, maintaining access, and covering tracks. Commit this to memory for your exam.

   ⊠ **A** is incorrect because, although this activity definitely occurs in the assessment phase of a pen test, the question is referencing the attack phase itself. Remember that all the attack phases occur during the assessment portion of the pen test. The preparation phase gets you an agreement and a scope, and the conclusion phase is your chance to present all your findings to the client. The assessment phase is where all the action happens.

   ⊠ **B** is incorrect because active reconnaissance is something that occurs *before* scanning and enumeration. During reconnaissance, you're gathering the high-level information you're going to need to make the rest of your test easy and smooth. Scanning devices for vulnerabilities is far removed from this.

   ⊠ **D** is incorrect because fingerprinting is another term for enumeration, but is not associated as a phase in the attack cycle. Most people associate the term *fingerprinting* with the operating system on the device—figuring out what the box is running and what ports are open on the machine. Several tools have been developed for fingerprinting, including SolarWinds, Queso, and Cheops.

18. While performing a pen test, you find success in exploiting a machine. Your attack vector took advantage of a common mistake—the Windows 7 installer script used to load the machine left the administrative account with a default password. Which attack did you successfully execute?

   A. Application level

   B. Operating system

   C. Shrink wrap

D. Social engineering

E. Misconfiguration

☑ **B.** Operating system (OS) attacks target common mistakes many people make when installing operating systems—accepting and leaving all the defaults. Examples usually include things such as administrator accounts with no passwords, ports left open, and guest accounts left behind. Another OS attack you may be asked about deals with versioning. Operating systems are never released fully secure and are consistently upgraded with hotfixes, security patches, and full releases. The potential for an old vulnerability within the enterprise is always high.

☒ **A** is incorrect because application-level attacks are centered on the actual programming codes of an application. These attacks are usually very successful in an overall pen test because many people simply discount the applications running on their OS and network, preferring to spend their time hardening the OS's and network devices. Many applications on a network aren't tested for vulnerabilities as part of their creation and, as such, have many vulnerabilities built in.

☒ **C** is incorrect because shrink-wrap attacks take advantage of the built-in code and scripts most *off-the-shelf applications* come with. These attacks allow hackers to take advantage of the very things designed to make installation and administration easier. These shrink-wrapped snippets make life easier for installation and administration, but they also make it easier for attackers to get in.

☒ **D** is incorrect because social engineering isn't relevant at all in this question. There is no human element here, so this one can be thrown out.

☒ **E** is incorrect because misconfiguration attacks take advantage of systems that are, on purpose or by accident, not configured appropriately for security. For example, suppose an administrator wants to make things as easy as possible for the users and, in keeping with security and usability being on opposite ends of the spectrum, leaves security settings at the lowest possible level, enabling services, opening firewall ports, and providing administrative privileges to all users. It's easier for the users, but creates a target-rich environment for the hacker.

19. A machine in your environment uses an open X-server to allow remote access. The X-server access control is disabled, allowing connections from almost anywhere and with little to no authentication measures. Which of the following are true statements regarding this situation? (Choose all that apply.)

A. An external vulnerability can take advantage of the misconfigured X-server threat.

B. An external threat can take advantage of the misconfigured X-server vulnerability.

C. An internal vulnerability can take advantage of the misconfigured X-server threat.

D. An internal threat can take advantage of the misconfigured X-server vulnerability.

☑ **B and D.** This is an easy one because all you have to understand are the definitions of threat and vulnerability. A *threat* is any agent, circumstance, or situation that could potentiality cause harm or loss to an IT asset. In this case, the implication is the threat is an individual (hacker) either inside or outside the network. A *vulnerability* is any weakness, such as a software flaw or logic design, that could be exploited by a threat to cause damage to an asset. In both these answers, the vulnerability—the access controls on X-server are not in place—can be exploited by the threat, whether internal or external.

☒ **A and C** are both incorrect because they list the terms backward. Threats take advantage of vulnerabilities and exploit them, not the other way around.

20. You are examining security logs snapshotted during a prior attack against the target. The target's IP address is 135.17.22.15, and the attack originated from 216.88.76.5. Which of the following correctly characterizes this attack?

    A. Inside attack

    B. Outside attack

    C. Black box attack

    D. Spoofing

    ☑ **B.** This is an example of one of those little definition questions you'll see on the exam and will be thankful for. An *inside attack* generates from inside the network boundary, whereas an *outside attack* comes from outside the border. Granted, anyone with any networking knowledge at all knows it's impossible to tell, solely from an IP address, whether one is inside or outside a company's network boundary. All sorts of things, such as VPNs, multiple nets, and subsidiaries, could make life miserable in figuring out where the inside versus outside line is. When faced with this on the exam, though, just take it at face value. Simple and easy.

    ☒ **A** is incorrect because the attack came from a different network—fully outside the enterprise's virtual walls. The only time this can become a tricky question is when subnetting is involved, in which case the question will have to point out where the enterprise network footprint stops.

    ☒ **C** is incorrect because we simply have no idea what type of attack—black, gray, or white—this is. True, it's starting from outside the network, leading us to believe it a black box attack, but that's not necessarily true, and there certainly isn't enough information here to make that call.

☒ **D** is incorrect because spoofing has to do with an attempt to fake a machine's identity (usually through MAC or IP). The question doesn't specify whether or not this is in play, so it can't be the answer we're looking for.

21. An ethical hacker needs to be aware of a variety of laws. What do Sections 1029 and 1030 of United States Code Title 18 specify?

    A. They criminalize the collection of personal information.

    B. They provide guidance on the right to obtain information from governmental agencies.

    C. They increase the government's ability to monitor communications.

    D. They define most of the U.S. laws concerning hacking and computer crime.

    ☑ **D.** Title 18, "Crimes and Criminal Procedure," Part 1, "Crimes," Chapter 47, "Fraud and false statements," Sections 1029 and 1030 address hacking and hacking-related criminal activity within the U.S. Section 1029 is titled "Fraud and related activity in connection with access devices," and Section 1030 is titled "Fraud and related activity in connection with computers." You'll need to know these.

    ☒ **A** is incorrect because this is in reference to the Spy Act (2007), which makes it unlawful for "any person who is not the owner, or authorized user, of a computer used for a financial institution, the U.S. Government, or in any interstate or foreign commerce or communication to engage in unfair or deceptive acts."

    ☒ **B** is incorrect because this is in reference to the Freedom of Information Act (1966), which doesn't actually state what information an individual is allowed to get, but rather states the nine instances in which one can't ask for it. These instances are generally things such as military, law enforcement, and classified secrets as well as information pertaining to trade secrets and interagency litigation.

    ☒ **C** is incorrect because this is in reference to the USA PATRIOT Act, the *Uniting and Strengthening America by Providing Appropriate Tools Required to Intercept and Obstruct Terrorism* act, which is designed to aid the United States Government in preventing terrorism by increasing the government's ability to monitor, intercept, and maintain records on almost every imaginable form of communication (telephone, networking, e-mail as well as medical and financial records are all addressed).

22. Which of the following should a security professional use as a possible means to verify the integrity of a data message from sender to receiver?

    A. Strong password requirements for encryption of the file

    B. Access controls on all network devices

C. Hash algorithm

D. Strong password requirements on operating system login

☑ **C.** A hash is the preferred method most in use for verifying the integrity of a file. Basically, before you send the file, you run it through a hash algorithm (such as MD5 or SHA-1) that generates a number. When it's received, you do the same. If the numbers match, voilà!

☒ **A** is incorrect because it's referencing confidentiality controls. Almost every time you see *password* referenced, you should think confidentiality, not integrity.

☒ **B** is incorrect because it's also referencing confidentiality controls. Access controls are exactly what they sound like: controls put in place to control access to something. In the context of network devices, they control things such as administrative access to the IOS.

☒ **D** is incorrect because it's also referencing confidentiality controls. Once again, passwords equate to confidentiality controls.

23. Which of the following describes activities taken in the conclusion phase of a penetration test?

A. Reports are prepared detailing security deficiencies.

B. Vulnerability assessment is conducted.

C. Security control audits are performed.

D. Contract and scope agreement is created.

☑ **A.** Pen tests consist of three major phases: preparation, assessment, and conclusion. The conclusion phase is where you wrap everything up and present your findings to the customer. The only tricky thing about this question is overthinking it. While you're testing and discovering things, you're documenting everything that's happening. Therefore, you could easily make an argument that, in a way, you're preparing reports during the *assessment* phase. Don't overthink this one—reports are done in the conclusion phase.

☒ **B** is incorrect because vulnerability assessment and all attacks and audits occur during the assessment phase of a pen test.

☒ **C** is incorrect because security control audits occur during the assessment phase of a pen test. Remember, all the action occurs in the middle, surrounding by planning for the action (preparation phase) and presenting it to the customer (conclusion phase).

☒ **D** is incorrect because contract and scope agreement are hammered out in the preparation phase. This is where you determine how far you can go, what the client actually wants to find out, and where they don't want you to be.

24. Which of the following best describes an ethical hacker?

    A. An ethical hacker never knowingly or unknowingly exceeds the boundaries of the scope agreement.

    B. An ethical hacker never performs a denial of service attack on a target machine.

    C. An ethical hacker never proceeds with an audit or test without written permission.

    D. An ethical hacker never performs social engineering on unsuspecting members of the target organization.

    ☑ **C.** I know you're tired of seeing this question. I'm tired of asking it. But you get the point now, right? This is important and you *will* see it on the exam. The only real difference between those bad guy crackers out there and us, the ethical hackers, is *written permission.* Bad guys want to steal and destroy stuff. They don't care about rules and don't bother to ask for permission. They will ruthlessly attack every avenue they can possibly think of in order to break into the target, and they don't care how far down the rabbit hole it takes them. The only difference between them and us is that we agree to do it only under certain controlled circumstances and guidelines. If, for one second, you think an ethical hacker won't take advantage of every single tool, loophole, loose lip, or technique available without regard to how bad it makes someone in the target organization feel, you are in the wrong field. We're just as dirty as the other guys; we just do it with permission.

    ☒ **A** is incorrect because, although the ethical hacker shouldn't ever knowingly exceed the scope or boundaries of his test, it's sometimes done unknowingly. Heck, sometimes there's almost no way around it, and it often occurs without the tester knowing about it until later. In several famous cases a pen test has gone awry and hit things outside the target organization. This doesn't mean the tester was unethical, however. It just happens.

    ☒ **B** is incorrect because your client may specifically ask you to perform a DoS attack. Oftentimes, they'll explicitly ask you *not* to perform a DoS attack, but the point is the same regardless: We will test everything we're told to, just as a bad guy would do in trying to affect or gain access to a resource.

    ☒ **D** is incorrect because social engineering is a big part of a true pen test. After all, the users are the weakest link in the chain, right? If you don't test them, you're not performing a full test. Because social engineering is on the table for the bad guys, it's on the table for us, too.

25. In which phase of the attack would a hacker set up and configure "zombie" machines?

    A. Reconnaissance

    B. Covering tracks

C. Gaining access

D. Maintaining access

☑ **D.** Zombies are basically machines the hacker has confiscated to do his work for him. If the attacker is really good, the owners of the zombie machines don't even know their machines have been drafted into the war.

☒ **A** is incorrect because the reconnaissance phase is all about gaining knowledge and information on a target. In reconnaissance you're learning about the target itself—what system types they may have in use, what operating hours they run, whether or not they use a shredder, and what personal information about their employees is available are all examples. Think of reconnaissance as the background information on a good character in a novel; it may not be completely necessary to know before you read the action scenes, but it sure makes it easier to understand why the character behaves in a certain manner during the conflict phase of the book. Setting up zombie systems goes far beyond the boundaries of gathering information.

☒ **B** is incorrect because this phase is where attackers attempt to conceal their success and avoid detection by security professionals. This can involve removing or altering log files, hiding files with hidden attributes or directories, and using tunneling protocols to communicate with the system.

☒ **C** is incorrect because in this phase attacks are leveled against the targets enumerated during the scanning and enumeration phase. Key words to look for in identifying this phase are the attacks themselves (such as buffer overflow and SQL injection). Finally, be careful about questions relating to elevating privileges. Sometimes this is counted as its own phase, so pay very close attention to the question's wording in choosing your answer.

Cryptography 101

This domain includes questions from the following topics:

- An overview of cryptography and encryption techniques
- Cryptographic algorithms
- How public and private keys are generated
- An overview of the MD5, SHA, RC4, RC5, and Blowfish algorithms
- The digital signature and its components
- Method and application of digital signature technology
- Overview of digital certificates
- Cryptanalysis and code-breaking methodologies
- A list of cryptography attacks

It's a glorious day in 1500 B.C. Mesopotamia, and the potter is elated. He has developed a new method of glazing—and as everyone in the area knows, longer lasting pottery could mean a lot more shekels in his pocket. But to complete this glaze, he needs help from a few close, trusted friends, which causes a problem for him: how to get messages about his glaze to those who can assist without tipping off everybody else? The clay tablets used to send messages back and forth across the kingdom provided no protection at all, but were the only way he knew to send this sort of meaningful communication back and forth.

So he sent tablets to his friends, with lots of symbols on them, with each symbol equating to a corresponding letter in the alphabet. He then wrote all new tablets, using his symbols instead of alphabet characters. Smiling at his cleverness, he relaxed in the knowledge that his new glazing process would be protected from prying eyes. The only real question is, did he realize he was one going to be one of the forefathers of cryptography?

This is one of the earliest and clearest known cryptography attempts in history. Sure, the Egyptians had some things going in hieroglyphics earlier than this, but their writing was based on symbols and weirdness. My kids will tell you they're not sure the Egyptians themselves understood half what they wrote to each other anyway. Cryptography and cryptanalysis are big parts of the security world, and have been ever since that dusty

Mesopotamian day. If you're going to be an ethical hacker, you're going to have to at least know the basics. The good news is, you are not required to break down the mathematics of the algorithms. The bad news, though, is that you need to know pretty much everything else about them.

 STUDY TIPS You'll be asked a variety of questions about cryptography on the exam, ranging from simple identification to mind-altering questions you won't even believe are part of this certification. The biggest thing you can do to prepare for the CEH cryptography questions is plain old organization. Also, make use of an old test-taking trick: eliminating those answers you absolutely know to be wrong is faster and easier than trying to figure out which one is right. As an example, if you simply remember which algorithms are symmetric and which are asymmetric, you can oftentimes eliminate half the answers based on that qualifier in the question itself. Key in on the characteristics of algorithms—symmetric versus asymmetric, block versus stream— and you're well on your way. And don't forget your key lengths—you'll be asked about them a lot. Lastly, when it comes to encrypted messaging, PKI is always going to be high on the testing list. Simply remembering that you encrypt with a public key and decrypt with a private key will nab you a couple questions without fail. And, for goodness sake, be sure to know the difference between a digital certificate and a digital signature.

1. Which of the following is a true statement concerning cryptography?

    A. Provides a means to protect data during storage but not transit.

    B. Provides a means to protect data in transit but not storage.

    C. Converts plaintext to ciphertext for protection during transit or in storage.

    D. Converts ciphertext to plaintext for protection during transit or in storage.

2. Which of the following would be the best choice to guarantee the integrity of messages in transit or storage?

    A. Block cipher

    B. Symmetric algorithm

    C. Asymmetric algorithm

    D. Hash algorithm

3. Which of the following encryption algorithms is your best choice if your primary need is bulk encryption, and you need fast, strong encryption?

    A. AES

    B. ECC

    C. RSA

    D. MD5

4. You're describing a basic PKI system to a new member of the team. He asks how the public key can be distributed within the system in an orderly, controlled fashion so that the users can be sure of the sender's identity. Which of the following would be your answer?

    A. Digital signature

    B. Hash value

    C. Private key

    D. Digital certificate

    E. Nonrepudiation

5. You are discussing hash values with a CEH instructor. Immediately after telling you the hash is a one-way algorithm and cannot be reversed, he explains that you can still discover the value entered into the hash, given enough time and resources. Which of the following hash anomalies might allow this?

    A. L0phtCrack

    B. Hash value compromise

    C. Chosen plaintext

    D. Collision

6. What is the standard format for digital certificates?

   A. X.500

   B. X.25

   C. XOR

   D. X.509

7. You're discussing cryptography and determine you need to ensure messages are safe from unauthorized observation. Also, you want to provide a way to ensure the identity of the sender and receiver during the communications process. Which of the following best suits your needs?

   A. Steganography

   B. Asymmetric encryption

   C. Hash

   D. Symmetric encryption

8. A hacker has gained access to several files. Many are encrypted, but one is not. Which of the following is the best choice for possibly providing a successful break into the encrypted files?

   A. Ciphertext only

   B. Known plaintext

   C. Chosen ciphertext

   D. Replay

9. You are discussing a steganography tool that takes advantage of the nature of "white space" to conceal information. Which tool are you referring to?

   A. Snow

   B. GifShuffle

   C. White Wipe

   D. Tripwire

10. At the basic core of encryption approaches, two main methods are in play: substitution and transposition. Which of the following best describes transposition?

    A. Bits are replaced with a different value.

    B. Bits are removed.

    C. The order of bits is changed.

    D. The parity bits are changed.

11. Jack and Jill work in an organization that has a PKI system in place for securing messaging. Jack encrypts a message for Jill and sends it on. Jill receives the message and decrypts it. Within a PKI system, which of the following statements is true?

A. Jack encrypts with his private key. Jill decrypts with her private key.

B. Jack encrypts with his public key. Jill decrypts with her public key.

C. Jack encrypts with Jill's private key. Jill decrypts with her public key.

D. Jack encrypts with Jill's public key. Jill decrypts with her private key.

12. Which of the following would you find in an X.509 digital certificate? (Choose all that apply.)

A. Version

B. Algorithm ID

C. Private key

D. Public key

E. Key usage

F. PTR record

13. Which of the following is secure substitute for telnet?

A. SHA-1

B. RSA

C. SSL

D. SSH

14. An SSL session requires a client and a server to handshake information between each other and agree on a secured channel. Which of the following best describes the session key creation during the setup of an SSL session?

A. The server creates the key after verifying the client's identity.

B. The server creates the key immediately on the client connection.

C. The client creates the key using the server's public key.

D. The client creates the key after verifying the server's identity.

15. Which encryption algorithm uses variable block sizes (from 32 to 128 bits)?

A. SHA-1

B. RC5

C. 3DES

D. AES

16. Which hash algorithm was developed by the NSA and produces output values up to 512 bits?

A. MD5

B. SHA-1

C. SHA-2

D. SSL

17. A hacker is attempting to uncover the key used in a cryptographic encryption scheme. Which attack vector is the most resource intensive and usually takes the longest amount of time?

    A. Social engineering

    B. Known plaintext

    C. Frequency analysis

    D. Brute force

18. In a discussion on symmetric encryption, a friend mentions that one of the drawbacks with this system is scalability. He goes on to say that for every person you add to the mix, the number of keys goes up exponentially. If seven people are in a symmetric encryption pool, how many keys are necessary?

    A. 7

    B. 14

    C. 21

    D. 28

19. Which of the following is a true statement?

    A. Symmetric encryption scales easily and provides for nonrepudiation.

    B. Symmetric encryption does not scale easily and does not provide for nonrepudiation.

    C. Symmetric encryption is not suited for bulk encryption.

    D. Symmetric encryption is slower than asymmetric encryption.

20. The PKI system you are auditing has a Certificate Authority (CA) at the top that creates and issues certificates. Users trust each other based on the CA itself. Which trust model is in use here?

    A. Standalone CA

    B. Web of Trust

    C. Single Authority

    D. Hierarchical Trust

21. A portion of a digital certificate is shown here:

```
Version                      V3
Serial Number                26 43 03 62 e9 6b 39 a4 9e 15 00 c7 cc 21 a2 20
Signature Algorithm          sha1RSA
Signature Hash Algorithm     sha1
Issuer                       VeriSign Class 3 Secure Server
Valid From                   Monday, October 17, 2011 8:00 PM
Valid To                     Wednesday, October 17, 2012 7:59:59 PM
...
Public Key                   RSA (2048)
...
```

Which of the following statements is true?

A. The hash created for the digital signature holds 160 bits.

B. The hash created for the digital signature holds 2,048 bits.

C. RSA is the hash algorithm used for the digital signature.

D. This certificate contains a private key.

22. Two bit strings are run through an XOR operation. Which of the following is a true statement for each bit pair regarding this function?

A. If the first value is 0 and the second value is 1, then the output is 0.

B. If the first value is 1 and the second value is 0, then the output is 0.

C. If the first value is 0 and the second value is 0, then the output is 1.

D. If the first value is 1 and the second value is 1, then the output is 0.

23. Which of the following attacks attempts to re-send a portion of a cryptographic exchange in hopes of setting up a communications channel?

A. Known plaintext

B. Chosen plaintext

C. Man in the middle

D. Replay

24. Within a PKI system, which of the following is an accurate statement?

A. Bill can be sure a message came from Sue by using his public key to decrypt it.

B. Bill can be sure a message came from Sue by using his private key to decrypt it.

C. Bill can be sure a message came from Sue by using her private key to decrypt the digital signature.

D. Bill can be sure a message came from Sue by using her public key to decrypt the digital signature.

25. One use of hash algorithms is for the secure storage of passwords: The password is run through a one-way hash, and the value is stored instead of the plaintext version. If a hacker gains access to these hash values and knows the hash algorithm used to create them, which of the following could be used to speed up his effort in cracking them?

A. Salt

B. Rainbow tables

C. Steganography

D. Collision

1. C

2. D

3. A

4. D

5. D

6. D

7. B

8. B

9. A

10. C

11. D

12. A, B, D, E

13. D

14. D

15. B

16. C

17. D

18. C

19. B

20. C

21. A

22. D

23. D

24. D

25. B

1. Which of the following is a true statement concerning cryptography?

   A. Provides a means to protect data during storage but not transit.

   B. Provides a means to protect data in transit but not storage.

   C. Converts plaintext to ciphertext for protection during transit or in storage.

   D. Converts ciphertext to plaintext for protection during transit or in storage.

   ☑ **C.** The whole point of cryptography is to put plaintext into an unreadable format (known as ciphertext) that only you and your intended recipient can translate (that is, decrypt). Cryptography is the science or study of protecting information, whether in transit or at rest, by using techniques to render the information unusable to anyone who does not possess the means to decrypt it. The overall process is simple: Take plaintext (something you can read) data, apply a cryptographic method, and turn it into ciphertext (something you can't read)—so long as there is some provision to allow you to bring the ciphertext back to plaintext.

   ☒ **A** is incorrect because cryptography is designed to protect data both at rest and in transit. Only protecting data in a resting state ignores the portion of its life when it's at the most risk—during transit between a sender and receiver. After all, what good would it do to protect your money in a vault but, once you take it out, to provide no protection at all while walking down the street?

   ☒ **B** is incorrect because cryptography is designed to protect data both in transit and at rest. Sure, data is most at risk when it's out of your hands, but ignoring it while in a resting state is folly. Data sitting on a hard drive somewhere unprotected is an open target, just waiting to be discovered.

   ☒ **D** is incorrect because converting ciphertext to plaintext is decrypting the message. Doing so before sending the message is cryptography in reverse and, frankly, makes no sense at all.

2. Which of the following would be the best choice to guarantee the integrity of messages in transit or storage?

   A. Block cipher

   B. Symmetric algorithm

   C. Asymmetric algorithm

   D. Hash algorithm

   ☑ **D.** Although it's nice to know the terms *block, stream, asymmetric,* and *asymmetric,* they're all irrelevant to this question. The key is the word *integrity,* and as you should already know from your study for this exam, that equates to a hash every time. Hash algorithms don't encrypt anything at all. They're *one-way* mathematical functions that take an input and typically produce a fixed-length string (usually a number), known as a *hash*, based on the arrangement of the data bits in the input. The sole purpose of a hash is to provide a means to verify the integrity of a piece of data—change a single bit in the arrangement of the original data, and you'll get a different response.

☒ **A** is incorrect because block ciphers are not designed for integrity checks. They use methods such as substitution and transposition in their algorithms and are considered simpler, and slower, than stream ciphers. Data bits are split up into blocks and fed into the cipher, with each block of data (usually 64 bits at a time) then encrypted with the key and algorithm.

☒ **B** is incorrect because a symmetric algorithm is not designed to provide integrity checks. Also known as "single key" and "shared key," *symmetric encryption* simply means one key is used both to encrypt and decrypt the data. Therefore, as long as both the sender and the receiver know and have the secret key, communication can be encrypted between the two.

☒ **C** is incorrect because asymmetric algorithms are not designed for integrity checks. Asymmetric encryption uses two keys—what the one key encrypts, the other key decrypts. The "public" key is the one used for encryption, whereas the "private" key is used for decryption.

3. Which of the following encryption algorithms is your best choice if your primary need is bulk encryption, and you need fast, strong encryption?

   A. AES

   B. ECC

   C. RSA

   D. MD5

☑ **A.** Questions like this on the exam are to be celebrated because they are easy—assuming you paid attention to my study tips at the beginning of this chapter. The question references bulk encryption—something fast and strong. This screams symmetric all the way, and the only symmetric algorithm listed here is AES.

☒ **B** is incorrect because ECC (Elliptic Curve Cryptosystem) is not symmetric in nature. It's primarily used for mobile devices and uses points on an elliptical curve, in conjunction with logarithmic problems, for encryption and signatures.

☒ **C** is incorrect because RSA is an asymmetric choice, not a symmetric one. RSA achieves strong encryption through the use of two large prime numbers: Factoring these numbers creates key sizes up to 4,096 bits. RSA can be used for encryption and digital signatures, and it's the modern de facto standard for those purposes.

☒ **D** is incorrect because MD5 is a hash algorithm and, as we all know, hash algorithms don't encrypt anything. Sure, they're great at integrity checks and, yes, you can pass a hash of something in place of the original (sending a hash of a stored password, for instance, instead of the password itself). However, this is not true encryption.

4. You're describing a basic PKI system to a new member of the team. He asks how the public key can be distributed within the system in an orderly, controlled fashion so that the users can be sure of the sender's identity. Which of the following would be your answer?

   A. Digital signature

   B. Hash value

   C. Private key

   D. Digital certificate

   E. Nonrepudiation

☑ **D.** This one's actually easy, yet is confusing to a lot of folks. You have to remember the goal of this little portion of a PKI system—how does one *know* this public key really belongs to User Joe and not User Mike, and how can it be delivered safely to everyone? A digital certificate is the answer because it contains the sender's public key and can be used to identify the sender. Because the CA provides the certificate and key (public), the user can be certain the public key actually belongs to the intended recipient. This simplifies distribution of keys as well, because users can go to a central authority—a key store, if you will—instead of directly to each user in the organization. Without central control and digital certificates, it would be a madhouse, with everyone chucking public keys at one another with wild abandon. And PKI is no place for Mardi Gras, my friend.

☒ **A** is incorrect because although a digital signature does provide a means for verifying an identity (encryption with your private key, which can only be decrypted with your corresponding public key, proves you are indeed you), it doesn't provide any means of sending keys anywhere. A digital signature is nothing more than an algorithmic output that is designed to ensure the authenticity (and integrity) of the sender. You need it to prove your certificate's authenticity, but you need the certificate in order to send keys around.

☒ **B** is incorrect because a hash value has nothing to do with sending public keys around anywhere. Yes, hash values are "signed" to verify authenticity, but that's it. There is no transport capability in a hash. It's just a number and, in this case, a distractor answer.

☒ **C** is incorrect for a number of reasons, but one should be screaming at you from the page right now: you never, *never*, send a private key anywhere. If you did send your private key off, it wouldn't be private anymore, now would it? The private key is simply the part of the pair used for encryption. It is never shared with anyone.

☒ **E** is incorrect because nonrepudiation is a definition term and has nothing to do with the transport of keys. Nonrepudiation is the means by which a recipient can ensure the identity of the sender and that neither party can deny having sent or received the message.

5. You are discussing hash values with a CEH instructor. Immediately after telling you the hash is a one-way algorithm and cannot be reversed, he explains that you can still discover the value entered into the hash, given enough time and resources. Which of the following hash anomalies might allow this?

   A. L0phtCrack

   B. Hash value compromise

   C. Chosen Plaintext

   D. Collision

☑ **D.** A collision, in the world of hashes, occurs when plaintext is fed into a hash until, eventually, two or more entries are found that create the same fixed-value hash result. In short, a collision occurs when two or more files create the same output. When a hacker can create a second file that produces the same hash value output as the original, he may be able to pass off the fake file as the original. This can obviously cause all sorts of problems, and when you think about what hashes are sometimes used for (such as storing hashes of passwords in a file instead of the passwords themselves), you can certainly understand where collisions are concerning. As an aside, it is just as likely you would find a *new* collision than the original collision, and without the knowledge of the original text, your results would be nothing more than an educated guess. For the purposes of the exam, though, just remember what a collision is and means.

☒ **A** is incorrect because L0phtCrack really has nothing to do with this question. It is a good-old password cracker in the Windows world, but it's not a collision of hash values in any sense. It's a "password auditing and recovery application" used to test password strength and "recover" lost passwords on Windows machines. It uses dictionary, brute-force, and hybrid attacks, as well as rainbow tables.

☒ **B** is incorrect for a couple of reasons. First, the term *hash value compromise* sounds really cool, but has no meaning in the CEH world. This term could be construed to mean lots of things, but if you'll run a quick Google check (go ahead, I'll wait) you'll see that it's not a definition term you'll need to know. Pretty good distractor, yes, but not a viable answer.

☒ **C** is incorrect because chosen plaintext is an attack used to determine the key used for encryption. It's a variant of "known plaintext," where the hacker has both plaintext and corresponding ciphertext messages and scans them for repeatable sequences. These are compared to the ciphertext versions and—*voilà*—key found.

6. What is the standard format for digital certificates?

   A. X.500

   B. X.25

   C. XOR

   D. X.509

   ☑ **D.** This is a quick, simple question you'll see on pretty much every study guide and practice test for CEH. It's just something you're going to have to have in your memory bank—one of those things you just know without thinking about it. The X.509 standard is a part of a much bigger series of standards, and it defines what should and should not be in a digital certificate. Because of the standard, any system complying with X.509 can exchange and use digital certificates to establish authenticity.

   ☒ **A** is incorrect because X.500 has nothing to do with digital certificates. It's actually a *series* of standards covering directory services, and it's more applicable to things such as Active Directory in Windows-based networks. As a related but completely worthless note, it was developed by ITU-T way back in 1988.

   ☒ **B** is incorrect because X.25 has nothing to do with digital certificates. X.25 is a protocol suite from ITU-T defining wide area network (WAN) communication.

   ☒ **C** is incorrect because XOR refers to a mathematical function. An XOR operation requires two inputs, which are compared by the operation. If the bits match, the output is 0; if they don't, it's 1.

7. You're discussing cryptography and determine you need to ensure messages are safe from unauthorized observation. Also, you want to provide a way to ensure the identity of the sender and receiver during the communications process. Which of the following best suits your needs?

   A. Steganography

   B. Asymmetric encryption

   C. Hash

   D. Symmetric encryption

   ☑ **B.** This one should be easy for you by now because it's right out of the definition book for asymmetric encryption. The other choices make no sense because the key to the answer is the repudiation aspect asked for in the question. Remember, asymmetric encryption came about because of the inherit problem with symmetric encryption and the single key to encrypt and decrypt messages—that is, how do you share the key efficiently and effectively without compromising security? The answer was to use two keys, and the machinations involved in that provide the means for nonrepudiation.

☒ **A** is incorrect because steganography is all about hiding messages inside images and other files. It's the practice of concealing a message inside another medium (such as another file or an image) in such a way that only the sender and recipient even know of its existence. It can be as simple as hiding the message in the text of a written correspondence or as complex as changing bits within a huge media file to carry a message.

☒ **C** is incorrect because a hash has nothing to do with this question. It's purely used as a distractor here, and you should be able to easily dismiss this one.

☒ **D** is incorrect because although symmetric encryption algorithms do a great job of protecting your data, they don't do a thing for you in the repudiation realm. Remember, symmetric uses only a single key, so there's nothing to identify the sender or receiver. It was this drawback that brought about asymmetric thinking for encryption in the first place.

8. A hacker has gained access to several files. Many are encrypted, but one is not. Which of the following is the best choice for possibly providing a successful break into the encrypted files?

   A. Ciphertext only

   B. Known plaintext

   C. Chosen ciphertext

   D. Replay

   ☑ **B.** There is definitely some room for argument on this question: Who's to say all the files were encrypted in the same way? However, of the options presented, known plaintext is the one that makes the most sense. In this attack, the hacker has both plaintext and ciphertext messages. Plaintext copies are scanned for repeatable sequences, which are then compared to the ciphertext versions. Over time, and with effort, this can be used to decipher the key.

   ☒ **A** is incorrect, but just barely so. I'm certain some of you are arguing that a ciphertext-only attack could also be used here, because in that attack several messages encrypted in the same way are run through statistical analysis to eventually reveal repeating code, which may be used to decode messages later on. Sure, an attacker might just ignore the plaintext copy in there, but the inference in the question is that he'd use both. You'll often see questions like this where you'll need to take into account the inference without overthinking the question.

⌧ **C** is incorrect because chosen ciphertext works almost exactly like a ciphertext-only attack. Statistical analysis without a plaintext version for comparison can be performed, but it's only for *portions* of gained ciphertext. That's the key word to look for.

⌧ **D** is incorrect because it's irrelevant to this scenario. Replay attacks catch streams of data and replay them to the intended recipient from another sender.

9. You are discussing a steganography tool that takes advantage of the nature of "white space" to conceal information. Which tool are you discussing?

   A. Snow

   B. GifShuffle

   C. White Wipe

   D. Tripwire

☑ **A.** Snow is one of the steganography tools the CEH exam covers. The following is from the Snow website: "The program snow is used to conceal messages in ASCII text by appending whitespace to the end of lines. Because spaces and tabs are generally not visible in text viewers, the message is effectively hidden from casual observers. And if the built-in encryption is used, the message cannot be read even if it is detected."

⌧ **B** is incorrect because GifShuffle is used to conceal messages in GIF images by shuffling bits in the color map. Because these changes are minutely small, GifShuffle leaves the image visibly unchanged. It's also an open source tool.

⌧ **C** is incorrect because White Wipe is not a steganography tool. In fact, as far as I know, it's not a tool at all. This is simply a distractor answer.

⌧ **D** is incorrect because Tripwire is not a steganography tool either. Rather, it's a conglomeration of tool actions that perform the overall IT security efforts for an enterprise. It provides for integrity checks, regulatory compliance, configuration management, and all other sorts of goodies.

10. At the basic core of encryption approaches, two main methods are in play: substitution and transposition. Which of the following best describes transposition?

    A. Bits are replaced with a different value.

    B. Bits are removed.

    C. The order of bits is changed.

    D. The parity bits are changed.

☑ **C.** This is just a different way of asking you to define substitution and transposition. Substitution is exactly what it sounds like. Transposition doesn't substitute at all; it changes the bit order altogether.

☒ **A** is incorrect because this is the definition for substitution. Substitution is exactly what it sounds like—bits are simply replaced by other bits.

☒ **B** is incorrect because bits aren't technically removed with either function. They may be replaced, or reordered, but they are not removed.

☒ **D** is incorrect because this answer has nothing, really, to do with encryption. *Parity bits* sounds sexy and exciting, but it's meaningless in this context. Parity bits are used for basic error correction, not encryption.

11. Jack and Jill work in an organization that has a PKI system in place for securing messaging. Jack encrypts a message for Jill and sends it on. Jill receives the message and decrypts it. Within a PKI system, which of the following statements is true?

    A. Jack encrypts with his private key. Jill decrypts with her private key.
    B. Jack encrypts with his public key. Jill decrypts with her public key.
    C. Jack encrypts with Jill's private key. Jill decrypts with her public key.
    D. Jack encrypts with Jill's public key. Jill decrypts with her private key.

    ☑ **D.** When it comes to PKI encryption questions, remember the golden rule: Encrypt with public, decrypt with private. In this instance, Jack wants to send a message to Jill. He will use Jill's public key—which everyone can get—to encrypt the message, knowing that only Jill, with her corresponding private key, can decrypt it.

    ☒ **A** is incorrect because you do not encrypt with a private key in a PKI system. Yes, you *can* encrypt with it, but what would be the point? Anyone with your public key—which everyone has—could decrypt it! Remember, private = decrypt, public = encrypt.

    ☒ **B** is incorrect because, in this case, Jack has gotten his end of the bargain correct, but Jill doesn't seem to know what she's doing. PKI encryption is done in key pairs—what one key encrypts, the other decrypts. So her use of her own public key to decrypt something encrypted with Jack's key—a key from a completely different pair—is baffling.

    ☒ **C** is incorrect because there is no way Jack should have anyone's private key, other than his own. That's kind of the point of a private key—you keep it to yourself and don't share it with anyone. As a note here, the stated steps would actually work—that is, one key encrypts, so the other decrypts—but it's completely backward for how the system is supposed to work. An abomination to security, if you will.

12. Which of the following would you find in an X.509 digital certificate? (Choose all that apply.)

   A. Version

   B. Algorithm ID

   C. Private key

   D. Public key

   E. Key usage

   F. PTR record

   ☑ **A, B, D, and E.** You are definitely going to need to know the digital certificate and what it contains. A *digital certificate* is an electronic file that is used to verify a user's identity, providing nonrepudiation throughout the system. The certificate contains standard fields used for specific purposes. Those fields are Version, Serial Number, Subject, Algorithm ID (or Signature Algorithm), Issuer, Valid From and Valid To, Key Usage, Subject's Public Key, and Optional.

   ☒ **C** is incorrect because a private key is never shared. The certificate usually is "signed" with an encrypted hash by the private key, but the key itself is never shared.

   ☒ **F** is incorrect because a PTR record is a part of the Domain Name System (DNS), not a digital certificate. A PTR record provides a reverse DNS lookup as a pointer to a canonical name.

13. Which of the following is a secure substitute for telnet?

   A. SHA-1

   B. RSA

   C. SSL

   D. SSH

   ☑ **D.** Secure Shell (SSH) was created to fill a security need. Telnet provides easy administrative access, but it's in the clear and ripe for theft. SSH performs the same functions—providing a channel for command execution and remote logging—but does so in a secured method, over a secured channel with strong authentication. As an aside, telnet can do lots of things SSH cannot (providing some marginal interaction with generic TCP services, serving as a poor hacker's web browser and so on). Therefore, SSH is to be thought of as a secure alternative to telnet, not a replacement.

   ☒ **A** is incorrect because SHA-1 is a hashing algorithm, not a means for encrypting a channel for communication exchange. It was published by NIST (National Institute of Standards and Technology) as a better, stronger hash alternative, and is now in its third cycle of development (SHA-2 and SHA-3 have been released).

☒ **B** is incorrect because RSA is an encryption algorithm, achieving strong encryption through the use of two large prime numbers. Factoring these numbers creates key sizes up to 4,096 bits. RSA can be used for encryption and digital signatures and is the modern de facto standard.

☒ **C** is incorrect because SSL is an application layer protocol for managing security on Internet message transit. It uses RSA asymmetric encryption to encrypt data transferred over its connection.

14. An SSL session requires a client and a server to handshake information between each other and agree on a secured channel. Which of the following best describes the session key creation during the setup of an SSL session?

   A. The server creates the key after verifying the client's identity.

   B. The server creates the key immediately on the client connection.

   C. The client creates the key using the server's public key.

   D. The client creates the key after verifying the server's identity.

   ☑ **D.** In the CEH world, SSL has six major steps (others claim seven or more, but we're studying for the CEH certification here, so we'll stick with theirs). The six steps are (1) Client hello, (2) Server hello and certificate, (3) Server hello done message, (4) Client verifies server identity and sends Client Key Exchange message, (5) Client sends Change Cipher Spec and Finish message, and (6) Server responds with Change Cipher Spec and Finish message. The session key is created by the client after it verifies the server identity (using the certificate provided in step 2).

   ☒ **A** is incorrect because the server does not create the session key.

   ☒ **B** is incorrect for the same reason—the client creates the key, not the server.

   ☒ **C** is incorrect because the client does not use a "public key" for an SSL session. It's a great distractor, trying to confuse you with PKI terms in an SSL question.

15. Which encryption algorithm uses variable block sizes (from 32 to 128 bits)?

   A. SHA-1

   B. RC5

   C. 3DES

   D. AES

   ☑ **B.** Questions on identifying encryption algorithms really come down to memorization of some key terms. Rivest Cipher (RC) encompasses several versions, from RC2 through RC6. It is an asymmetric block cipher that uses a variable key length up to 2,040 bits. RC6, the latest version, uses 128-bit blocks, whereas RC5 uses variable block sizes (32, 64, or 128).

☒ **A** is incorrect because SHA-1 is a hash algorithm, not an encryption algorithm. If this question were about verifying integrity, this would be a good choice. However, in this case, it is a distractor.

☒ **C** is incorrect because although 3DES is a symmetric block cipher, it does not use variable block sizes. 3DES (called *triple* DES) uses a 168-bit key and can use up to three keys in a multiple-encryption method. It's much more effective than DES, but is much slower.

☒ **D** is incorrect because AES, another symmetric block cipher, uses key lengths of 128, 192, or 256 bits. It effectively replaces DES and is much faster than either DES or its triplicate cousin (3DES).

16. Which hash algorithm was developed by the NSA and produces output values up to 512 bits?

   A. MD5

   B. SHA-1

   C. SHA-2

   D. SSL

☑ **C.** Both SHA-1 and SHA-2 were developed by the NSA; however, SHA-1 only produced a 160-bit output value. SHA-2 was developed to rectify the shortcomings of its predecessor and is capable of producing outputs of 224, 256, 384, and 512 bits. Although it was designed as a replacement for SHA-1 (which was supposed to have been phased out in 2010), SHA-2 is still not as widely used.

☒ **A** is incorrect because MD5 produces 128-bit output. It was created by Ronald Rivest for ensuring file integrity; however, serious flaws in the algorithm, and the advancement of other hashes, have resulted in this hash being rendered obsolete (U.S. CERT, August 2010). Despite this, you'll find MD5 is still used for file verification on downloads and, in many cases, to store passwords.

☒ **B** is incorrect because SHA-1 produces a 160-bit value output. It was created by NSA and used to be required by law for use in U.S. Government applications. However, serious flaws became apparent in late 2005, and the U.S. Government began recommending the replacement of SHA-1 with SHA-2 after 2010 (see FIPS PUB 180-1).

☒ **D** is incorrect because SSL isn't even a hash algorithm. If you picked this one, you have some serious studying to do.

17. A hacker is attempting to uncover the key used in a cryptographic encryption scheme. Which attack vector is the most resource intensive and usually takes the longest amount of time?

   A. Social engineering

   B. Known plaintext

   C. Frequency analysis

   D. Brute force

   ☑ **D.** I know you probably weren't expecting a brute force definition to show up so early, but sometimes this exam will throw terms in and out of objectives to see if you're paying attention. Brute force attacks—whether attempting to crack a password or, in this case, to determine a key used in cryptography—are the longest and most resource intensive. If you think about what the attack is doing, this makes perfect sense. Although, eventually, every brute force attack will be successful, the length of the key can make the length of time necessary to go through all possible iterations unacceptable. For example, if it takes your supercomputer 12 years to crack an algorithm key, it's probably a safe bet that the target has changed it within that timespan.

   ☒ **A** is incorrect because social engineering requires little to no resources at all, and given the right individual on the phone (or sitting behind a desk), it could be pretty quick. Granted, this is a ridiculous answer here—who is actually going to hand over a cryptographic key to someone—but stranger things have happened.

   ☒ **B** is incorrect because known plaintext takes at least some of the time-crunching out for you. Remember in this attack that the hacker has both plaintext and ciphertext messages. Plaintext copies are scanned for repeatable sequences, which are then compared to the ciphertext versions. Over time, and with effort, this can be used to decipher the key; however, it is not as resource intensive as brute force.

   ☒ **C** is incorrect because, although this answer sounds really cool, it doesn't fit with the question criteria (time and resource intensive). Frequency analysis relies on the fact that, in any given sample of English writing, there will be certain letters (and combinations of letters) that occur with more frequency than others. This kind of attack appeals to the math geeks in our field—and to those who tech-edit hacking books.

18. In a discussion on symmetric encryption, a friend mentions that one of the drawbacks with this system is scalability. He goes on to say that for every person you add to the mix, the number of keys goes up exponentially. If seven people are in a symmetric encryption pool, how many keys are necessary?

A. 7

B. 14

C. 21

D. 28

☑ **C.** Symmetric encryption is really fast and works great with bulk encryption; however, scalability and key exchange are huge drawbacks. To determine the number of keys you need, use the formula N (N – 1) / 2. Plugging in the number 7 into this, we have 7 (7 – 1) / 2 = 21.

☒ **A** is incorrect because although symmetric key does use the same key for encryption and decryption, each new node requires a different key. Seven keys simply isn't enough.

☒ **B** is incorrect because 14 keys isn't enough.

☒ **D** is incorrect because 28 keys is too many. Stick with the formula N (N – 1) / 2.

19. Which of the following is a true statement?

A. Symmetric encryption scales easily and provides for nonrepudiation.

B. Symmetric encryption does not scale easily and does not provide for nonrepudiation.

C. Symmetric encryption is not suited for bulk encryption.

D. Symmetric encryption is slower than asymmetric encryption.

☑ **B.** Symmetric encryption has always been known for strength and speed; however, scalability and key exchange are big drawbacks. Additionally, there is no way to provide for nonrepudiation (within the confines of the encryption system). Symmetric encryption is good for a great many things when you don't want all the overhead of key management.

☒ **A** is incorrect because symmetric encryption does not scale easily and does not provide for nonrepudiation. The single key used for each channel makes scalability an issue. Remember, the formula for number of keys is N (N – 1) / 2.

☒ **C** is incorrect because symmetric encryption is perfectly designed for bulk encryption. Assuming you can find a way to ensure the key exchange is protected, speed makes this the best choice.

☒ **D** is incorrect because one of the benefits of symmetric encryption is its speed. It is much faster than asymmetric encryption, but doesn't provide some of the benefits asymmetric provides us (scalability, nonrepudiation, and so on).

20. The PKI system you are auditing has a Certificate Authority (CA) at the top that creates and issues certificates. Users trust each other based on the CA itself. Which trust model is in use here?

A. Standalone CA

B. Web of Trust

C. Single Authority

D. Hierarchical Trust

☑ C. Trust models within PKI systems provide a standardized method for certificate and key exchanges. The valid trust models include Web of Trust, Single Authority, and Hierarchical. The Single Authority system has a CA at the top that creates and issues certs. Users then trust each other based on the CA at the top vouching for them. Assuming a Single Authority model is used, it's of vital importance to protect it. After all, if it is compromised, your whole system is kaput.

☒ A is incorrect because "Standalone CA" doesn't refer to a trust model. It instead defines a single CA that is usually set up as a Trusted Offline Root in a hierarchy, or when extranets and the Internet are involved.

☒ B is incorrect because Web of Trust refers to a model where users create and manage their own certificates and key exchange and multiple entities sign certificates for one another. In other words, users within this system trust each other based on certificates they receive from other users on the same system.

☒ D is incorrect because although a Hierarchical Trust system also has a CA at the top (which is known as the *root CA)*, it makes use of one or more inter-mediate CAs underneath it—known as *RAs*—to issue and manage certifi-cates. This system is the most secure because users can track the certificate back to the root to ensure authenticity without a single point of failure.

21. A portion of a digital certificate is shown here:

```
Version                    V3
Serial Number              26 43 03 62 e9 6b 39 a4 9e 15 00 c7 cc 21 a2 20
Signature Algorithm        sha1RSA
Signature Hash Algorithm   sha1
Issuer                     VeriSign Class 3 Secure Server
Valid From                 Monday, October 17, 2011 8:00 PM
Valid To                   Wednesday, ⊠October ⊠17, ⊠2012 7:59:59 PM
...
Public Key                 RSA (2048)
...
```

Which of the following statements is true?

A. The hash created for the digital signature holds 160 bits.

B. The hash created for the digital signature holds 2,048 bits.

C. RSA is the hash algorithm used for the digital signature.

D. This certificate contains a private key.

☑ **A.** Questions on the digital certificate are usually easy enough, and this is no exception. The algorithm used to create the hash is clearly defined (Signature Hash Algorithm) as SHA-1 and, as we already know, SHA-1 creates a 160-bit hash output. This will then be encrypted by the sender's private key and decrypted on the recipient's end with the public key, thus verifying identity.

☒ **B** is incorrect as a distractor, because the RSA key size of 2,048 is listed in the Public Key section of the certificate.

☒ **C** incorrect because RSA is not a hash algorithm. It is, without doubt, used as an encryption algorithm with this certificate (and uses a 2,048-bit key to do so), but does not hash anything.

☒ **D** is incorrect because (as I'm certain you are already aware) a private key is *never* shared. The public key is contained for recipients to use if they wish to encrypt something to send back to the originator, but the private key is never shared.

22. Two bit strings are run through an XOR operation. Which of the following is a true statement for each bit pair regarding this function?

   A. If the first value is 0 and the second value is 1, then the output is 0.

   B. If the first value is 1 and the second value is 0, then the output is 0.

   C. If the first value is 0 and the second value is 0, then the output is 1.

   D. If the first value is 1 and the second value is 1, then the output is 0.

☑ **D.** An XOR operation requires two inputs, and in the case of encryption algorithms, this would be the data bits and the key bits. Each bit is fed into the operation—one from the data, the next from the key—and then XOR makes a determination: If the bits match, the output is 0; if they don't, it's 1.

☒ **A** is incorrect because the two values being compared are different; therefore, the output would be 1.

☒ **B** is incorrect because the two values being compared are different; therefore, the output would be 1.

☒ **C** is incorrect because the two values being compared are the same; therefore, the output should be 0.

23. Which of the following attacks attempts to re-send a portion of a cryptographic exchange in hopes of setting up a communications channel?

   A. Known plaintext

   B. Chosen plaintext

   C. Man in the middle

   D. Replay

☑ **D.** Replay attacks are most often performed within the context of a man-in-the-middle attack and not necessarily just for comm channel setup: They're also used for DoS attacks against a system, to feed bad data in hope of corrupting a system, to try to overflow a buffer (send more encrypted data than expected), and so on. The hacker repeats a portion of a cryptographic exchange in hopes of fooling the system into setting up a communications channel. The attacker doesn't really have to know the actual data (such as the password) being exchanged; he just has to get the timing right in copying and then replaying the bit stream. Session tokens can be used in the communications process to combat this attack.

☒ **A** is incorrect because known plaintext doesn't really have anything to do with this scenario. Known plaintext refers to having both plaintext and corresponding ciphertext messages, which are scanned for repeatable sequences and then compared to the ciphertext versions.

☒ **B** is incorrect for the same reason as **A**: This answer simply doesn't apply to this scenario. In a chosen plaintext attack, a hacker puts several encrypted messages through statistical analysis to determine repeating code.

☒ **C** is incorrect because, in this instance, replay refers to the attack being described in the question, not man in the middle. I know you think this is confusing, and I do understand. However, this is an example of CEH word-play you'll need to be familiar with. Man in the middle is usually listed as an attack by every security guide; however, within the context of the exam, it may also refer solely to where the attacker has positioned himself. From this location, he can launch a variety of attacks—replay being one of them.

24. Within a PKI system, which of the following is an accurate statement?

A. Bill can be sure a message came from Sue by using his public key to decrypt it.

B. Bill can be sure a message came from Sue by using his private key to decrypt it.

C. Bill can be sure a message came from Sue by using her private key to decrypt the digital signature.

D. Bill can be sure a message came from Sue by using her public key to decrypt the digital signature.

☑ **D.** Remember, a digital signature is a hash value that is encrypted with the user's private key. Because the corresponding public key can decrypt it, this provides the nonrepudiation feature we're looking for. This is the only instance on the exam where the private key is used for encryption. In general, public encrypts, private decrypts.

☒ **A** is incorrect because not only does this have nothing to do with proving identity, but it also cannot work. Bill can't use his own public key to decrypt a message sent to him. The keys work in pairs—if the message is encrypted with his public key, only his private key can decrypt it.

⊠ **B** is incorrect because this has nothing to do with proving Sue's identity. Sure, Bill will be using his own private key to decrypt messages sent to him by other users; however, it doesn't provide any help in proving identity.

⊠ **C** is incorrect because there is no way Bill should have Sue's private key. Remember, private keys are not shared with anyone, for any reason. This is why encrypting a hash with it works so well for the digital signing process.

25. One use of hash algorithms is for the secure storage of passwords: The password is run through a one-way hash, and the value is stored instead of the plaintext version. If a hacker gains access to these hash values, and knows the hash algorithm used to create them, which of the following could be used to speed up his effort in cracking them?

   A. Salt
   B. Rainbow tables
   C. Steganography
   D. Collision

   ☑ **B.** Rainbow tables are the result of a lot of effort in putting all known combinations of plaintext entries into a hash, one at a time, and capturing the hash value that's created. Then, instead of having to brute force your way in and spending countless computational cycles, you can simply compare the hash value you stole from the password file to the rainbow table—once you find a match, *voilà*!

   ⊠ **A** is incorrect because a salt is used to increase security on a password hash, not to crack it. A *salt* is a collection of random bits used as a key in addition to the hashing algorithm. Because the bits, and length, are random, a good salt makes a collision attack very difficult to pull off.

   ⊠ **C** is incorrect because steganography simply makes no sense here. *Steganography* involves hiding messages inside another medium—for example, hiding a message inside a .jpg file.

   ⊠ **D** is incorrect because although the entire effort is in finding the correct collision to unlock the plaintext version, the collision itself isn't an effort to speed things up.

Reconnaissance: Information Gathering for the Ethical Hacker

This chapter includes questions from the following topics:

- Defining footprinting
- Describing information-gathering methodology
- Understanding the use of whois, ARIN, and nslookup
- Describing DNS record types
- Defining and describing Google hacking
- Using Google hacking

A friend of mine invited me to go "offshore" kayak fishing with him a couple weeks back. By *offshore*, he meant launching from the beach right down the road from my house and paddling out less than a mile. Some great fishing can be found right off the reef out there, and I almost immediately said yes. However, considering this was in the middle of *Shark Week* on the Discovery Channel and I had just watched a guy get torn in half by a giant great white, I thought I'd do some research first.

I looked into news reports online referencing any shark attacks in my local area. I then checked the local fishing magazines for anything shark and kayak related. I even went around asking other fishermen about it, and from all sources I got almost all positive remarks. I then spent time researching baits, fishing methods, and protective measures right outside the surf zone. Sure, I read the story of a spear-fisherman who had seen what appeared to be a great white a few dozen miles south of here, and the story about the bonito being ripped from the kayaker's hand by a larger blacktip, but all my reconnaissance in preparing to attack the reef for larger fish told me it was a relatively safe trip. And once I get the courage to actually go do it, I'll let you know how it goes.

In the meantime, this chapter is also all about reconnaissance and footprinting—the methods and tools for gathering information about your targets before you even try to attack them.

STUDY TIPS Tons of questions come from this particular segment of hacking, mainly because it's so important to gather good intelligence before starting to attack. Make sure you spend lots of time getting very familiar with DNS, and by all means start practicing your Google hacking right now—you'll definitely need it. Most Google hacking questions require you to know exact syntax, so be very careful in your study and practice.

1. The result of a "whois" search on a target is listed here:

```
Registrant:
        AnyBusiness Inc.
        1377 somewhere street
New York, NY 10013
        US
Phone: +13219667786
        Email: noemailhere@anybus.com

    Domain Name: anybusiness.com
        Created on.............: Mon, Jul 07, 1997
        Expires on.............: Sat, Jul 06, 2013
        Record last updated on..: Mon, Jul 02, 2012

    Administrative Contact:
    anybusiness.com
    P. O. Box 8799 615 N. Riverside Dr
    Somewhere, FL 32903
    US
    Phone: +1.3215550587
    Email: admin@anybus.com

    Technical  Contact:
    Mark Sensei
    187 Someplace drive
    Indialantic, FL 32903
    US
    Phone: +1.3215550879
    Email: M.sensei@gmail.com

DNS Servers:
    ns2.anybus.com
    ns1.anybus.com
```

Which of the following is a true statement regarding this output?

A. Anybusiness.com was registered using GoDaddy.com.

B. The technical contact for this website may have entered personal information at registration.

C. There is no information within this output useful for a zone transfer.

D. The administrative and technical contacts are the same.

2. Your client's business is headquartered in Japan. Which regional registry would be the best place to look for footprinting information?

A. APNIC

B. RIPE

C. ASIANIC

D. ARIN

E. LACNIC

3. Which of the following are footprinting tools? (Choose all that apply.)

   A. Sam Spade

   B. Nslookup

   C. Traceroute

   D. NetCraft

   E. Nessus

4. You are looking for files with the terms "Apache" and "Version" in their titles. Which Google hack is the appropriate one?

   A. inurl:apacheinurl:version

   B. allintitle:apache version

   C. intitle:apacheinurl:version

   D. allinurl:apache version

5. You've just kicked off a penetration test against a target organization and have decided to perform a little passive footprinting. One of the first sites you visit are job boards, where the company has listed various openings. What is the primary useful footprinting information to be gained through this particular search?

   A. Insight into the HR processes of the company

   B. Insight into the operating systems, hardware, and applications in use

   C. Insight into corporate security policy

   D. None of the above

6. Which of the following activities is not considered passive footprinting?

   A. Dumpster diving

   B. Reviewing financial sites for company information

   C. Clicking links within the company's public website

   D. Calling the company's help desk line

7. As fate would have it, you are contracted to pen test an organization you are already familiar with. You start your passive reconnaissance by perusing the company website. Several months ago, the public-facing website had a listing of all staff members, including phone numbers, e-mail addresses, and other useful information. Since that time, the listing has been removed from the website. Which of the following is the best option to provide access to the listing?

   A. Use a tool such as BlackWidow or Wget.

   B. Perform Google hack incache:staff.

   C. Use whois to discover the information.

   D. Use Google Cache.

   E. Use www.archive.org.

8. You are footprinting information for a pen test. Social engineering is part of your reconnaissance efforts, and some of it will be active in nature. You take steps to ensure that if the social engineering efforts are discovered at this early stage, any trace efforts point to another organization. Which of the following terms best describes what you are participating in?

   A. Anonymous footprinting

   B. Pseudonymous footprinting

   C. Passive footprinting

   D. Redirective footprinting

9. You are setting up DNS for your enterprise. Server A is both a web server and an FTP server. You wish to advertise both services for this machine. Which DNS record type would you use to accomplish this?

   A. CNAME

   B. SOA

   C. MX

   D. PTR

   E. NS

10. You are shoulder-surfing one of your team members. You see him type in the following:

```
nslookup
>server 202.27.55.64
>set type = any
>ls -d anyorg.com
```

   What is being accomplished here?

   A. He is attempting DNS poisoning.

   B. He is attempting DNS spoofing.

   C. He is attempting a zone transfer.

   D. He is resetting the DNS cache.

11. Within the DNS system, a primary server (SOA) holds and maintains all records for the zone. Secondary servers will periodically ask the primary whether there have been any updates. If updates have occurred, they will ask for a zone transfer to update their own copies. Under what conditions will a secondary name server request a zone transfer from a primary?

   A. When the primary SOA record serial number is higher that the secondary's

   B. When the secondary SOA record serial number is higher that the primary's

   C. Only when the secondary reboots or restarts services

   D. Only when manually prompted to do so

12. Examine the following SOA record:

```
@   IN  SOARTDNSRV1.somebiz.com.  postmaster.somebiz.com. (
200408097    ; serial number
                              3600        ; refresh   [1h]
                              600         ; retry     [10m]
                              86400       ; expire    [1d]
7200 )        ; min TTL    [2h]
```

If a secondary server in the enterprise is unable to check in for a zone update within an hour, what happens to the zone copy on the secondary?

A. The zone copy is dumped.

B. The zone copy is unchanged.

C. The serial number of the zone copy is decremented.

D. The serial number of the zone copy is incremented.

13. Which of the following footprinting tools uses ICMP to provide information on network pathways?

A. Whois

B. Sam Spade

C. Nmap

D. Traceroute

E. AngryIP

14. Examine the following command-line entry:

```
C:\>nslookup
   Default Server:  ns1.somewhere.com
   Address:  128.189.72.5
> set q=mx
>mailhost
```

Which two statements are true regarding this command sequence?

A. Nslookup is in noninteractive mode.

B. Nslookup is in interactive mode.

C. The output will show all mail servers in the zone somewhere.com.

D. The output will show all name servers in the zone somewhere.com.

15. Joe accesses the company website, www.anybusi.com, from his home computer and is presented with a defaced site containing disturbing images. He calls the IT department to report the website hack and is told they do not see any problem with the site: No files have been changed, and when the site is accessed from their terminals (inside the company) it appears normally. Joe connects over VPN into the company website and notices the site appears normally. Which of the following might explain the issue?

A. DNS poisoning

B. Route poisoning

C. SQL injection

D. ARP poisoning

16. One way to mitigate against DNS poisoning is to restrict or limit the amount of time records can stay in cache before they're updated. Which DNS record type allows you to set this restriction?

   A. NS

   B. PTR

   C. MX

   D. CNAME

   E. SOA

17. You are gathering reconnaissance on your target organization whose website has a .com extension. With no other information to go on, which regional Internet registry would be the best place to begin your search?

   A. ARIN

   B. APNIC

   C. LACNIC

   D. RIPE

   E. AfriNIC

18. Which of the following is a good footprinting tool for discovering information on a company's founding, history, and financial status?

   A. SpiderFoot

   B. EDGAR database

   C. Sam Spade

   D. Pipl.com

19. How does traceroute map the routes traveled by a packet?

   A. By carrying a hello packet in the payload, forcing the host to respond

   B. By using DNS queries at each hop

   C. By manipulating the time to live (TTL) parameter

   D. Using ICMP type 5, code 0 packets

20. You are footprinting a target headquartered in the Dominican Republic. You have gathered some competitive intelligence and have engaged in both passive and active reconnaissance. Your next step is to define the network range this organization uses. What is the best way to accomplish this?

   A. Call the company help desk and ask them

   B. Use the EDGAR database

   C. Use LACNIC to look up the company range

   D. Use ARIN to look up the company range

21. A zone file consists of which types of records? (Choose all that apply.)

   A. PTR

   B. MX

   C. SN

   D. SOA

   E. DNS

   F. A

   G. AX

22. Examine the following SOA record:

```
@   IN  SOARTDNSRV1.somebiz.com.  postmaster.somebiz.com. (
200408097    ; serial number
                         3600           ; refresh    [1h]
                         600            ; retry      [10m]
                         86400          ; expire     [1d]
7200 )          ; min TTL    [2h]
```

   How long will the secondary server wait before asking for an update to the zone file?

   A. One hour

   B. Two hours

   C. Ten minutes

   D. One day

23. A colleague enters the following into a Google search string:

```
intitle:intranetinurl:intranet+intext:"human resources"
```

   Which of the following statements is most correct concerning this attempt?

   A. The search engine will not respond with any result because you cannot combine Google hacks on one line.

   B. The search engine will respond with all pages having "intranet" in their title and "human resources" in the URL.

C. The search engine will respond with all pages having "intranet" in the title and in the URL.

D. The search engine will respond with only pages having "intranet" in the title and URL and with "human resources" in the text.

24. A good footprinting method is to track e-mail messages and see what kind of information you can pull back. Which tool is useful in this scenario?

   A. Nmap

   B. BlackWidow

   C. Snow

   D. eMailTrackerPro

   E. MailMan

25. You are footprinting DNS information using dig. What command syntax should be used to discover all name servers listed by DNS server 202.55.77.12 in the anybiz.com namespace?

   A. dig @www.anybiz.com NS 202.55.77.12

   B. dig NS @www.anybiz.com 202.55.77.12

   C. dig NS @202.55.77.12 www.anybiz.com

   D. dig @202.55.77.12 www.anybiz.com NS

1. B
2. A
3. A, B, C, D
4. B
5. B
6. D
7. E
8. B
9. A
10. C
11. A
12. B
13. D
14. B, C
15. A
16. E
17. A
18. B
19. C
20. C
21. A, B, D, F
22. A
23. D
24. D
25. D

1. The result of a "whois" search on a target is listed here:

```
Registrant:
        AnyBusiness Inc.
        1377 somewhere street
New York, NY 10013
        US
Phone: +13219667786
        Email: noemailhere@anybus.com

    Domain Name: anybusiness.com
        Created on..............: Mon, Jul 07, 1997
        Expires on..............: Sat, Jul 06, 2013
        Record last updated on..: Mon, Jul 02, 2012

    Administrative Contact:
        anybusiness.com
        P. O. Box 8799
Somewhere, FL 32937
        US
        Phone: +1.3215550587
        Email: admin@anybus.com

    Technical  Contact:
        Mark Sensei
        187 Someplace drive
        Thistown, FL 32903
        US
        Phone: +1.3212970879
        Email: M.sensei@gmail.com

DNS Servers:
        ns2.anybus.com
        ns1.anybus.com
```

Which of the following is a true statement regarding this output?

A. Anybusiness.com was registered using GoDaddy.com.

B. The technical contact for this website may have entered personal information at registration.

C. There is no information within this output useful for a zone transfer.

D. The administrative and technical contacts are the same.

☑ B. The Technical Contact listing displays the technical contact's name as well as what may be their personal phone number. The address? Probably where they work, but you never know. This could turn out to be nothing, but it might provide you with an "in" for social engineering efforts later.

☒ A is incorrect because the registrant is clearly listed as anybusiness.com. You'll find these whois searches to be hit and miss sometimes. Every once in a while you'll find tons of information. Other times, it's bare-bones basics.

Had this site been registered with GoDaddy.com, it would look something like this:

```
Registrant:
    Domains By Proxy, LLC
    Registered through: GoDaddy.com, LLC (http://www.godaddy.com)
    Domain Name: anybusiness.COM
```

☒ **C** is incorrect because the target's DNS servers are listed right at the bottom. If you're going to pull a zone transfer, you'll need to know the DNS servers holding the proper information.

☒ **D** is incorrect because these two contacts are clearly different. The administrative contact is listed as a business name (smart idea). The technical contact, however, may be personal in nature.

2. Your client's business is headquartered in Japan. Which regional registry would be the best place to look for footprinting information?

   A. APNIC

   B. RIPE

   C. ASIANIC

   D. ARIN

   E. LACNIC

☑ **A.** This one is easy as pie, and should be a freebie if you see it on the test. Five regional Internet registries provide overall management of public IP address space within a given geographic region. APNIC handles the Asia and Pacific realms.

☒ **B** is incorrect because RIPE handles Europe, Middle East, and parts of Central Asia/Northern Africa. If you're wondering, the name is French and stands for Réseaux IP Européens.

☒ **C** is incorrect because ASIANIC is not a regional registry. It's purely a distractor in this case.

☒ **D** is incorrect because the ARIN service region includes Canada, many Caribbean and North Atlantic islands, and the United States. Caribbean islands falling under ARIN include Puerto Rico, the Bahamas, Antigua, American and British Virgin Islands, Turks and Caicos Islands, and the Cayman Islands (among others).

☒ **E** is incorrect because LACNIC handles Latin America and some of the Caribbean. It stands for Latin America and Caribbean Network Information Center. LACNIC coverage includes most of South America, Guatemala, French Guiana, the Dominican Republic, and Cuba (among others). This one and ARIN most often get confused.

3. Which of the following are footprinting tools? (Choose all that apply.)

   A. Sam Spade

   B. Nslookup

   C. Traceroute

   D. NetCraft

   E. Nessus

   ☑ **A, B, C,** and **D.** Although Sam Spade is, for all intents and purposes, defunct, it's still listed as a DNS footprinting tool within the CEH exam. Nslookup is a command that's part of virtually every operating system in the world, and provides a means to query DNS servers for information. NetCraft is one of those neat little tools to help you find *internal* links within a site, which may provide information on employees and business partners. Traceroute (syntax on Windows systems is *tracert host name*) is a command-line tool that tracks a packet across the Internet and provides a route path and transit times. Speaking of traceroute, it's important for you to remember that the Windows and Linux versions are different animals. The Windows version is ICMP based, whereas the Linux/UNIX version is, by default, a UDP-based tool that manipulates TTL to elicit an ICMP response. This makes the Linux/UNIX version a valuable tool in trying to get into places that might block all external-to-internal ICMP.

   ☒ **E** is incorrect because Nessus isn't considered a part of footprinting, per se. It is an integral part of vulnerability management, but we're not talking about finding a vulnerability on the target you've already footprinted and enumerated in this scenario. That comes much later in the phases of hacking. Don't confuse vulnerability research (gaining knowledge on what vulnerabilities exist by using hackerstorm, secunia, and so on) with footprinting tools. Yes, you need to keep up to speed with what vulnerabilities are present in the networking world, but using Nessus to discover which ones are present on a particular machine isn't footprinting.

4. You are looking for files with the terms "Apache" and "Version" in their titles. Which Google hack is the appropriate one?

   A. inurl:apacheinurl:version

   B. allintitle:apache version

   C. intitle:apacheinurl:version

   D. allinurl:apache version

   ☑ **B.** The Google search operator *allintitle* searches for pages that contain the string, or strings, you specify. It also allows for the combination of strings in the title, so you can search for more than one term within the title of a page.

☒ **A** is incorrect because the operator *inurl* only looks in the URL of the site, not the page title. In this example, the search might bring you to a page such as http://anyplace.com/apache_Version/pdfs.html.

☒ **C** is incorrect because the *apacheinurl* operator doesn't exist. The legitimate operator for searching in a URL would be *"inurl"*. Yes, you can combine operators, but the two used here just won't get the job done—even if the correct version of URL lookup was used.

☒ **D** is incorrect because *allinurl* does not look at page titles—it's only concerned with the URL itself. As with the title searches, the allinurl operator allows you to combine search strings.

5. You've just kicked off a penetration test against a target organization and have decided to perform a little passive footprinting. One of the first sites you visit are job boards, where the company has listed various openings. What is the primary useful footprinting information to be gained through this particular search?

   A. Insight into the HR processes of the company

   B. Insight into the operating systems, hardware, and applications in use

   C. Insight into corporate security policy

   D. None of the above

   ☑ **B.** Jobs boards are great sources of information. You probably wouldn't get much of a response if you called the business up and said, "Hi! I'll be attempting a hack into your network. Would you be so kind as to tell me your server infrastructure and whether you're using Microsoft Exchange for your e-mail?" However, go out to a job board, and the listing will provide all that information for you anyway. If they're asking for system administrator experience on Linux RHEL 8, you're already ahead of the game. Job postings list the set of skills, technical knowledge, and system experience required, so why not use them in preparation?

   ☒ **A** is incorrect because although the HR processes may be useable in a long-term attack—for social engineering purposes—you're probably not going to get too much actual policy/process information here. And, frankly, that's not what you'd be looking for.

   ☒ **C** is incorrect because corporate security policy information simply isn't provided in a job listing. If it is, they've got serious problems a pen test isn't going to fix.

   ☒ **D** is incorrect because ignoring job listings as part of your reconnaissance efforts is folly. Why ignore such a gold mine of easily obtainable information? Depending on how deeply they go into describing job duties and knowledge requirement, you might be able to build a pretty good picture of your attack before you even leave the living room (or wherever you do your recon from).

6. Which of the following activities is not considered passive footprinting?

    A. Dumpster diving

    B. Reviewing financial sites for company information

    C. Clicking links within the company's public website

    D. Calling the company's help desk line

    ☑ **D.** So this one may be a little tricky, but it's really pretty easy when you think about it. Remember, active and passive footprinting can be defined by two things: what you touch and how much discovery risk you put yourself in. Social engineering in and of itself is not all passive or active in nature. Dumpster diving, for example, is considered passive. Pick up a phone and call someone inside the company, or talk to people in the parking lot, however, and you've exposed yourself to discovery and are now practicing active footprinting.

    ☒ **A** is incorrect because digging through the trash for useful information is passive footprinting defined: According to the EC Council and this exam, your discovery risk is negligible and you're not touching the company's network or personnel. Now, in the real world rummaging through someone's trash on private property with no authorization and in full view of security personnel is probably going to get you caught, and is about as passive as a Tasmanian Devil; however, for your exam, ditch your hold on the real world and please remember that dumpster diving is passive.

    ☒ **B** is incorrect because reviewing financial sites for company information is a method of gaining competitive intelligence. As you know, *competitive intelligence* refers to the information gathered by a business entity about their competitor's customers, products, and marketing. Most of this information is readily available and can be acquired through a host of different means.

    ☒ **C** is incorrect because although you are actively participating in moving around inside the company's website, you are not necessarily putting yourself at discovery risk, nor are you touching anything the company doesn't want you to. The public website is put in place for people to use, and the odds of someone picking up your click-throughs out of the thousands they receive every day are minimal. Granted, if you keep digging through their site and get deep enough (for example, you dig your way to an admin portal on a SAP site), you can, and should, be detected.

7. As fate would have it, you are contracted to pen test an organization you are already familiar with. You start your passive reconnaissance by perusing the company website. Several months ago, the public-facing website had a listing of all staff members, including phone numbers, e-mail addresses, and other useful information. Since that time, the listing has been removed from the website. Which of the following is the best option to provide access to the listing?

    A. Use a tool such as BlackWidow or Wget.

    B. Perform Google hack incache:staff.

C. Use whois to discover the information.

D. Use Google Cache.

E. Use www.archive.org.

☑ **E.** Archive.org keeps archival copies of web pages. If information relevant to your efforts was posted on the site at some point in the past but has since been updated or removed, and the change was not recent, using Archive.org is your best option.

☒ **A** is incorrect because BlackWidow and Wget are tools used to pull a full copy of the current version of the site to your machine for analysis. Sure, this provides great insight into buried links and other hidden information, but it's not going to pull any information that has been removed.

☒ **B** is incorrect because although a Google hack may be a good option to locate this information (maybe search for the company name+staff+listing and so on), it's not apropos in this scenario. The question clearly points to an archival copy of the site. Additionally, "incache" is not a Google hack operator that I'm aware of.

☒ **C** is incorrect because whois doesn't provide this type of information. If you want registration information on the site, whois is your vector, but it's not going to help in this scenario.

☒ **D** is incorrect because although Google Cache does provide an archival copy of the site, it's not a very old copy. From Goggle's description, "Google takes a snapshot of each page it examines and caches (stores) that version as a back-up. The cached version is what Google uses to judge if a page is a good match for your query." In other words, a cache of the page is taken repeatedly throughout the day, not stored for months on end.

8. You are footprinting information for a pen test. Social engineering is part of your reconnaissance efforts, and some of it will be active in nature. You take steps to ensure that if the social engineering efforts are discovered at this early stage, any trace efforts point to another organization. Which of the following terms best describes what you are participating in?

A. Anonymous footprinting

B. Pseudonymous footprinting

C. Passive footprinting

D. Redirective footprinting

☑ **B.** *Pseudonymous footprinting* is a relatively new term in the CEH realm, so you'll probably see it on your exam. It refers to obfuscating your footprinting efforts in such a way that anyone trying to trace things back to you would instead be pointed to a different person (usually to look like a competitor's business). I understand there's probably a large segment of readers (like my tech editor) screaming that this term sounds fabricated and shouldn't be here. I won't argue for or against it. All I'll say is that this term is on your exam, so you better memorize it. As a side note for those of you getting ready for a real-world job in pen testing, the scenario presented here may sound like a great idea, but you better be very, very careful in practicing it. In many ways, this could be illegal: pointing to another organization without authorization could make you liable both criminally and civilly.

☒ **A** is incorrect because *anonymous footprinting* refers to footprinting efforts that can't be traced back to you. These don't redirect a search to someone else; they're just efforts to hide your footprinting in the first place.

☒ **C** is incorrect because *passive footprinting* is generally gathering competitive intelligence and doesn't put you at risk of discovery anyway.

☒ **D** is incorrect because the term *redirective footprinting* is made up. It's here purely as a distractor.

9. You are setting up DNS for your enterprise. Server A is both a web server and an FTP server. You wish to advertise both services for this machine. Which DNS record type would you use to accomplish this?

   A. CNAME

   B. SOA

   C. MX

   D. PTR

   E. NS

☑ **A.** You know—or should know by now—that a host name can be mapped to an IP using an "A" record within DNS. CNAME records provide for aliases within the zone on that name. For instance, your server might be named mattserver1.matt.com. A sample DNS zone entry to provide HTTP and FTP access might look like this:

```
NAME                       TYPE    VALUE
-------------------------------------------------------
ftp.matt.com.              CNAME   mattserver.matt.com
www.matt.com               CNAME   mattserver.matt.com
mattserver1.matt.com.      A       202.17.77.5
```

☒ **B** is incorrect because the SOA (Start of Authority) entry identifies the primary name server for the zone. The SOA record contains the host name of the server responsible for all DNS records within the namespace, as well as the basic properties of the domain.

☒ **C** is incorrect because the MX (Mail Exchange) record identifies the e-mail servers within your domain.

☒ **D** is incorrect because a PTR (Pointer Record) works the opposite of an A record. The pointer maps an IP address to a host name, and is generally used for reverse lookups.

☒ **E** is incorrect because an NS (Name Server) record shows the name servers within your zone. These servers are the ones that respond to your client's requests for name resolution.

10. You are shoulder-surfing one of your team members. You see him type in the following:

```
nslookup
>server 202.27.55.64
>set type = any
>ls -d anyorg.com
```

What is being accomplished here?

A. He is attempted DNS poisoning.

B. He is attempting DNS spoofing.

C. He is attempting a zone transfer.

D. He is resetting the DNS cache.

☑ **C.** DNS records are maintained and managed by the authoritative server for your namespace (the SOA), which shares them with your other DNS servers (name servers) so your clients can perform lookups and name resolutions. The process of replicating all these records is known as a *zone transfer*. Nslookup is a really cool tool that lets you peruse the DNS system, and to sometimes ask for a zone transfer to you—even though you're not a name server within the zone. This effectively gives you a map of the network. A quick note, to dash the hopes of those who think this stuff is going to be super easy: Zone transfers are rarely, if ever, successful from outside of an organization. Also, there has been at least one court case where the judge ruled that a zone transfer constituted hacking. So although nslookup can be used for all sorts of things, including sometimes asking a server for a zone transfer, don't sit at home and try it on a whim—you may find yourself in hot water.

☒ **A** is incorrect because DNS poisoning is not accomplished with this command string. *DNS poisoning* refers to information introduced into a name server's cache to purposefully reroute a request. This causes the NS to return an incorrect IP address, which diverts traffic to another system—usually the hacker's machine.

☒ **B** is incorrect for the same reason. *DNS spoofing* is another term used interchangeably with DNS poisoning, although they can sometimes refer to different attacks. In general, DNS poisoning refers to server attacks—altering the cache on a name server and such—whereas DNS spoofing can refer to all sorts of shenanigans involving the clients.

☒ **D** is incorrect because there is no alteration of any records here. Your team member is simply using nslookup to ask for all records in the zone to be dumped here, so he can go through them and plan out an attack.

11. Within the DNS system, a primary server (SOA) holds and maintains all records for the zone. Secondary servers will periodically ask the primary whether there have been any updates. If updates have occurred, they will ask for a zone transfer to update their own copies. Under what conditions will a secondary name server request a zone transfer from a primary?

    A. When the primary SOA record serial number is higher that the secondary's

    B. When the secondary SOA record serial number is higher that the primary's

    C. Only when the secondary reboots or restarts services

    D. Only when manually prompted to do so

    ☑ **A.** Occasionally you'll get a question that's not necessarily hacking in nature, but more about how the DNS system works in general. The serial number on an SOA is incremented each time the zone file is changed. So, when the secondary checks in with the primary, if the serial number is higher than its own, the secondary knows there has been a change and asks for a full zone transfer.

    ☒ **B** is incorrect because the serial number increments with each change, not decrements. If the secondary checked in and the numbers were reversed— that is, the secondary had a serial number higher than the primary—it would either leave its own record unchanged or most likely dump the zone altogether.

    ☒ **C** is incorrect because a zone transfer does not occur on startup. Additionally—and this is a free test-taking tip here—any time you see the word *only* in an answer, that answer is usually wrong. In this case, that's definitely true, because the servers are configured to check in with each other on occasion to ensure the zone is consistent across the enterprise.

    ☒ **D** is incorrect because this is just a ridiculous answer. Could you imagine having to manually update every DNS server? I can think of worse jobs, but this one would definitely stink.

12. Examine the following SOA record:

```
@    IN   SOARTDNSRV1.somebiz.com.   postmaster.somebiz.com. (
200408097     ; serial number
                              3600          ; refresh   [1h]
                              600           ; retry     [10m]
                              86400         ; expire    [1d]
7200 )          ; min TTL    [2h]
```

If a secondary server in the enterprise is unable to check in for a zone update within an hour, what happens to the zone copy on the secondary?

A. The zone copy is dumped.

B. The zone copy is unchanged.

C. The serial number of the zone copy is decremented.

D. The serial number of the zone copy is incremented.

☑ **B.** You will definitely see questions about the SOA record. In this question, the key portion you're looking for is the TTL at the bottom, currently set to 2 hours (7,200 seconds). This sets the time a secondary server has to verify its records are good. If it can't check in, this Time to Live for zone records will expire, and they'll all be dumped. Considering, though, that this TTL is set to 2 hours and the question states it has only been 1 hour since the update, the zone copy on the secondary will remain unchanged.

☒ **A** is incorrect because the secondary is still well within its window for verifying the zone copy it holds. It only dumps the records when TTL is exceeded.

☒ **C** is incorrect because serial numbers are never decremented; they're always incremented. Also, the serial number of the zone copy is only changed when a connection to the primary occurs and a copy is updated.

☒ **D** is incorrect because although serial numbers are incremented upon changes (secondary copies number from the primary's copy when records are transferred), the serial number of the zone copy is only changed when a connection to the primary occurs and a copy is updated. That has not occurred in this case.

13. Which of the following footprinting tools uses ICMP to provide information on network pathways?

A. Whois

B. Sam Spade

C. Nmap

D. Traceroute

E. AngryIP

☑ **D.** Traceroute is a command-line tool that tracks a packet across the Internet and provides route path and transit times. It accomplishes this by using ICMP ECHO packets to report information on each "hop" (router) from the source to destination. The TTL on each packet increments by one after each hop is hit and, ensuring the response comes back explicitly from that hop, returns its name and IP address.

☒ **A** is incorrect because this tool doesn't work that way and isn't used for that purpose. Whois originally started in Unix, but has become ubiquitous in operating systems everywhere. It has generated any number of websites set up specifically for the purpose of gathering registration information. It queries the registries and returns all sorts of information, including domain ownership, addresses, locations, and phone numbers.

☒ **B** is incorrect because Sam Spade is a DNS enumeration tool—not a path determination.

☒ **C** is incorrect because nmap is a scanning and enumeration tool. It isn't used in the same manner as traceroute. It is one of the more widely used tools that CEH covers, so you'll need to know it very well.

☒ **E** is incorrect because although AngryIP does use ICMP, it's not used for path determination. It provides a very quick method to scan a subnet and see what hosts are "alive."

14. Examine the following command-line entry:

```
C:\>nslookup
   Default Server:  ns1.somewhere.com
   Address:  128.189.72.5
> set q=mx
>mailhost
```

Which two statements are true regarding this command sequence?

A. Nslookup is in noninteractive mode.

B. Nslookup is in interactive mode.

C. The output will show all mail servers in the zone somewhere.com.

D. The output will show all name servers in the zone somewhere.com.

☑ **B and C.** Nslookup runs in one of two modes: interactive or noninteractive. Noninteractive mode is simply the use of the command followed by an output: For example, nslookupwww.google.com will return the IP address your server can find for Google. Interactive mode is started by simply typing **nslookup** and pressing ENTER. Your default server name will display, along with its IP address, and a carrot (>) will await entry of your next command. In this scenario, we've entered interactive mode and set the type to MX, which we all know means, "Please provide me with all the mail exchange servers you know about."

☒ **A** is incorrect because we are definitely in interactive mode.

☒ **D** is incorrect because the type was set to MX, not NS.

15. Joe accesses the company website, www.anybusi.com, from his home computer and is presented with a defaced site contained disturbing images. He calls the IT department to report the website hack and is told they do not see any problem with the site: No files have been changed, and when the site is accessed from their terminals (inside the company) it appears normally. Joe connects over VPN into the company website and notices the site appears normally. Which of the following might explain the issue?

A. DNS poisoning

B. Route poisoning

C. SQL injection

D. ARP poisoning

☑ **A.** DNS poisoning makes the most sense here. Joe's connection from home uses a different DNS server for lookups than that of the business network. It's entirely possible someone has changed the cache entries in his local server to point to a different IP than the one hosting the real website—one that the hackers have set up to provide the defaced version. The fact the web files haven't changed and the site seems to be displaying just fine from inside the network also bears this out. What's more, for those of you paying close attention, in a case like this, it's important to note VPN access. If it turns out Joe's DNS modification is the only one in place, there is a strong likelihood that Joe is being specifically targeted for exploitation—something Joe should take very seriously.

☒ **B** is incorrect because route poisoning has nothing to do with this scenario. Route poisoning is used in distance vector routing protocols to prevent route loops in routing tables.

☒ **C** is incorrect because although SQL injection is indeed a hacking attack, it's not relevant here. The fact the website files remain intact and unchanged prove that access to the site through a SQL weakness isn't what occurred here.

☒ **D** is incorrect because ARP poisoning is relevant inside a particular subnet, not outside it (granted, you can have ARP forwarded by a router configured to do so, but that simply isn't the case for this question). ARP poisoning will redirect a request from one machine to another inside the same subnet, and has little to do with the scenario described here.

16. One way to mitigate against DNS poisoning is to restrict or limit the amount of time records can stay in cache before they're updated. Which DNS record type allows you to set this restriction?

A. NS

B. PTR

C. MX

D. CNAME

E. SOA

☑ **E.** The SOA record holds all sorts of information, and when it comes to DNS poisoning, the TTL is of primary interest. The shorter the TTL, the less time records are held in cache. Although it won't prevent DNS poisoning altogether, it can limit the problems a successful cache poisoning attack causes.

☒ **A** is incorrect because an NS record shows the name server(s) found in the domain.

☒ **B** is incorrect because a PTR record provides for reverse lookup capability—an IP-address-to-host-name mapping.

☒ **C** is incorrect because an MX record shows the mail exchange server(s) in the zone.

☒ **D** is incorrect because a CNAME record is used to provide alias entries for your zone (usually for multiple services or sites on one IP address).

17. You are gathering reconnaissance on your target organization whose website has a .com extension. With no other information to go on, which regional Internet registry would be the best place to begin your search?

   A. ARIN

   B. APNIC

   C. LACNIC

   D. RIPE

   E. AfriNIC

☑ **A.** I knew as soon as I typed this that it would be the one question in this chapter you would all lose your minds over. And trust me, I do understand it may seem totally without merit. But I promise you it's legitimate. Most (not all, but *most*) .com registries occur in North America. For loads of reasons, registrations from other areas of the world tend to use their country designator. Because this one is a .com, we can reasonably assume it was registered in North America and, as we all know, ARIN takes care of registries for North America. In some instances a site will show "com.au" or something similar, but the country designator should be a dead giveaway in such as case. In short, .com without the country designator is ARIN controlled.

☒ **B** is incorrect because APNIC handles registries for Asia and Pacific areas.

☒ **C** is incorrect because LACNIC handles registries for Latin America and some of the Caribbean.

☒ **D** is incorrect because RIPE handles registries for Europe (and some of central Asia).

☒ **E** is incorrect because AfriNIC handles registries for Africa.

18. Which of the following is a good footprinting tool for discovering information on a company's founding, history, and financial status?

   A. SpiderFoot

   B. EDGAR database

   C. Sam Spade

   D. Pipl.com

☑ **B.** The EDGAR database—www.sec.gov/edgar.shtml—holds all sorts of competitive intelligence information on businesses. The following is from the website: "All companies, foreign and domestic, are required to file registration statements, periodic reports, and other forms electronically through EDGAR. Anyone can access and download this information for free. Here you'll find links to a complete list of filings available through EDGAR and instructions for searching the EDGAR database." Note that EDGAR and the SEC only have purview over publicly traded companies. Privately held companies are not regulated or obligated to put information in EDGAR. Additionally, even publicly traded companies might not provide information about privately owned subsidiaries, so be careful and diligent.

☒ **A** is incorrect because SpiderFoot is a free, open-source, domain-footprinting tool. According to the SpiderFoot website, SpiderFoot scrapes the websites on a domain, as well as searches Google, NetCraft, whois, and DNS, to collect information.

☒ **C** is incorrect because Sam Spade is a DNS footprinting tool.

☒ **D** is incorrect because pipl.com is a site used for "people search." When footprinting, pipl.com can employ so-called "deep web searching" for loads of information you can use. According to the website, the term *deep web* (or *invisible web*) "refers to a vast repository of underlying content, such as documents in online databases, that general-purpose web crawlers cannot reach. The deep web content is estimated at 500 times that of the surface web, yet has remained mostly untapped due to the limitations of traditional search engines."

19. How does traceroute map the routes traveled by a packet?

   A. By carrying a hello packet in the payload, forcing the host to respond

   B. By using DNS queries at each hop

   C. By manipulating the time to live (TTL) parameter

   D. Using ICMP type 5, code 0 packets

☑ **C.** Traceroute tracks a packet across the Internet by incrementing the TTL on each packet it sends by one after each hop is hit and returns, thus ensuring the response comes back explicitly from that hop and returns its name and IP address. This provides route path and transit times. It accomplishes this by using ICMP ECHO packets to report information on each hop (router) from the source to destination.

☒ **A** is incorrect because ICMP simply doesn't work that way. A hello packet is generally used between clients and servers as a check-in/health mechanism—not a route-tracing method.

☒ **B** is incorrect because a DNS lookup at each hop is pointless and does you no good. DNS isn't for route tracing; it's for matching host names and IP addresses.

☒ **D** is incorrect because an ICMP type 5, code 0 packet is all about message redirection and not about a ping request (type 8).

20. You are footprinting a target headquartered in the Dominican Republic. You have gathered some competitive intelligence and have engaged in both passive and active reconnaissance. Your next step is to define the network range this organization uses. What is the best way to accomplish this?

    A. Call the company help desk and ask them

    B. Use the EDGAR database

    C. Use LACNIC to look up the company range

    D. Use ARIN to look up the company range

    ☑ **C.** LACNIC covers Latin America, Cuba, and some Caribbean islands. The regional registry can provide all sorts of information, and chief among all that data is the IP address range owned by the organization.

    ☒ **A** is incorrect, but only because LACNIC can provide the information passively. Otherwise, you'd be surprised what kind of information you can get by simply calling and asking. I'd like to say the technician on the other end of the line would either hang up or alert security to try and catch you, but I'd bet at least some technicians would go try and look it up for you.

    ☒ **B** is incorrect because the EDGAR database, managed within the Security and Exchange Commission (SEC), doesn't hold this information. It's great for all sorts of other competitive intelligence (financial info, company data, and so on), but it doesn't provide network ranges.

    ☒ **D** is incorrect because ARIN doesn't cover the Dominican Republic—it covers North America and several Caribbean islands.

21. A zone file consists of which types of records? (Choose all that apply.)

    A. PTR

    B. MX

    C. SN

    D. SOA

    E. DNS

    F. A

    G. AX

☑ **A, B, D,** and **F.** A zone file contains a list of all the resource records in the namespace zone. Here are the valid resource records:

SRV	**Service:** Defines the host name and port number of servers providing specific services, such as a Directory Services server.
SOA	**Start of Authority:** This record identifies the primary name server for the zone. The SOA record contains the host name of the server responsible for all DNS records within the namespace as well as the basic properties of the domain.
PTR	**Pointer:** Maps an IP address to a host name (providing for reverse DNS lookups). You don't absolutely need a PTR record for every entry in your DNS namespace, but they are usually associated with e-mail server records.
NS	**Name Server:** This record defines the name servers within your namespace. These servers are the ones that respond to your client's requests for name resolution.
MX	**Mail Exchange:** This record identifies your e-mail servers within your domain.
CNAME	**Canonical Name:** This record provides for domain name aliases within your zone. For example, you may have an FTP and a web service running on the same IP address. CNAME records could be used to list both within DNS for you.
A	**Address:** This record maps an IP address to a host name and is used most often for DNS lookups.

☒ **C, E,** and **G** are incorrect because these are not valid DNS resource records.

22. Examine the following SOA record:

```
@   IN  SOARTDNSRV1.somebiz.com.  postmaster.somebiz.com. (
200408097    ; serial number
                              3600         ; refresh   [1h]
                              600          ; retry     [10m]
                              86400        ; expire    [1d]
7200 )      ; min TTL   [2h]
```

How long will the secondary server wait before asking for an update to the zone file?

A. One hour

B. Two hours

C. Ten minutes

D. One day

☑ **A.** The refresh interval defines the amount of time a secondary will wait before checking in to see if it needs a zone update.

☒ **B** is incorrect because the refresh interval is set to 3,600 seconds (one hour). If you chose this answer because the TTL interval appealed to you, note that the TTL interval is the minimum time to live for all records in the zone (if not updated by a zone transfer, they will perish).

  ☒ **C** is incorrect because the refresh interval is set to 3,600 seconds (one hour). If you chose this answer because the retry interval appealed to you, note that the retry interval is the amount of time a secondary server will wait to retry *if the zone transfer fails*.

  ☒ **D** is incorrect because the refresh interval is set to 3,600 seconds (one hour). If you chose this answer because the expire interval appealed to you, note that the expire interval is the maximum amount of time a secondary server will spend trying to complete a zone transfer.

23. A colleague enters the following into a Google search string:

    ```
    intitle:intranet inurl:intranet +intext:"finance"
    ```

    Which of the following statements is most correct concerning this attempt?

    A. The search engine will not respond with any result because you cannot combine Google hacks on one line.

    B. The search engine will respond with all pages having "intranet" in their title and "human resources" in the URL.

    C. The search engine will respond with all pages having "intranet" in the title and in the URL.

    D. The search engine will respond with only pages having "intranet" in the title and URL and with "human resources" in the text.

  ☑ **D.** This is a great Google hack that's listed on several websites providing Google hacking examples. Think about what your colleague is looking for here—an internal page (intranet in title and URL) possibly containing finance data. Don't you think that would be valuable? This example shows the beauty of combining Google hacks to really burrow down to what you want to grab. Granted, an intranet being available from the Internet, indexed by Google, and open enough for your colleague to touch it is unlikely, but these are questions concerning syntax, not reality.

  ☒ **A** is incorrect because Google hack operators *can* be combined. As a matter of fact, once you get used to them, you'll spend more time combining them to narrow an attack than launching them one by one.

  ☒ **B** is incorrect because the operator does not say to look for "human resources" in the URL. It specifically states this should be looked for in the text of the page.

  ☒ **C** is incorrect because there is more to the operation string than just "intranet" in the URL and title. Don't just glaze over the intext:"human resources" operator—it makes answer **D** more correct.

24. A good footprinting method is to track e-mail messages and see what kind of information you can pull back. Which tool is useful in this scenario?

   A. Nmap

   B. BlackWidow

   C. Snow

   D. eMailTrackerPro

   E. MailMan

   ☑ **D.** eMailTrackerPro, from Visualware, is an e-mail-tracking application that displays all sorts of information on where an e-mail originated from, where it's going, and how it will get there. It can track origin, misdirection detection, whois, and IP data as well as abuse.

   ☒ **A** is incorrect because nmap is not an e-mail-tracking tool. However, it's a tool you'll really need to know well for the scanning and enumeration phase.

   ☒ **B** is incorrect because BlackWidow is a website-copying tool designed to pull a full copy of a site to your machine so you can analyze it at your leisure.

   ☒ **C** is incorrect because snow is a steganography tool.

   ☒ **E** is incorrect because MailMan isn't an e-mail-tracking tool. It is included here solely as a distractor.

25. You are footprinting DNS information using dig. What command syntax should be used to discover all name servers listed by DNS server 202.55.77.12 in the anybiz.com namespace?

   A. dig @www.anybiz.com NS 202.55.77.12

   B. dig NS @www.anybiz.com 202.55.77.12

   C. dig NS @202.55.77.12 www.anybiz.com

   D. dig @202.55.77.12 www.anybiz.com NS

   ☑ **D.** Dig syntax is dig @*server name type* (where *server* is the name or IP of the DNS name server, *name* is the name of the resource you're looking for, and *type* is the type of record you wish to pull). In this case, the server IP is 202.55.77.12, the resource is www.anybiz.com, and the type is NS.

   ☒ **A, B,** and **C** are incorrect because the syntax does not match the command usage.

Scanning and Enumeration

This chapter includes questions from the following topics:
- Describing the CEH scanning methodology, scan types, and the objectives of scanning
- Describing the use of various scanning and enumeration tools
- Scan types, such as ping sweep, SYN, stealth, XMAS, NULL, and many more
- Describing TCP communication (three-way handshake and flag types)
- OS fingerprinting through banner grabbing
- Scanning countermeasures
- Enumerating and its techniques
- NULL sessions and their countermeasures
- SNMP enumeration and its countermeasures
- Describing the steps involved in performing enumeration

Have you seen the movie *The Waterboy?* If I were a film critic, I might say it's a heart-warming tale of self-discovery involving a young man learning to face his past, present, and future. But the reality is it's just a funny movie designed to lighten things up and provide a laugh or two. At the climatic end of the movie, the football team that the waterboy is playing on desperately needs the ball back in order to attempt a game tying—or even winning—play. In one of the pivotal scenes in this sequence, the two teams have lined up and the kicker is preparing to launch an on-side kick.

The kicker has performed reconnaissance, as he can clearly see which men are on the line and which are deep. He also knows his own side, and where the "good hands" guys are. He knows some basics about the other team and has learned through—dare I say it—passive footprinting (from the bench) which players are going to see the field on special team's play and which aren't. Now, he needs to identify which of these targets might have a vulnerability—which man on the other side of the ball represents the weak link in the line. After a couple seconds of "enumerating" his possibilities, he finds his target and prepares to launch the attack.

As stated in the companion book to this study guide, you know how to footprint your client; now it's time to learn how to dig around what you found for relevant, salient information. After footprinting, you'll need to scan for basics—the equivalent of knocking on all your neighbors' doors to see who is home and what they look like.

Then, when you find a machine up and about, you'll need to get to know it really well, asking some rather personal questions.

 STUDY TIPS First and foremost, get your basic network knowledge down pat. Know your port numbers, protocols, and communications handshakes like the back of your hand, and learn how routing/switching basics can affect your efforts. And definitely get to know the scanning and enumeration tools *very* well. You're going to be quizzed on their use, output, and syntax, so prep by practicing—it's the absolute best way to prepare for this exam.

1. What is the second step in the TCP three-way handshake?

    A. SYN

    B. ACK

    C. SYN/ACK

    D. ACK-SYN

    E. FIN

2. You wish to perform a ping sweep of a subnet within your target organization. Which of the following nmap command lines is your best option?

    A. `nmap 192.168.1.0/24`

    B. `nmap -sT 192.168.1.0/24`

    C. `nmap -sP 192.168.1.0/24`

    D. `nmap -P0 192.168.1.0/24`

3. Which of the following TCP flags is used to reset a connection?

    A. SYN

    B. ACK

    C. PSH

    D. URG

    E. FIN

    F. RST

4. A pen test team member is attempting to enumerate a Windows machine and uses a tool called enum to enumerate user accounts on the device. Doubtful this can be done, a junior team member is shocked to see the local users enumerated. The output of his enum use is provided here:

```
C:\>enum -U 192.168.17.5
server 192.168.17.5
setting up session... success.
gettings user list (pass 1, index 0)... success, got 6
Admin  JfiedlerMsander Poop  Guest  Support123
cleaning up... success.
```

    The junior team member asks what type of connection is used by this tool to accomplish its task and is told it requires a "null session" to be established first. If the machine allows null connections, which of the following command strings will successfully connect?

    A. `net use "" /u: \\192.169.5.12\share ""`

    B. `net use \\192.168.5.12\c$ /u:""`

    C. `net use \\192.168.5.12\share "" /u:""`

    D. `net use \\192.168.5.12\c$ /u:""`

5. A colleague enters the following command:

```
root@mybox: # hping3 -A 192.168.2.x -p 80
```

What is being attempted here?

A. An ACK scan using hping3 on port 80 for a single address

B. An ACK scan using hping3 on port 80 for a group of addresses

C. Address validation using hping3 on port 80 for a single address

D. Address validation using hping3 on port 80 for a group of addresses

6. You are examining traffic between hosts and note the following exchange:

Source	Prot	Port	Flag	Destination
192.168.5.12	TCP	4082	FIN/URG/PSH	192.168.5.50
192.168.5.12	TCP	4083	FIN/URG/PSH	192.168.5.50
192.168.5.12	TCP	4084	FIN/URG/PSH	192.168.5.50
192.168.5.50	TCP	4083	RST/ACK	192.168.5.12
192.168.5.12	TCP	4085	FIN/URG/PSH	192.168.5.50

Which of the following statements are true regarding this traffic? (Choose all that apply.)

A. It appears to be part of an ACK scan.

B. It appears to be part of an XMAS scan.

C. It appears port 4083 is open.

D. It appears port 4083 is closed.

7. You are examining traffic and notice an ICMP type 3, code 13 response. What does this normally indicate?

A. The network is unreachable.

B. The host is unknown.

C. Congestion control is enacted for traffic to this host.

D. A firewall is prohibiting connection.

8. You have a zombie system ready and begin an IDLE scan. As the scan moves along, you notice that fragment identification numbers gleaned from the zombie machine are incrementing randomly. What does this mean?

A. Your IDLE scan results will not be useful to you.

B. The zombie system is a honeypot.

C. There is a misbehaving firewall between you and the zombie machine.

D. This is an expected result during an IDLE scan.

9. As a pen test on a major international business moves along, a colleague discovers an IIS server and a mail exchange server on a DMZ subnet. You review a ping sweep accomplished earlier in the day on that subnet and note neither machine responded to the ping. What is the most likely reason for the lack of response?

A. The hosts might be turned off or disconnected.

B. ICMP is being filtered.

C. The destination network might be down.

D. The servers are Linux based and do not respond to ping requests.

10. Which of the following tools is not a good choice for determining possible vulnerabilities on live targets you have identified?

A. SAINT

B. Nmap

C. Nessus

D. Retina

11. Which of the following tools can be used for operating system prediction? (Choose all that apply.)

A. Nmap

B. Whois

C. Queso

D. ToneLoc

E. MBSA

12. You are in training for your new pen test assignment. Your trainer enters the following command:

```
telnet 192.168.12.5 80
```

After typing the command, he hits ENTER a few times. What is being attempted?

A. A DoS attack against a web server

B. A zone transfer

C. Banner grabbing

D. Configuring a port to "listening" state

13. What is being attempted with the following command?

```
nc –u –v –w2 192.168.1.100 1-1024
```

A. A full connect scan on ports 1–1024 for a single address

B. A full connect scan on ports 1–1024 for a subnet

C. A UDP port scan of ports 1–1024 on a single address

D. A UDP scan of ports 1–1024 on a subnet

14. You are told to monitor a packet capture for any attempted DNS zone transfer. Which port should you key your search on?

    A. TCP 22

    B. TCP 53

    C. UDP 22

    D. UDP 53

15. In the scanning and enumeration phase of your attack, you put tools such as ToneLoc, THC-Scan, and WarVox to use. What are you attempting to accomplish?

    A. War dialing

    B. War driving

    C. Proxy discovery

    D. Ping sweeping

16. Which of the following are SNMP enumeration tools? (Choose all that apply.)

    A. Nmap

    B. SNMPUtil

    C. ToneLoc

    D. OpUtils

    E. Solar Winds

    F. NSAuditor

17. The following results are from an nmap scan:

    ```
    Starting nmap V. 3.10A ( www.insecure.org/nmap/
    <http://www.insecure.org/nmap/> )
    Interesting ports on 192.168.15.12:
    (The 1592 ports scanned but not shown below are in state: filtered)
    Port State Service
    21/tcp open ftp
    25/tcp open smtp
    53/tcp closed domain
    80/tcp open http
    443/tcp open https
    Remote operating system guess: Too many signatures match to
        reliably guess the OS.
    Nmap run completed -- 1 IP address (1 host up) scanned in 263.47 seconds
    ```

    Which of the following is the best option to assist in identifying the operating system?

    A. Attempt an ACK scan

    B. Traceroute to the system

C. Run the same nmap scan with the -vv option

D. Attempt banner grabbing

18. You wish to run a scan against a target network. You're concerned about it being a reliable scan, with legitimate results, but want to take steps to ensure it is as stealthy as possible. Which scan type is best in this situation?

    A. `nmap -sN targetIPaddress`

    B. `nmap -sO targetIPaddress`

    C. `nmap -sS targetIPaddress`

    D. `nmap -sT targetIPaddress`

19. Which of the following ports are not required for a null session connection? (Choose all that apply.)

    A. 135

    B. 137

    C. 139

    D. 161

    E. 443

    F. 445

20. You are enumerating a subnet. Examining message traffic, you discover SNMP is enabled on multiple targets. If you assume default settings in setting up enumeration tools to use SNMP, which community strings should you use?

    A. Public (read-only) and Private (read/write)

    B. Private (read-only) and Public (read/write)

    C. Read (read-only) and Write (read/write)

    D. Default (both read and read/write)

21. Nmap is a powerful scanning and enumeration tool. What does the following nmap command attempt to accomplish?

    `nmap -sA -T4 192.168.15.0/24`

    A. A serial, slow operating system discovery scan of a Class C subnet

    B. A parallel, fast operating system discovery scan of a Class C subnet

    C. A serial, slow ACK scan of a Class C subnet

    D. A parallel, fast ACK scan of a Class C subnet

22. You are examining a packet capture of all traffic from a host on the subnet. The host sends a segment with the SYN flag set, in order to set up a TCP communications channel. The destination port is 80, and the sequence number is set to 10. Which of the following statements are *not* true regarding this communications channel? (Choose all that apply.)

    A. The host will be attempting to retrieve an HTML file.

    B. The source port field on this packet can be any number between 1023 and 65535.

    C. The first packet from the destination in answer back to this host will have the SYN and ACK flags set.

    D. The packet returned in answer to this SYN request will acknowledge the sequence number by returning "10."

23. Which TCP flag instructs the recipient to ignore buffering constraints and immediately send all data?

    A. URG

    B. PSH

    C. RST

    D. BUF

24. You receive a RST-ACK from a port during a SYN scan. What is the state of the port?

    A. Open

    B. Closed

    C. Filtered

    D. Unknown

25. Which port-scanning method presents the most risk of discovery, but provides the most reliable results?

    A. Full-connect

    B. Half-open

    C. Null scan

    D. XMAS scan

1. C
2. C
3. F
4. C
5. B
6. B, C
7. D
8. A
9. B
10. B
11. A, C
12. C
13. C
14. B
15. A
16. B, D, E, F
17. D
18. C
19. A, B, C, F
20. A
21. D
22. A, D
23. B
24. B
25. A

1. What is the second step in the TCP three-way handshake?

    A. SYN

    B. ACK

    C. SYN/ACK

    D. ACK-SYN

    E. FIN

    ☑ **C.** Admittedly, this is an easy one, but I'd bet dollars to doughnuts you see it in some form on your exam. It's such an important part of scanning and enumeration because, without understanding this basic principle of communication channel setup, you're almost doomed to failure. A three-way TCP handshake has the originator forward a SYN. The recipient, in step 2, sends a SYN and an ACK. In step 3, the originator responds with an ACK. The steps are referred to as SYN, SYN/ACK, ACK.

    ☒ **A** is incorrect because SYN is the first step (flag set) in the three-way handshake.

    ☒ **B** is incorrect because ACK is the last step (flag set) in the three-way handshake.

    ☒ **D** is incorrect because of the order listed. True, both these flags are the flags set in the three-way handshake. However in discussion of this step-by-step process, it's SYN/ACK, not the other way around. And, yes, this distractor, in some form, will most likely be on your exam.

    ☒ **E** is incorrect because the FIN flag brings an orderly close to a communication session.

2. You wish to perform a ping sweep of a subnet within your target organization. Which of the following nmap command lines is your best option?

    A. `nmap 192.168.1.0/24`

    B. `nmap -sT 192.168.1.0/24`

    C. `nmap -sP 192.168.1.0/24`

    D. `nmap -P0 192.168.1.0/24`

    ☑ **C.** The –sP switch within nmap is designed for a ping sweep. Nmap syntax is fairly straightforward: nmap<scan options><target>. If you don't define a switch, nmap performs a basic enumeration scan of the target(s). The switches, though, provide the real power with this tool.

    ☒ **A** is incorrect because this syntax will not perform a ping sweep. This syntax will run a basic scan against the entire subnet.

    ☒ **B** is incorrect because the –sT switch does not run a ping sweep. It stands for a TCP Connect scan, which is the slowest—but most productive and loud—scan option.

D is incorrect because this syntax will not perform a ping sweep. The –P0 switch actually runs the scan without ping (ICMP). This is a good switch to use when you don't seem to be getting responses from your target(s). It forces nmap to start the scan even if it thinks that the target doesn't exist (useful if the computer is blocked by a firewall).

3. Which of the following TCP flags is used to reset a connection?

   A. SYN

   B. ACK

   C. PSH

   D. URG

   E. FIN

   F. RST

   ☑ **F.** The RST flag, when set, indicates to both parties that communications need to be closed and restarted. It forces a termination of communications in both directions, and is used to reset a connection.

   ☒ **A** is incorrect because the SYN flag is used to initiate a connection between hosts. The synchronize flag is set during initial communication establishment and indicates negotiation of parameters and sequence numbers.

   ☒ **B** is incorrect because the ACK flag is used to acknowledge receipt of a packet. It is set as an acknowledgement to SYN flags, and is set on all segments after the initial SYN flag.

   ☒ **C** is incorrect because the PSH flag is used to instruct the sender to immediately send all buffered data: It forces delivery of data without concern for any buffering.

   ☒ **D** is incorrect because the URG flag is used to indicate a packet that needs to be processed immediately. When this flag is set, it indicates the data inside is being sent out of band.

   ☒ **E** is incorrect because the FIN flag is used to tell the recipient there will be no more traffic. It signifies an ordered close to communications.

4. A pen test team member is attempting to enumerate a Windows machine and uses a tool called enum to enumerate user accounts on the device. Doubtful this can be done, a junior team member is shocked to see the local users enumerated. The output of his enum use is provided here:

```
C:\>enum -U 192.168.17.5
server 192.168.17.5
setting up session... success.
gettings user list (pass 1, index 0)... success, got 6
Admin  JfiedlerMsander Poop  Guest  Support123
cleaning up... success.
```

The junior team member asks what type of connection is used by this tool to accomplish its task and is told it requires a "null session" to be established first. If the machine allows null connections, which of the following command strings will successfully connect?

A. `net use "" /u: \\192.169.5.12\share ""`

B. `net use \\192.168.5.12\c$ /u:""`

C. `net use \\192.168.5.12\share "" /u:""`

D. `net use \\192.168.5.12\c$ /u:""`

☑ **C.** You will definitely be asked about null sessions on the exam, and will need to know the syntax very well. A null session occurs when you log into a system with no user ID and password at all. This type of connection can't be made to a regular share, but it can be done to the Interprocess Communication (IPC) administrative share, which is used by Windows processes uses the SYSTEM username to communicate with other processes across the network. Some tools that make use of the null session are enum, SuperScan, User2SID, and SID2User. `net use \\IPAddress\share "" /u: ""` is the correct syntax for establishing a null session.

☒ **A** is incorrect because the correct syntax is not used.

☒ **B** is incorrect because the correct syntax is not used. Additionally, see the C$ entry there? That's a dead giveaway, and CEH test question writers love using it to confuse you—especially if the question has something about "a null session to exploit an administrative share." This, of course, is referencing the IPC$, but some candidates immediately see that term and go for C$ every time. Don't fall for it—remember, null sessions = IPC$ share.

☒ **D** is incorrect because the correct syntax is not used.

5. A colleague enters the following command:

   `root@mybox: # hping3 -A 192.168.2.x -p 80`

   What is being attempted here?

   A. An ACK scan using hping3 on port 80 for a single address

   B. An ACK scan using hping3 on port 80 for a group of addresses

   C. Address validation using hping3 on port 80 for a single address

   D. Address validation using hping3 on port 80 for a group of addresses

   ☑ **B.** Hping is a great tool providing all sorts of options. You can craft packets with it, audit and test firewalls, and do all sorts of crazy man-in-the-middle stuff with it. In this example, you're simply performing a basic ACK scan (the –A switch) using port 80 (–p 80) on an entire Class C subnet (the "x" in the address runs through all 254 possibilities). Hping3, the latest version, is scriptable (TCL language) and implements an engine that allows human-readable description of TCP/IP packets.

☒ **A** is incorrect because the syntax is for an entire subnet (or, I guess to be technically specific, all 254 addresses that all start with 192.168.2). The "x" in the last octet tells hping to fire away at all those available addresses.

☒ **C** and **D** are both incorrect because "address validation" is not a scan type.

6. You are examining traffic between hosts and note the following exchange:

```
Source              Prot   Port   Flag          Destination
192.168.5.12        TCP    4082   FIN/URG/PSH   192.168.5.50
192.168.5.12        TCP    4083   FIN/URG/PSH   192.168.5.50
192.168.5.12        TCP    4084   FIN/URG/PSH   192.168.5.50
192.168.5.50        TCP    4083   RST/ACK       192.168.5.12
192.168.5.12        TCP    4085   FIN/URG/PSH   192.168.5.50
```

Which of the following statements are true regarding this traffic? (Choose all that apply.)

A. It appears to be part of an ACK scan.

B. It appears to be part of an XMAS scan.

C. It appears port 4083 is open.

D. It appears port 4083 is closed.

☑ **B** and **C.** The exam will ask you to define scan types in many, many ways. It may be a simple definition match; sometimes it'll be some crazy Wireshark or tcpdump listing. In this example, you see a cleaned-up traffic exchange showing packets from one host being sent one after another to the second host, indicating a scan attempt. The packets have the FIN, URG, and PSH flags all set, which tells you it's an XMAS scan. If the destination port is open, you should receive an RST/ACK response—if it's closed, we get nothing. This tells us port 4083 looks like it's open. As an addendum, did you know there are two reasons why it's called an XMAS scan? The first is because it lights up an IDS like a Christmas tree, and the second is because the flags themselves are all lit.

☒ **A** is incorrect because there is no indication this is an ACK scan. An ACK scan has only the ACK flag set, and is generally used in firewall filter tests: No response means a firewall is present, and RST means the firewall is not there (or the port is not filtered).

☒ **D** is incorrect because you did receive an answer from the port (a RST/ACK was sent in the fourth line of the capture).

7. You are examining traffic and notice an ICMP type 3, code 13 response. What does this normally indicate?

A. The network is unreachable.

B. The host is unknown.

C. Congestion control is enacted for traffic to this host.

D. A firewall is prohibiting connection.

☑ **D.** ICMP types will be covered in depth on your exam, so know them well. Type 3 messages are all about "destination unreachable," and the code in each packet tells you why it's unreachable. A code 13 indicates "communication administratively prohibited," which indicates a firewall filtering traffic. Granted, this only occurs when a network designer is nice enough to configure the device to respond in such a way, and you'll probably never get that nicety in the real world, but the definition of what the "type" and "code" mean are relevant here.

☒ **A** is incorrect because "network unreachable" is type 3, code 0. It's generated by a router to inform the source that the destination address is unreachable, that is, it does not have an entry in the route table to send the message to.

☒ **B** is incorrect because "host unknown" is type 3, code 7. There's a route to the network the router knows about, but that host is not there (this sometimes refers to a naming or DNS issue).

☒ **C** is incorrect because "congestion control" ICMP messaging is type 4.

8. You have a zombie system ready and begin an IDLE scan. As the scan moves along, you notice that fragment identification numbers gleaned from the zombie machine are incrementing randomly. What does this mean?

   A. Your IDLE scan results will not be useful to you.

   B. The zombie system is a honeypot.

   C. There is a misbehaving firewall between you and the zombie machine.

   D. This is an expected result during an IDLE scan.

   ☑ **A.** An IDLE scan makes use of a zombie machine and IP's knack for incrementing fragment identifiers (IPIDs). However, it is absolutely essential the zombie remain idle to all other traffic during the scan. The attacker will send packets to the target with the (spoofed) source address of the zombie. If the port is open, the target will respond to the SYN packet with a SYN/ACK, but this will be sent to the zombie. The zombie system will then craft a RST packet in answer to the unsolicited SYN/ACK, and the IPID will increase. If this occurs randomly, then it's very probable your zombie is not, in fact, idle, and your results are moot. See, if it's not idle, it's going to increment haphazardly, as communications from the device will be shooting hither and yon with wild abandon. You're banking on the fact the machine is quietly doing your bidding—and nothing else.

   ☒ **B** is incorrect because there is not enough information here to identify the zombie machine as anything at all—much less a machine set up as a "honeypot."

   ☒ **C** is incorrect because a firewall between you and the zombie won't have any effect at all on the zombie's IPIDs.

☒ **D** is incorrect because this is definitely *not* expected behavior during an IDLE scan. Expected behavior is for the IPID to increase regularly. With each discovered open port; not randomly, as occurs with traffic on an active system.

9. As a pen test on a major international business moves along, a colleague discovers an IIS server and a mail exchange server on a DMZ subnet. You review a ping sweep accomplished earlier in the day on that subnet and note neither machine responded to the ping. What is the most likely reason for the lack of response?

   A. The hosts might be turned off or disconnected.

   B. ICMP is being filtered.

   C. The destination network might be down.

   D. The servers are Linux based and do not respond to ping requests.

   ☑ **B.** Admittedly, this one is a little tricky, and, yes, I purposefully wrote it this way (mainly because I've seen questions like this before). The key here is the "most likely" designator. It's entirely possible—dare I say, even *expected*—that the Systems Administrator on those two very important machines would turn off ICMP. Of the choices provided, this one is the most likely explanation.

   ☒ **A** is incorrect, but only because there is a better answer. This is a major firm that undoubtedly does business at all times of day and with customers and employees around the world (the question did state it was an international business). Is it possible that both these servers are down? Sure, you might have timed your ping sweep so poorly that you happened to hit a maintenance window or something, but it's highly unlikely.

   ☒ **C** is incorrect because, frankly, the odds of an entire DMZ subnet being down while you're pen testing are very slim. And I can promise you if the subnet did drop while you were testing, your test is over.

   ☒ **D** is incorrect because this is simply not true.

10. Which of the following tools is not a good choice for determining possible vulnerabilities on live targets you have identified?

    A. SAINT

    B. Nmap

    C. Nessus

    D. Retina

    ☑ **B.** Nmap is a great scanning tool, providing all sorts of options for you. It can do a great job of identifying "live" machines and letting you know what ports a machine has open—not to mention helping you to identify the operating system in use on the machine. But when it comes to identifying actual vulnerabilities the machine may be open to, other tools are designed for that purpose.

- ☒ **A** is incorrect because SAINT (Security Administrator's Integrated Network Tool) is a vulnerability-scanning tool. It's now commercially available (used to be free and open source, but no longer) and runs on Linux and Mac OS X. SAINT is one of the few scanners that doesn't provide a Windows version at all.

- ☒ **C** is incorrect because Nessus is a very well-known and popular vulnerability assessment scanner. Also once free and open source, Nessus can now be purchased commercially. It is continually updated and has thousands of "plug-ins" available for almost any usage you can think of.

- ☒ **D** is incorrect because Retina is a vulnerability-scanning application. Owned by eEye, Retina is a popular choice on Department of Defense (DoD) and government networks.

11. Which of the following tools can be used for operating system prediction? (Choose all that apply.)

   A. Nmap

   B. Whois

   C. Queso

   D. ToneLoc

   E. MBSA

   - ☑ **A and C.** Operating system guessing—also known as *fingerprinting,* or if you're really trying to impress someone, *stack fingerprinting*—can be accomplished by either nmap or Queso. Granted, Queso is an older tool, but it's still a staple of this certification.

   - ☒ **B** is incorrect because whois is used to look up registrar information for a web registration.

   - ☒ **D** is incorrect because ToneLoc is a war dialing tool used to look for open modems on an enterprise.

   - ☒ **E** is incorrect because MBSA (Microsoft Baseline Security Advisor) is a tool for examining the security posture of a Windows machine. MBSA can provide vulnerability information on the host, locally or remotely.

12. You are in training for your new pen test assignment. Your trainer enters the following command:

    ```
    telnet 192.168.12.5 80
    ```

After typing the command, he hits ENTER a few times. What is being attempted?

A. A DoS attack against a web server

B. A zone transfer

C. Banner grabbing

D. Configuring a port to "listening" state

☑ C. Banner grabbing is a great enumerating method. The tactic involves sending an unsolicited request to an open port to see what, if any, default message is returned. The returned banner can provide all sorts of details, depending on what application is actually on the port. Things such as error messages, HTTP headers, and login messages can indicate potential vulnerabilities. There are lots of ways to accomplish this. For example, with netcat you can use the following command:

```
nc -v -n 212.77.64.88 80
```

However, telnet (to a port other than 23) is one of the easiest methods for accomplishing the task.

☒ A is incorrect because the worse that can happen on this attempt is a closed session with no banner return. Nothing about this will create or bolster a DoS attack.

☒ B is incorrect because this attempt is clearly not a zone transfer (accomplished on command line using nslookup or dig).

☒ D is incorrect because telnet is not used in this fashion.

13. What is being attempted with the following command:

```
nc -u -v -w2 192.168.1.100 1-1024
```

A. A full connect scan on ports 1–1024 for a single address

B. A full connect scan on ports 1–1024 for a subnet

C. A UDP port scan of ports 1–1024 on a single address

D. A UDP scan of ports 1–1024 on a subnet

☑ C. In this example, netcat is being used to run a scan on UDP ports (the –u switch gives this away) from 1 to 1024. The address provided is a single address, not a subnet. Other switches in use here are –v (for verbose) and –w2 (defines the two-second timeout for connection, where netcat will wait for a response).

☒ A is incorrect because the –u switch shows this as a UDP scan. By default (that is, no switch in place), netcat runs in TCP.

☒ B is incorrect because the –u switch shows this as a UDP scan. Additionally, this is aimed at a single address, not a subnet.

☒ D is incorrect because this is aimed at a single address, not a subnet.

14. You are told to monitor a packet capture for any attempted DNS zone transfer. Which port should you key your search on?

    A. TCP 22

    B. TCP 53

    C. UDP 22

    D. UDP 53

    ☑ **B.** DNS uses port 53 in both UDP and TCP. Port 53 over UDP is used for DNS lookups. Zone transfers are accomplished using port 53 over TCP. Considering the reliability and error correction available with TCP, this makes perfect sense.

    ☒ **A** is incorrect because TCP port 22 is for SSH, not DNS.

    ☒ **C** is incorrect because UDP port 22 simply doesn't exist (SSH is TCP based).

    ☒ **D** is incorrect because UDP port 53 is used for DNS lookups. Because lookups are generally a packet or two, and we're concerned with speed on a lookup, UDP's fire-and-forget speed advantage is put to use here.

15. In the scanning and enumeration phase of your attack, you put tools such as ToneLoc, THC-Scan, and WarVox to use. What are you attempting to accomplish?

    A. War dialing

    B. War driving

    C. Proxy discovery

    D. Ping sweeping

    ☑ **A.** ToneLoc, THC-Scan, and WarVox are all war-dialing applications. In war dialing, the attacker dials an entire set of phone numbers looking for an open modem. Modems are designed to answer the call, and despite the fact they are for the most part outdated, they can easily provide backdoor access to a system otherwise completely secured from attack.

    ☒ **B** is incorrect because war driving refers to a method of discovering wireless access points. Although you may not need a vehicle any longer to do so, war driving used to refer to, quite literally, driving around in a car looking for open access points. In the ethical hacking realm, it still indicates a search for open WAPs.

    ☒ **C** is incorrect because the tools listed here have nothing to do with locating and identifying proxies.

    ☒ **D** is incorrect because the tools listed here have nothing to do with ping sweeping. Tools such as Angry IP, nmap, Solar Winds, and PingScannerPro are ping sweepers.

16. Which of the following are SNMP enumeration tools? (Choose all that apply.)

   A. Nmap

   B. SNMPUtil

   C. ToneLoc

   D. OpUtils

   E. Solar Winds

   F. NSAuditor

   ☑ **B, D, E,** and **F.** SNMP (in all its versions) is a great protocol designed to help network managers get the most out of their devices and nets. Unfortunately, it's so powerful and easy to use that hackers abuse it frequently, leading to many administrators simply turning it off. Enumerating a device using SNMP—crawling the Management Information Base (MIB) for the device— is relatively easy. SNMPUtil, Solar Winds, and OpUtils are probably the most well-known of this group. NSAuditor is probably better known for its vulnerability-scanning features, but it is listed by CEH as an SNMP enumerator.

   ☒ **A** is incorrect because nmap is not an SNMP enumerator—it's a scanning tool.

   ☒ **C** is incorrect because ToneLoc is a war-dialing tool used for discovering open modems.

17. The following results are from an nmap scan:

```
Starting nmap V. 3.10A ( www.insecure.org/nmap/
<http://www.insecure.org/nmap/> )
Interesting ports on 192.168.15.12:
(The 1592 ports scanned but not shown below are in state: filtered)
Port State Service
21/tcp open ftp
25/tcp open smtp
53/tcp closed domain
80/tcp open http
443/tcp open https
Remote operating system guess: Too many signatures match to reliably
guess the OS.
Nmap run completed -- 1 IP address (1 host up) scanned in 263.47 seconds
```

   Which of the following is the best option to assist in identifying the operating system?

   A. Attempt an ACK scan

   B. Traceroute to the system

   C. Run the same nmap scan with the -vv option

   D. Attempt banner grabbing

☑ **D.** Of the options presented, banner grabbing is probably your best bet. In fact, it's a good *start* for operating system fingerprinting. You can telnet to any of these active ports or run an nmap banner grab. Either way, the returning banner may help in identifying the OS.

☒ **A** is incorrect because an ACK scan isn't necessarily going to help here. For that matter, it may have already been run.

☒ **B** is incorrect because traceroute does not provide any information on fingerprinting. It will show you a network map, hop by hop, to the target, but it won't help tell you whether it's a Windows machine.

☒ **C** is incorrect because the –vv switch only provides more (verbose) information on what namp already has. Note that the original run presented this message on the OS fingerprinting effort: "Remote operating system guess: Too many signatures match to reliably guess the OS."

18. You wish to run a scan against a target network. You're concerned about it being a reliable scan, with legitimate results, but want to take steps to ensure it is as stealthy as possible. Which scan type is best in this situation?

    A. `nmap -sN targetIPaddress`

    B. `nmap -sO targetIPaddress`

    C. `nmap -sS targetIPaddress`

    D. `nmap -sT targetIPaddress`

    ☑ **C.** A half-open scan, as defined by this nmap command line, is the best option in this case. The SYN scan was created with stealth in mind, because the full connect scan was simply too noisy (or created more entries in an application-level logging system, whichever your preference). Granted, most IDSs can pick it up; however, if you go slow enough, it is almost invisible.

    ☒ **A** is incorrect because a null scan may not provide the reliability you're looking for. Remember, this scan won't work on a Windows host at all.

    ☒ **B** is incorrect because the –sO switch tells you this is a operating system scan. Fingerprinting scans are not stealthy by anyone's imagination, and they won't provide the full information you're looking for here.

    ☒ **D** is incorrect because the –sT option indicates a full connect scan. Although this is very reliable, it is very noisy, and you will most likely be discovered during the scan.

19. Which of the following ports are required for a null session connection? (Choose all that apply.)

    A. 135

    B. 137

    C. 139

D. 161

E. 443

F. 445

☑ **A, B, C,** and **F.** Null sessions have been virtually eliminated from the hacking arsenal since Windows XP was released; however, many machine are still vulnerable to this attack and—more importantly to you—the CEH test loves covering it. Null session connections make use of TCP ports 135, 137, 139, and 445.

☒ **D** is incorrect because port 161 is used for SNMP, which has nothing to do with null session connections.

☒ **E** is incorrect because port 443 is used for SSL connections, and has nothing to do with null sessions.

20. You are enumerating a subnet. Examining message traffic you discover SNMP is enabled on multiple targets. If you assume default settings in setting up enumeration tools to use SNMP, which community strings should you use?

A. Public (read-only) and Private (read/write)

B. Private (read-only) and Public (read/write)

C. Read (read-only) and Write (read/write)

D. Default (both read and read/write)

☑ **A.** SNMP uses a community string as a form of a password. The read-only version of the community string allows a requester to read virtually anything SNMP can drag out of the device, whereas the read/write version is used to control access for the SNMP SET requests. The read-only default community string is *public*, whereas the read/write string is *private*. If you happen upon a network segment using SNMPv3, though, keep in mind that SNMPv3 can use a hashed form of the password in transit versus the clear text.

☒ **B** is incorrect because the community strings are listed in reverse here.

☒ **C** is incorrect because "Read" and "Write" are not community strings.

☒ **D** is incorrect because "Default" is not a community string in SNMP.

21. Nmap is a powerful scanning and enumeration tool. What does this nmap command attempt to accomplish?

```
nmap –sA –T4 192.168.15.0/24
```

A. A serial, slow operating system discovery scan of a Class C subnet

B. A parallel, fast operating system discovery scan of a Class C subnet

C. A serial, slow ACK scan of a Class C subnet

D. A parallel, fast ACK scan of a Class C subnet

☑ **D.** You are going to need to know nmap switches very well for your exam. In this example, the –A switch indicates an ACK scan (the only scan that returns no response on a closed port), and the –T4 switch indicates an "aggressive" scan, which runs fast and in parallel.

☒ **A** is incorrect because a slow, serial scan would use the –T, -T0, or –T! switch. Additionally, the OS detection switch is –O, not -A.

☒ **B** is incorrect because although this answer got the speed of the scan correct, the operating system detection portion is off.

☒ **C** is incorrect because although this answer correctly identified the ACK scan switch, the –T4 switch was incorrectly identified.

22. You are examining a packet capture of all traffic from a host on the subnet. The host sends a segment with the SYN flag set, in order to set up a TCP communications channel. The destination port is 80, and the sequence number is set to 10. Which of the following statements are *not* true regarding this communications channel? (Choose all that apply.)

   A. The host will be attempting to retrieve an HTML file.

   B. The source port field on this packet can be any number between 1023 and 65535.

   C. The first packet from the destination in answer back to this host will have the SYN and ACK flags set.

   D. The packet returned in answer to this SYN request will acknowledge the sequence number by returning "10."

   ☑ **A and D.** Yes, it is true that port 80 traffic is HTTP; however, there are two problems with this statement. The first is all that is happening here is an arbitrary connection to something on port 80. For all we know, it's a listener, telnet connection, or anything at all. Second, assuming it's actually an HTTP server, the sequence described here would do nothing but make a connection—not necessarily transfer anything. Sure, this is picky, but it's the truth. Next, sequence numbers are acknowledged between systems during the three-way handshake by incrementing by 1. In this example, the source sent an opening sequence number of "10" to the recipient. The recipient, in crafting the SYN/ACK response, will first acknowledge the opening sequence number by incrementing it to 11. After this, it will add its own sequence number to the packet (a random number it will pick) and send both off.

   ☒ **B** is incorrect because it's a true statement. Source port fields are dynamically assigned using anything other than the "well-known" port range (0–1023). IANA has defined the following port number ranges: Ports 1024 to 49151 are the registered ports (assigned by IANA for specific service upon application by a requesting entity) and ports 49152 to 65535 are dynamic or private ports that cannot be registered with IANA.

☒ **C** incorrect because it's a true statement. The requesting machine has sent the first packet in the three-way handshake exchange—a SYN packet. The recipient will respond with a SYN/ACK and wait patiently for the last step—the ACK packet.

23. Which TCP flag instructs the recipient to ignore buffering constraints and immediately send all data?

    A. URG

    B. PSH

    C. RST

    D. BUF

    ☑ **B.** This answer normally gets mixed up with the URG flag, because we all read it as *urgent*. However, just remember the key word with PSH is "buffering." In TCP, buffering is used to maintain a steady, harmonious flow of traffic. Every so often, though, the buffer itself becomes a problem, slowing things down. A PSH flag tells the recipient stack that the data should be pushed up to the receiving application immediately.

    ☒ **A** is incorrect because the URG flag is used to inform the receiving stack that certain data within a segment is urgent and should be prioritized. As an aside, URG isn't used very much by modern protocols.

    ☒ **C** is incorrect the RST flag forces a termination of communications (in both directions).

    ☒ **D** is incorrect because BUF isn't a TCP flag at all.

24. You receive a RST-ACK from a port during a SYN scan. What is the state of the port?

    A. Open

    B. Closed

    C. Filtered

    D. Unknown

    ☑ **B.** Remember, a SYN scan occurs when you send a SYN packet to all open ports. If the port is open, you'll obviously get a SYN/ACK back. However, if the port is closed, you'll get a RST-ACK.

    ☒ **A** is incorrect because an open port would respond differently (SYN/ACK).

    ☒ **C** is incorrect because a filtered port would likely not respond at all. (The firewall wouldn't allow the packet through, so no response would be generated.)

    ☒ **D** is incorrect because you know exactly what state the port is in, due to the RST-ACK response.

25. Which port-scanning method presents the most risk of discovery, but provides the most reliable results?

    A. Full-connect

    B. Half-open

    C. Null scan

    D. XMAS scan

    ☑ A. Full-connect scan runs through an entire TCP three-way handshake on all ports you aim at. It's loud and easy to see happening, but the results are indisputable. As an aside, the –sT switch in nmap runs a full-connect scan (you should go ahead and memorize that one).

    ☒ B is incorrect because a half-open scan involves sending only the SYN packet and watching for responses. It is designed for stealth, but may be picked up on IDS sensors (both network and most host-based IDSs).

    ☒ C is incorrect because a null scan sends packets with no flags set at all. Responses will vary, depending on the OS and version, so reliability is spotty. As an aside, null scans are designed for UNIX/Linux machines and don't work on Windows systems.

    ☒ D is incorrect because although an XMAS scan is very easily detectable (as our celebrated technical editor put it, "a fairly well-trained monkey would see it"), the results are oftentimes sketchy. The XMAS scan is great for test questions, but won't result in much more than a derisive snort and an immediate disconnection in the real world.

Sniffers and Evasion

This chapter includes questions from the following topics:

- Sniffing and protocols that are susceptible to sniffing
- Describing active and passive sniffing
- Describing ethical hacking techniques for layer 2 traffic
- Sniffing tools and displays
- Describing sniffing countermeasures
- Intrusion detection system (IDS) types, use, and placement
- Describing signature analysis within Snort
- Listing IDS evasion techniques
- Firewall types, use, and placement
- Describing firewall hacking tools and techniques
- Use and placement of a honeypot

When I joined the Air Force many, many years ago, our basic training in San Antonio, Texas was somewhat unique: We were one of the first to have a "sister" flight right next door (I guess while we had billions of dollars to develop new planes, we didn't have the cash to build separate dormitory buildings for men and women). So, basically, one side of the building was men and the other side women—with nothing but a wall between the two flights. As you can imagine, being locked in a dorm for 13 weeks with 40 other guys—and only guys—left a little to be desired, and the impediment a mere 6 to 8 inches of wood, sheetrock, and nails separating us from the fairer sex wasn't much of an impediment at all.

We spent a lot of our time trying to figure out where they would be, when they would be there, and how long they would be hanging out. We even identified specific "targets" of our individual attention and in our spare moments of free time enumerated what she liked and didn't like (making this entire scenario some real-world but oddly twisted corollary for the beginning stages of a pen test, but that's getting off target). One of the best avenues for information we had was a small pinhole one of the guy was successful in cutting through the wall (we couldn't make it too big—our training instructor would've noticed it and killed us via pushups, sit-ups, and bad Air Force dining hall food). If you were quiet enough and cupped your hands around that little hole, you could hear what the ladies were saying and what they were planning on doing. In effect, we were sniffing traffic without their knowledge, and that's what we'll be studying in this chapter.

STUDY TIPS Just as with the previous chapter, review your basic network knowledge thoroughly. You'll see lots of questions designed to test your knowledge on how networking devices handle traffic, how addressing affects packet flow, and which protocols are susceptible to sniffing. Additionally, learn Wireshark *really* well. Pay particular attention to filters within Wireshark—how to set them up, and what syntax they follow—and how to read a capture (not to mention the "follow TCP stream" option). If you haven't already, download Wireshark and start playing with it. Right now, before you even read the questions that follow.

Snort is another tool you'll need to know inside and out. Be very well versed in configuring rules and reading output from a Snort capture/alert. And when it comes to those captures, oftentimes you can peruse an answer just by pulling out port numbers and such, so don't panic when you see them.

Lastly, don't forget your firewall types—you won't see many questions on identifying a definition, but you'll probably see a least a couple of scenario questions where this knowledge comes in handy.

1. A target machine (with a MAC of 12:34:56:AB:CD:EF) is connected to a switch port. An attacker (with a MAC of 78:91:00:ED:BC:A1) is attached to a separate port on the same switch with a packet capture running. There is no spanning of ports or port security in place. Two packets leave the target machine. Message 1 has a destination MAC of E1:22:BA:87:AC:12. Message 2 has a destination MAC of FF:FF:FF:FF:FF:FF. Which of the following statements is true regarding the messages being sent?

   A. The attacker will see message 1.

   B. The attacker will see message 2.

   C. The attacker will see both messages.

   D. The attacker will see neither message

2. You have successfully tapped into a network subnet of your target organization. You begin an attack by learning all significant MAC addresses on the subnet. After some time, you decide to intercept messages between two hosts. You begin by sending broadcast messages to Host A showing your MAC address as belonging to Host B. Simultaneously, you send messages to Host B showing your MAC address as belonging to Host A. What is being accomplished here?

   A. ARP poisoning to allow you to see all messages from both sides without interrupting their communications process

   B. ARP poisoning to allow you to see messages from Host A to Host B, and vice versa

   C. ARP poisoning to allow you to see messages from Host A destined to any address

   D. ARP poisoning to allow you to see messages from Host B destined to any address

   E. Failed ARP poisoning—you will not be able to see any traffic

3. Sniffing network traffic can sometimes be a function of an investigation run by a law enforcement agency (LEA). Within the confines of the lawful intercept, what provides most of the processing of the information and is usually provided by a third party?

   A. IAP

   B. Collection function

   C. Wiretap

   D. Mediation device

4. An attacker has successfully tapped into a network segment and has configured port spanning for his connection, which allows him to see all traffic passing through the switch. Which of the following protocols protects any sensitive data from being seen by this attacker?

   A. FTP

   B. IMAP

   C. Telnet

   D. POP

   E. SMTP

   F. SSH

5. You have a large packet capture file in Wireshark to review. You wish to filter traffic to show all packets with an IP address of 192.168.22.5 that contain the string HR_admin. Which of the following filters would accomplish this task?

   A. `ip.addr==192.168.22.5 &&tcp contains HR_admin`

   B. `ip.addr 192.168.22.5 && "HR_admin"`

   C. `ip.addr 192.168.22.5 &&tcp string ==HR_admin`

   D. `ip.addr==192.168.22.5 + tcp contains tide`

6. Which of the following is a tool used for MAC spoofing?

   A. PromiScan

   B. NetWitness

   C. CACE

   D. SMAC

7. You are attempting to sniff traffic on a switch. Which of the following are good methods to ensure you are successful? (Choose all that apply.)

   A. Reboot the switch immediately after connecting.

   B. Implement port security.

   C. Configure a span port.

   D. Use MAC flooding.

8. Which of the following are modes Snort can operate in? (Choose all that apply.)

   A. Sniffer

   B. Spoofing

   C. Packet Logger

   D. Network IDS

9. Examine the following Snort rule:

```
alerttcp !$HOME_NET any -> $HOME_NET 23 (content:
"admin";msg:"Telnet attempt..admin access";)
```

Which of the following are true regarding the rule? (Choose all that apply.)

A. This rule will alert on packets coming from the designated home network.

B. This rule will alert on packets coming from outside the designated home address.

C. This rule will alert on packets designated for any port, from port 23, containing the "admin" string.

D. This rule will alert on packets designated on port 23, from any port, containing the "admin" string.

10. You wish to begin sniffing, and you have a Windows 7 laptop. You download and install Wireshark, but quickly discover your NIC needs to be in "promiscuous mode." What allows you to put your NIC into promiscuous mode?

A. Installing lmpcap

B. Installing npcap

C. Installing winPcap

D. Installing libPcap

E. Manipulating the NIC properties through Control Panel, Network and Internet, Change Adapter Settings.

11. You are attempting to deliver a payload to a target inside the organization; however, it is behind an IDS. You are concerned about successfully accomplishing your task without alerting the IDS monitoring team. Which of the following methods are possible options? (Choose all that apply.)

A. Flood the network with fake attacks.

B. Encrypt the traffic between you and the host.

C. Session hijacking.

D. Session splicing.

12. A pen test member has gained access to an open switch port. He configures his NIC for promiscuous mode and sets up a sniffer, plugging his laptop directly into the switch port. He watches traffic as it arrives at the system, looking for specific information to possibly use later. What type of sniffing is being practiced?

A. Active

B. Promiscuous

C. Blind

D. Passive

E. Session

13. Tcpdump is a popular packet capture sniffer. Examine the following segment of a tcpdump capture (note the capture only shows one side of the communication):

```
18:53:24.872785 IP ubuntu.local.38656 > 192.168.5.12.ftp:
S 4155592273:4155592273(0) win 5840
...g....................
............
18:53:24.879473 IP ubuntu.local.38656 > 192.168.5.12.ftp:
.ack 1228937421 win 170
....g.I@.............
.........
18:53:24.881654 IP ubuntu.local.38656 > 192.168.5.12.ftp:
.ack 47 win 170
....g.I@.......8.....
......EN
18:53:26.401846 IP ubuntu.local.38656 > 192.168.5.12.ftp:
P 0:10(10) ack 43 win 170
....g.I@......`$.....
...=..ENUSER user1

18:53:26.403802 IP ubuntu.local.38656 > 192.168.5.12.ftp:
.ack 72 win 170
....h.I@.............
...>..E^
18:53:29.169036 IP ubuntu.local.38656 > 192.168.5.12.ftp:
P 10:25(15) ack 76 win 170
....h.I@......#c.....
......E^PASS nothing

18:53:29.171553 IP ubuntu.local.38656 > 192.168.5.12.ftp:
.ack 94 win 170
....h.I@.,...........
......Ez
18:53:29.171649 IP ubuntu.local.38656 > 192.168.5.12.ftp:
P 25:31(6) ack 96 win 170
....h.I@.,...........
......EzSYST

18:53:29.211607 IP ubuntu.local.38656 > 192.168.5.12.ftp:
.ack 113 win 170
....h.I@.?.....j.....
......Ez
18:53:31.367619 IP ubuntu.local.38656 > 192.168.5.12.ftp:
P 31:37(6) ack 115 win 170
....h.I@.?...........
......EzQUIT

18:53:31.369316 IP ubuntu.local.38656 > 192.168.5.12.ftp:
.ack 152 win 170
....h.I@.g...........
......E.
18:53:31.369759 IP ubuntu.local.38656 > 192.168.5.12.ftp:
```

```
F 37:37(0) ack 156 win 170
....h.I@.h.....e.....
......E.
```

What can you gather from this capture? (Choose all that apply.)

A. The FTP connection is from 192.168.1.12 to the local host.

B. The FTP connection is from the local host to 192.168.5.12.

C. The FTP connection was unsuccessful.

D. The FTP authentication credentials are clearly visible.

14. What does this line from the Snort configuration file indicate?

```
var RULE_PATH c:\etc\snort\rules
```

A. The configuration variable is not in proper syntax.

B. It instructs the Snort engine to write rule violations in this location.

C. It instructs the Snort engine to compare packets to the rule set named "rules."

D. It defines the location of the Snort rules.

15. As part of a security monitoring team, Joe is reacting to an incursion into the network. The attacker successfully exploited a vulnerability on an internal machine, and Joe is examining how the attacker succeeded. He reviews the IDS logs but sees no alerts for the time period; however, there is definitive proof of the attack. Which IDS shortcoming does this refer to?

A. False acceptance rate

B. False negative

C. Session splicing

D. False positive

16. Examine the Snort output shown here:

```
08/28-12:23:13.014491 01:10:BB:17:E3:C5 ->A5:12:B7:55:57:AB type:0x800
len:0x3C
190.168.5.12:33541 ->213.132.44.56:23 TCP TTL:128 TOS:0x0 ID:12365

IpLen:20 DgmLen:48 DF
***A**S* Seq: 0xA153BD Ack: 0xA01657 Win: 0x2000 TcpLen: 28
TCP Options (4) => MSS: 1460 NOP NOPSackOK
0x0000: 00 02 B3 87 84 25 00 10 5A 01 0D 5B 08 00 45 00  ...%..Z..[..E.
0x0010: 00 30 98 43 40 00 80 06 DE EC C0 A8 01 04 C0 A8  .0.C@........
0x0020: 01 43 04 DC 01 BB 00 A1 8B BD 00 00 00 00 70 02  .C..........p.
0x0030: 20 00 4C 92 00 00 02 04 05 B4 01 01 04 02        .L..........
```

Which of the following is true regarding the packet capture?

A. The capture indicates a NOP sled attack.

B. The capture shows step 2 of a TCP handshake.

C. The packet source is 213.132.44.56.

D. The packet capture shows an SSH session attempt.

17. Your IDS sits on the network perimeter and has been analyzing traffic for a couple of weeks. On arrival one morning, you find the IDS has alerted on a spike in network traffic late the previous evening. Which type of IDS are you using?

    A. Stateful

    B. Snort

    C. Passive

    D. Signature based

    E. Anomaly based

18. You are performing an ACK scan against a target subnet. You previously verified connectivity to several hosts within the subnet, but want to verify all live hosts on the subnet. Your scan, however, is not receiving any replies. Which type of firewall is most likely in use at your location?

    A. Packet filtering

    B. IPS

    C. Stateful

    D. Active

19. You are separated from your target subnet by a firewall. The firewall is correctly configured and only allows requests through to ports opened by the administrator. In firewalking the device, you find that port 80 is open. Which technique could you employ to send data and commands to or from the target system?

    A. Encrypt the data to hide it from the firewall.

    B. Use session splicing.

    C. Use MAC flooding.

    D. Use HTTP tunneling.

20. Which of the following tools are useful in identifying potential honeypots on a subnet? (Choose all that apply.)

    A. Wireshark

    B. Ettercap

    C. Nessus

    D. Send-Safe HH

    E. Nmap

21. Examine the Wireshark filter shown here:

    ```
    ip.src == 192.168.1.1 &&tcp.srcport == 80
    ```

    Which of the following correctly describes the capture filter?

    A. The results will display all traffic from 192.168.1.1 destined for port 80.

    B. The results will display all HTTP traffic to 192.168.1.1.

C. The results will display all Http traffic from 192.168.1.1.

D. No results will display due to invalid syntax.

22. You need to put the NIC into listening mode on your Linux box, capture packets, and write the results to a log file named my.log. How do you accomplish this with tcpdump?

A. `tcpdump -i eth0 -w my.log`

B. `tcpdump -l eth0 -c my.log.`

C. `tcpdump /i eth0 /w my.log`

D. `tcpdump /l eth0 /c my.log`

23. Which of the following tools can assist with IDS evasion? (Choose all that apply.)

A. Whisker

B. Fragroute

C. Capsa

D. Wireshark

E. ADMmutate

F. Inundator

24. Which command puts Snort into packet logger mode?

A. `./snort -dev -l ./log`

B. `./snort -v`

C. `./snort -dev -l ./log -h 192.168.1.0/24 -c snort.conf`

D. None of the above

25. Examine the following hex dump of a packet capture:

```
0000 00 13 10 fece 6c 18 3d a2 5b 67 64 08 00 45 00    ....l.= .[gd..E.
0010 00 36 0b 48 40 00 80 06 fd 5e c0 a8 01 65 0f c0    .6.H@... .^...e..
0020 20 4e c2 73 00 15 0a 15 36 47 d9 0b 0b 4c 50 18    N.s21.. 6G...LP.
0030 0f 91 0a b2 00 00 55 53 45 52 20 75 73 65 72 5f    ......US ER user_
0040 31 33 0d 0a                                        13..
0000 00 13 10 fece 6c 18 3d a2 5b 67 64 08 00 45 00    ....l.= .[gd..E.
0010 00 37 0b 49 40 00 80 06 fd 5c c0 a8 01 65 0f c0    .7.I@... .\...e..
0020 20 4e c2 73 00 15 0a 15 36 55 d9 0b 0b 6f 50 18    N.s.... 6U...oP.
0030 0f 89 be 88 00 00 50 41 53 53 20 31 32 33 34 5f    ......PA SS 1234_
0040 35 36 37 0d 0a                                     567..
```

What does this packet capture show?

A. An ARP spoofing attempt

B. A Unicode IDS evasion attempt

C. An FTP session authentication

D. A ping sweep

1. B
2. B
3. D
4. F
5. A
6. D
7. C, D
8. A, C, D
9. B, D
10. C
11. B, D
12. D
13. B, D
14. D
15. B
16. B
17. E
18. C
19. D
20. C, D
21. C
22. A
23. A, B, E, F
24. A
25. C

1. A target machine (with a MAC of 12:34:56:AB:CD:EF) is connected to a switch port. An attacker (with a MAC of 78:91:00:ED:BC:A1) is attached to a separate port on the same switch with a packet capture running. There is no spanning of ports or port security in place. Two packets leave the target machine. Message 1 has a destination MAC of E1:22:BA:87:AC:12. Message 2 has a destination MAC of FF:FF:FF:FF:FF:FF. Which of the following statements is true regarding the messages being sent?

   A. The attacker will see message 1.

   B. The attacker will see message 2.

   C. The attacker will see both messages.

   D. The attacker will see neither message.

   ☑ **B.** *This question is all about how a switch works*, with a little MAC knowledge thrown in. Remember that switches are designed to filter unicast messages but to flood multicast and broadcast messages (filtering goes only to one port, whereas flooding sends to all). Broadcast MAC addresses in the frame are very easy to spot—they're always all F's, indicating all 48 bits turned on in the address. In this case, message 1 is a unicast address and went off to its destination, whereas message 2 is clearly a broadcast message, which the switch will gladly flood to all ports, including the attacker's.

   ☒ **A** is incorrect because the unicast destination MAC does not match the attacker's machine. When the frame is read by the switch and compared to the internal address list (CAM table), it will be filtered and sent to the appropriate destination port.

   ☒ **C** is incorrect because the switch will not flood both messages to the attacker's port—it only floods broadcast and multicast.

   ☒ **D** is incorrect because the broadcast address will definitely be seen by the attacker.

2. You have successfully tapped into a network subnet of your target organization. You begin an attack by learning all significant MAC addresses on the subnet. After some time, you decide to intercept messages between two hosts. You begin by sending broadcast messages to Host A showing your MAC address as belonging to Host B. Simultaneously, you send messages to Host B showing your MAC address as belonging to Host A. What is being accomplished here?

   A. ARP poisoning to allow you to see all messages from both sides without interrupting their communications process

   B. ARP poisoning to allow you to see messages from Host A to Host B, and vice versa

C. ARP poisoning to allow you to see messages from Host A destined to any address

D. ARP poisoning to allow you to see messages from Host B destined to any address

E. Failed ARP poisoning—you will not be able to see any traffic

☑ **B.** ARP poisoning is a relatively simple way to place yourself as the "man in the middle" and spy on traffic. (By the way, be careful with the term *man in the middle* because it usually refers to a position where you are not interrupting traffic). The ARP cache is updated whenever your machine does a name lookup, or when ARP (a broadcast protocol) receives an unsolicited message advertising a MAC-to-IP match. In this example, you've told Host A and Host B that you hold the MAC address for Host B and Host A, respectively. Both machines will update their cache, and when a message is being crafted by the OS, it will happily put the spoofed address in its place. Just remember that ARP poisoning is oftentimes noisy and may be easy to discover if port security is enabled. Additionally, watch out for denial of service side effects of attempting ARP poisoning—you may very well bring down a target without even trying to.

☒ **A** is incorrect for a couple reasons. First, you won't receive messages from each host addressed to anywhere in the world—you'll only receive messages addressed from one to the other, and vice versa. Second, the communications flow between the two hosts will be affected by this. As a matter of fact, neither machine can talk to the other, even if you wanted to: The ARP poisoning has all messages going to the hacker.

☒ **C** is incorrect for a couple reasons. First, it's only referencing one host when the ARP poisoning is in both directions. Second, you would not get messages from Host A to any destination—only those that are addressed to Host B.

☒ **D** is incorrect for a couple reasons. First, it's only referencing one host when the ARP poisoning is in both directions. Second, you would not get messages from Host B to everywhere—only those that are addressed to Host A.

☒ **E** is incorrect because the ARP poisoning should work fine here, and you will see traffic between the two hosts.

3. Sniffing network traffic can sometimes be a function of an investigation run by a law enforcement agency (LEA). Within the confines of the lawful intercept, what provides most of the processing of the information and is usually provided by a third party?

A. IAP

B. Collection function

C. Wiretap

D. Mediation device

☑ **D.** So this question comes straight out of the EC Council's definitions of a *lawful intercept*, which is a process allowing an LEA to sniff traffic based on a judicial order. A lot of approvals and whatnot are needed to set up this tap, but within the confines of the entire intercept, you have a judicial order allowing it, a tap (usually the service provider allows a port opening for this), something to process all the data (the mediation device) and a collection area where everything is stored and parsed/processed further. The key in this is the third-party portion—a mediation device is usually provided by a third party, whereas the tap and the collection are not.

☒ **A** is incorrect because the IAP (intercept access point) is the device providing all the raw data—the tap being used to capture everything.

☒ **B** is incorrect because the collection function is an application that stores and parses the information gleaned from the tap and mediation devices.

☒ **C** is incorrect because a wiretap is simply a device that connects to a communications circuit allowing for the sniffing of traffic.

4. An attacker has successfully tapped into a network segment and has configured port spanning for his connection, which allows him to see all traffic passing through the switch. Which of the following protocols protects any sensitive data from being seen by this attacker?

   A. FTP

   B. IMAP

   C. Telnet

   D. POP

   E. SMTP

   F. SSH

☑ **F.** The biggest deterrent you have to sniffing is encryption (as an aside, it's also the biggest threat to an IDS, but that's for a different question). All the protocols listed here are susceptible to sniffing in one way or another because they pass information in the clear—that is, with no encryption. SSH is the only one listed that provides secured transmission and is, therefore, the only correct answer. The CEH exam objective here is to ensure you know which protocols pass information in the clear—and thus making them easy to sniff—and which do not.

☒ **A** is incorrect because FTP sends its passwords and all data in clear text. If you're sniffing the wire and someone logs in with FTP— *voilà!*—you've got it all.

☒ **B** is incorrect because IMAP also passes all information—including passwords—in the clear.

⊠ **C** is incorrect because telnet is another open protocol, passing everything in the clear.

⊠ **D** is incorrect because POP sends all information in clear text.

⊠ **E** is incorrect because SMTP also sends everything in clear text—just look at your e-mail headers if you doubt me.

5. You have a large packet capture file in Wireshark to review. You wish to filter traffic to show all packets with an IP address of 192.168.22.5 that contain the string HR_admin. Which of the following filters would accomplish this task?

A. `ip.addr==192.168.22.5 &&tcp contains HR_admin`

B. `ip.addr 192.168.22.5 && "HR_admin"`

C. `ip.addr 192.168.22.5 &&tcp string ==HR_admin`

D. `ip.addr==192.168.22.5 + tcp contains tide`

☑ **A.** This is a perfect example of a typical Wireshark question on your exam (and you will see a couple). This is the only answer that sticks to Wireshark filter syntax. Definitely know the ip.addr, ip.src, and ip.dst filters; the "tcp contains" filter is another favorite of test question writers. When you combine filters in one search, use the && designator.

⊠ **B, C,** and **D** are all incorrect because the syntax is wrong for Wireshark filters. As an aside, a great way to learn the syntax of these filters is to use the expression builder directly beside the filter entry box. It's self-explanatory and contains literally thousands of possible expression builds.

6. Which of the following is a tool used for MAC spoofing?

A. PromiScan

B. NetWitness

C. CACE

D. SMAC

☑ **D.** SMAC is a great tool for spoofing MAC addresses. It's free (at least initially) and easy to use. It's also powerful and works on Windows systems. As an interesting aside, if you change the MAC address, it will remain in the altered condition through reboot until you stop spoofing—in other words, the MAC spoof will remain in place until you manually change it back to the original value, even after a reboot.

☒ **A** is incorrect because PromiScan is a tool designed specifically to help you detect promiscuous NIC use on your subnet. In other words, it can help you find sniffers on your network. It's an older tool, developed by Microsoft, that carries a hefty price tag. However, it's the de facto standard sniffing node-detection tool, which is recommended by SANS and has been used worldwide ever since its release.

☒ **B** is incorrect because NetWitness is an all-in-one sniffer from RSA's Advanced Security Management Solutions. It's not designed to spoof MAC addresses.

☒ **C** is incorrect because CACE Pilot is another sniffing tool.

7. You are attempting to sniff traffic on a switch. Which of the following is a good method to ensure you are successful? (Choose all that apply.)

   A. Reboot the switch immediately after connecting.

   B. Implement port security.

   C. Configure a span port.

   D. Use MAC flooding.

   ☑ **C and D.** Switches *filter* unicast traffic, so your attached sniffer would only receive traffic intended for its MAC address as well as any broadcast traffic. To get around this, there are two things you can do. One, if you can gain administrative access to the IOS, you can configure a span port (which sends copies of messages from all ports to yours). Legitimate span ports are designed for things such as network IDS. Second, you can use MAC flooding. Using a tool such as MacOF or Yersinia, you can send thousands and thousands of fake MAC addresses to the switch's CAM table. Once the table gets full, the switch effectively turns into a hub, flooding all packets out all ports. Just know that MAC flooding is harder to pull off with modern network switches and will, most likely, be noticed. Lastly, don't get port spanning and sniffing confused with spoofing. Port spanning will allow you to sniff traffic but doesn't do a thing for you in spoofing your own traffic.

   ☒ **A** is incorrect because rebooting the switch will not help. Usually switches have two configuration files—one in use while the switch is up and running, and the other used to load policies and such at startup. Generally these are the same: to protect the switch in case of a power outage or forced shutdown.

   ☒ **B** is incorrect because port security would actually frustrate your efforts even further. Port security refers to a method by which the administrator defines only specific MAC addresses that the port will allow to connect.

8. Which of the following are modes Snort can operate in? (Choose all that apply.)

   A. Sniffer

   B. Spoofing

   C. Packet Logger

   D. Network IDS

   ☑ **A, C,** and **D.** Snort is more than just a network intrusion detection system. It can run in three different modes. *Sniffer* mode is exactly what it sounds like, and lets you watch packets in real time as they come across your network tap. *Packet Logger* mode saves packets to disk for review at a later time. And, finally, what it's most famous for, *Network Intrusion Detection System* mode analyzes network traffic against various rule sets you pick from, depending on your network's situation.

   ☒ **B** is incorrect because there is not a "Spoofing" mode in Snort.

9. Examine the following Snort rule:

   ```
   alerttcp !$HOME_NET any -> $HOME_NET 23 (content:
   "admin";msg:"Telnet attempt..admin access";)
   ```

   Which of the following are true regarding the rule? (Choose all that apply.)

   A. This rule will alert on packets coming from the designated home network.

   B. This rule will alert on packets coming from outside the designated home address.

   C. This rule will alert on packets designated for any port, from port 23, containing the "admin" string.

   D. This rule will alert on packets designated on port 23, from any port, containing the "admin" string.

   ☑ **B** and **D.** Snort rules, logs, entries, and configuration files will definitely be a part of your exam. This particular rule takes into account a lot of things you'll see. First, note the exclamation mark (!) just before the HOME_NET variable. Any time you see this, it indicates the opposite of the following variable—in this case, any packet from an address *not* in the home network and using any source port number, intended for any address that is within the home network. Following that variable is a spot for a port number, and the word "any" indicates we don't care what the source port is. Next, we spell out the destination information: anything in the home network and destined for port 23. Lastly, we add one more little search before spelling out the message we want to receive: The "content" designator allows us to spell out strings we're looking for.

   ☒ **A** and **C** are incorrect because these statements are polar opposite to what the rule is stating.

10. You wish to begin sniffing, and you have a Windows 7 laptop. You download and install Wireshark, but quickly discover your NIC needs to be in "promiscuous mode." What allows you to put your NIC into promiscuous mode?

A. Installing lmpcap

B. Installing npcap

C. Installing winPcap

D. Installing libPcap

E. Manipulating the NIC properties through Control Panel, Network and Internet, Change Adapter Settings

☑ **C.** To understand this, you've got to know how a NIC is designed to work. The NIC "sees" lots of traffic, but only pulls in traffic it knows belongs to you. It does this by comparing the MAC address of each frame against its own: If they match, it pulls the frame in and works on it; if they don't match, the frame is ignored. If you plug a sniffer into a NIC that only looks at traffic designated for the machine you're on, you've kind of missed the point, wouldn't you say? Promiscuous mode tells the NIC to pull in *everything*. This allows you to see all those packets moving to and fro inside your collision domain. WinPcap is a library that allows NICs on Windows machines to operate in promiscuous mode.

☒ **A** is incorrect because "lmpcap" does not exist.

☒ **B** is incorrect because "npcap" does not exist.

☒ **D** is incorrect because libPcap is used on Linux machines for the same purpose—putting cards into promiscuous mode.

☒ **E** is incorrect because accessing the Change Adapter Setting window does not allow you to put the card into promiscuous mode—you still need winPcap for this.

11. You are attempting to deliver a payload to a target inside the organization; however, it is behind an IDS. You are concerned about successfully accomplishing your task without alerting the IDS monitoring team. Which of the following methods are possible options? (Choose all that apply.)

A. Flood the network with fake attacks.

B. Encrypt the traffic between you and the host.

C. Session hijacking.

D. Session splicing.

☑ **B and D.** Encryption has always been the enemy of network IDS. After all, if the traffic is encrypted and we can't see it, what good does it do to have a monitoring system look at the garbled bits? Granted, it would seem difficult to set up encryption between the target host and yourself, but it is plausible and, therefore, a good answer. Session splicing is a great tool to use as well. In session splicing, you put a payload into packets the IDS usually ignores, such as SYN segments. The fragments can then be reassembled later on the target machine. (If you want to get real sneaky, send them out of order.)

☒ **A** is incorrect, but just barely so. Yes, flooding a network with fake attacks can definitely work. The cover fire from all the other attacks *should* allow you to sneak by. However, there is no way to accomplish this without alerting the monitoring team—after all, the objective is to keep them busy looking at all those fake attacks long enough for you to pull off a real one. Keep in mind that if you're going to attempt this method, you'll need a block of sacrificial IP addresses you won't mind losing. The security staff will, no doubt, see your initial attempts and start blocking those IPs from network access. If you're hoping to provide cover fire for a "real" attack, you'll need to have plenty of "pawn" IPs to sacrifice.

☒ **C** is incorrect because session hijacking has almost nothing to do with IDS evasion. It has a lot to do with guessing sequence numbers and leaping into the middle of an existing, already-authenticated communications channel, but we're not on that chapter yet. Granted, you may be able to make use of some firewall applications or web sessions to bypass some IDS filters, but that's not the intent of this question (nor is that how it will be phrased on your exam).

12. A pen test member has gained access to an open switch port. He configures his NIC for promiscuous mode and sets up a sniffer, plugging his laptop directly into the switch port. He watches traffic as it arrives at the system, looking for specific information to possibly use later. What type of sniffing is being practiced?

    A. Active

    B. Promiscuous

    C. Blind

    D. Passive

    E. Session

    ☑ **D.** This is one of those weird CEH definitions that drive us all crazy on the exam. Knowing the definition of *passive* versus *active* isn't really going to make you a better pen tester, but it may save you a question on the test. When it comes to sniffing, if you are not injecting packets into the stream, it's a passive exercise. Tools such as Wireshark are passive in nature. A tool such as Ettercap, though, has built-in features to trick switches into sending all traffic their way, and all sorts of other sniffing hilarity. This type of sniffing, where you use packet interjection to force a response, is active in nature.

☒ **A** is incorrect because in the example given, no packet injection is being performed. The pen tester is simply hooking up a sniffer and watching what comes by. The only way this can be more passive is if he has a hammock nearby.

☒ **B** is incorrect because the term *promiscuous* is not a sniffing type. Instead, it refers to the NIC's ability to pull in frames that are not addressed specifically for it.

☒ **C** is incorrect because the term *blind* is not a sniffing type. This is included as a distractor.

☒ **E** is incorrect because the term *session* is not a sniffing type. This is included as a distractor.

13. Tcpdump is a popular packet capture sniffer. Examine the following segment of a tcpdump capture (note the capture only shows one side of the communication):

```
18:53:24.872785 IP ubuntu.local.38656 > 192.168.5.12.ftp:
S 4155592273:4155592273(0) win 5840
...g..................
...........
18:53:24.879473 IP ubuntu.local.38656 > 192.168.5.12.ftp:
.ack 1228937421 win 170
....g.I@............
........
18:53:24.881654 IP ubuntu.local.38656 > 192.168.5.12.ftp:
.ack 47 win 170
....g.I@.......8.....
......EN
18:53:26.401846 IP ubuntu.local.38656 > 192.168.5.12.ftp:
P 0:10(10) ack 43 win 170
....g.I@......`$.....
...=..ENUSER user1

18:53:26.403802 IP ubuntu.local.38656 > 192.168.5.12.ftp:
.ack 72 win 170
....h.I@............
...>..E^
18:53:29.169036 IP ubuntu.local.38656 > 192.168.5.12.ftp:
P 10:25(15) ack 76 win 170
....h.I@......#c.....
......E^PASS nothing

18:53:29.171553 IP ubuntu.local.38656 > 192.168.5.12.ftp:
.ack 94 win 170
....h.I@.,..........
......Ez
18:53:29.171649 IP ubuntu.local.38656 > 192.168.5.12.ftp:
P 25:31(6) ack 96 win 170
....h.I@.,..........
......EzSYST
```

```
18:53:29.211607 IP ubuntu.local.38656 > 192.168.5.12.ftp:
.ack 113 win 170
....h.I@.?.....j....
......Ez
18:53:31.367619 IP ubuntu.local.38656 > 192.168.5.12.ftp:
P 31:37(6) ack 115 win 170
....h.I@.?..........
......EzQUIT

18:53:31.369316 IP ubuntu.local.38656 > 192.168.5.12.ftp:
.ack 152 win 170
....h.I@.g..........
......E.
18:53:31.369759 IP ubuntu.local.38656 > 192.168.5.12.ftp:
F 37:37(0) ack 156 win 170
....h.I@.h.....e.....
......E.
```

What can you gather from this capture? (Choose all that apply.)

A. The FTP connection is from 192.168.1.12 to the local host.

B. The FTP connection is from the local host to 192.168.5.12.

C. The FTP connection was unsuccessful.

D. The FTP authentication credentials are clearly visible.

☑ **B and D.** Tcpdump is a great packet capture tool, but I personally hate going through all those lines of captured code. Wireshark, Cain and Abel, and a variety of other tools do this work for me; however, you will see snippets like this on your exam, so it's worthy of a look. First, note the "from-to" in each captured packet line, clearly showing packets from the host to the destination. Next, remember when we discussed protocols that were susceptible to sniffing, and FTP was mentioned as one of them? The user ID (user1) and password (nothing) shown in clear text should provide ample explanation why that is true.

☒ **A** is incorrect because the order is listed backward.

☒ **C** is incorrect because the authentication credentials were passed successfully.

14. What does this line from the Snort configuration file indicate?

```
var RULE_PATH c:\etc\snort\rules
```

A. The configuration variable is not in proper syntax.

B. It instructs the Snort engine to write rule violations in this location.

C. It instructs the Snort engine to compare packets to the rule set named "rules."

D. It defines the location of the Snort rules.

☑ **D.** The var RULE_PATH entry in the config file defines the path to the rules for the IDS—in this case, they will be located in C:\etc\snort\rules. The rules container will hold tons of rule sets, with each available for you to "turn on."

If you were configuring Snort to watch for fantasy football traffic, for example, you would tell it to look for all the rules in this container and then turn on the rule set you defined for fantasy football connection attempts.

☒ **A** is incorrect because this configuration line is in proper syntax.

☒ **B** is incorrect because this variable is not designed for that purpose. The rule violations will be written to a log file that you designate when starting the Snort engine. For example, the command

```
snort -l c:\snort\log\ -c c:\snort\etc\snort.conf
```

starts Snort and has the log file located at c:\snort\log.

☒ **C** is incorrect because the "include" variable is the one used for this purpose. Within this same configuration file, for example, you may have a rule set name fantasy.rules. To get Snort to alert on them, you point the configuration files to where all the rules are (accomplished by the variable RULE_PATH), then you tell it which of the rule sets to bring into play:

```
include $RULE_PATH/fantasy.rules
```

15. As part of a security monitoring team, Joe is reacting to an incursion into the network. The attacker successfully exploited a vulnerability on an internal machine, and Joe is examining how the attacker succeeded. He reviews the IDS logs but sees no alerts for the time period; however, there is definitive proof of the attack. Which IDS shortcoming does this refer to?

A. False acceptance rate

B. False negative

C. Session splicing

D. False positive

☑ **B.** A *false negative* occurs when an IDS reports a particular stream of traffic is just fine when, in fact, an intrusion attempt did occur. False negatives are considered far worse than false positives, and are many times not discovered until well after an attack has occurred—just like in this scenario. There are multiple reasons a false negative can occur.

☒ **A** is incorrect because the term *false acceptance rate (FAR)* refers to a short-coming with biometric authentication systems. The FAR is the rate at which a biometric system will incorrectly accept an attempt at authentication: The lower the rate, the better the security.

☒ **C** is incorrect because although session splicing can be used to evade the IDS, this question is referring to the shortcoming of the IDS itself. There are two big ones: false positive and false negative.

☒ **D** is incorrect because a false positive occurs when the IDS triggers on "normal" traffic when it is not malicious. False positives are a bigger problem with behavior-based IDS.

16. Examine the Snort output shown here:

```
08/28-12:23:13.014491 01:10:BB:17:E3:C5 ->A5:12:B7:55:57:AB type:0x800
len:0x3C
190.168.5.12:33541 ->213.132.44.56:23 TCP TTL:128 TOS:0x0 ID:12365

IpLen:20 DgmLen:48 DF
***A**S* Seq: 0xA153BD Ack: 0xA01657 Win: 0x2000 TcpLen: 28
TCP Options (4) => MSS: 1460 NOP NOPSackOK
0x0000: 00 02 B3 87 84 25 00 10 5A 01 0D 5B 08 00 45 00 ...%..Z..[..E.
0x0010: 00 30 98 43 40 00 80 06 DE EC C0 A8 01 04 C0 A8 .0.C@........
0x0020: 01 43 04 DC 01 BB 00 A1 8B BD 00 00 00 00 70 02 .C..........p.
0x0030: 20 00 4C 92 00 00 02 04 05 B4 01 01 04 02 .L..........
```

Which of the following is true regarding the packet capture?

A. The capture indicates a NOP sled attack.

B. The capture shows step 2 of a TCP handshake.

C. The packet source is 213.132.44.56.

D. The packet capture shows an SSH session attempt.

☑ B. You'll probably see at least one or two Snort capture logs on the exam, and most of them are just this easy. If you examine the capture log, it shows a TCP port 23 packet from 190.168.5.12 headed toward 213.132.44.56. The TCP flags are clearly shown in line 5 as "***A**S*," indicating the SYN and ACK flags are set. Because the three-way handshake is SYN, SYN/ACK, and ACK—*voilà!*—we've solved another one!

☒ A is incorrect because this is a single packet that is not attempting a NOP sled in any shape or form.

☒ C is incorrect because this answer has it in reverse—the source is 190.168.5.12.

☒ D is incorrect because the port number shown in the capture is 23 (telnet), not 22 (SSH).

17. Your IDS sits on the network perimeter and has been analyzing traffic for a couple of weeks. On arrival one morning, you find the IDS has alerted on a spike in network traffic late the previous evening. Which type of IDS are you using?

A. Stateful

B. Snort

C. Passive

D. Signature based

E. Anomaly based

☑ **E.** The scenario described here is precisely what an anomaly- or behavior-based system is designed for. The system watches traffic and, over time, develops an idea of what "normal" traffic looks like—everything from source and destinations, ports in use, and times of higher data flows. In one sense, it's better than a plain signature-based system because it can find things heuristically based on behavior; however, anomaly-based systems are notorious for the amount of false positives they spin off—especially early on.

☒ **A** is incorrect because *stateful* refers to a firewall type, not an IDS.

☒ **B** is incorrect because Snort is a signature-based IDS.

☒ **C** is incorrect because the term *passive* isn't associated with IDS. Now, an IDS *can* react to an alert by taking action to stop or prevent an attack, but this is referred to as an *intrusion prevention system (IPS)*, not active or passive.

☒ **D** is incorrect because a signature-based IDS isn't going to care about the amount of traffic going by, nor what time it decides to do so. A signature-based IDS simply compares each packet against a list (signature file) you configure it to look at. If it doesn't match anything in the signature file, then no action is taken.

18. You are performing an ACK scan against a target subnet. You previously verified connectivity to several hosts within the subnet, but want to verify all live hosts on the subnet. Your scan, however, is not receiving any replies. Which type of firewall is most likely in use at your location?

    A. Packet filtering

    B. IPS

    C. Stateful

    D. Active

☑ **C.** Most people think of a firewall as a simple packet filter, examining packets as they are coming in against an access list—if the port is allowed, let the packet through. However, the stateful inspection firewall has the ability to examine all sorts of information about a packet—including the payload—and make a determination on the state of the packet. For a very common (dare I say, textbook) example, if a stateful firewall receives an ACK packet, it's smart enough to know whether there is an associated SYN packet that originated from inside the network to go along with it. If there isn't not—that is, if communications did not start from inside the subnet—it'll drop the packet.

☒ **A** is incorrect because a packet-filtering firewall wouldn't bother with the flags. It would be concerned about what port the packet was headed to. If, for instance, you host a web page out of that subnet, but not an FTP server, your firewall should be set up to allow port 80 in, but not port 21.

☒ **B** is incorrect because an IPS (intrusion prevention system) isn't a firewall at all. It's a network-monitoring solution that has the capability of recognizing malicious traffic and taking action to prevent or stop the attack.

☒ **D** is incorrect because the term *active* is not associated with a firewall type. This is included as a distractor.

19. You are separated from your target subnet by a firewall. The firewall is correctly configured and only allows requests through to ports opened by the administrator. In firewalking the device, you find that port 80 is open. Which technique could you employ to send data and commands to or from the target system?

    A. Encrypt the data to hide it from the firewall.

    B. Use session splicing.

    C. Use MAC flooding.

    D. Use HTTP tunneling.

    ☑ **D.** Okay, so HTTP tunneling is a successful "hacking" technique, but it's hardly new. Microsoft makes use of HTTP tunneling for lots of things, and they've been doing it for years. The tactic is fairly simple: Because port 80 is almost never filtered by a firewall, you can craft port 80 segments to carry a payload for protocols the firewall may have otherwise blocked. Of course, you'll need something on the other end to pull the payload out of all those port 80 packets that IIS is desperately wanting to answer, but that's not altogether difficult.

    ☒ **A** is incorrect because encryption won't do a thing for you here. The firewall isn't looking necessarily at content/payload—it's looking at the packet/frame header and port information. Encryption is a good choice to get around an IDS, not a firewall.

    ☒ **B** is incorrect because session splicing is a technique for evading an IDS, not a firewall. Again, the firewall is interested in the packet and frame header, not what fragments of code you've hidden in the payload.

    ☒ **C** is incorrect because MAC flooding is a technique for sniffing switches. The idea is to fill the CAM table to the brim with thousands of useless MAC addresses. This effectively turns the switch into a hub, because it is too confused to filter and just begins flooding all traffic to all ports.

20. Which of the following tools are useful in identifying potential honeypots on a subnet? (Choose all that apply.)

    A. Wireshark

    B. Ettercap

    C. Nessus

    D. Send-Safe HH

    E. Nmap

☑ **C and D.** A *honeypot* is a system set up as a decoy to entice attackers. The idea is to load it up with all sorts of fake goodies, with not-*too*-easy vulnerabilities a hacker may exploit. After all that scanning and enumeration, this one is sure to show up as a possible target. Both Nessus (better known as a vulnerability assessment tool) and Send-Safe Honeypot Hunter (HH) are tools you can use to help point out potential honeypots to avoid. Nessus has a plug-in for an older honeypot (LaBrea Tarpit), and can be used to identify vulnerabilities on systems within the network. Sometimes—not always, but sometimes—a list of vulnerabilities on a particular machine can be a dead giveaway it's a honeypot (if 95 percent of the machines on the network are fully patched but one shows up with 200 Category 1 vulnerabilities, you should hear bells ringing). Send-Safe HH (http://www.send-safe.com/honeypot-hunter.html) is a shareware tool that may be useful in identifying honeypots using "lists of HTTPS and SOCKS proxies." As an aside, you can use honeypots to your advantage if you know where they are by turning them into proverbial double-agents. Security monitoring will have all sorts of time spent watching you hack away at the honeypot, while your real attack goes on elsewhere. Just a thought.

☒ **A is incorrect** because Wireshark is simply a network sniffer.

☒ **B is incorrect** because Ettercap is also a network sniffer. Granted, you can have lots of fun with the active sniffing features in Ettercap, but it's not designed to find and label a honeypot for you.

☒ **E is incorrect** because although nmap *is* a network-scanning tool, it's not designed to point out a honeypot. Granted, you may be able to discern that identity by nmap results, but that's more of a job for your gray matter, not nmap itself.

21. Examine the Wireshark filter shown here:

```
ip.src == 192.168.1.1 &&tcp.srcport == 80
```

Which of the following correctly describes the capture filter?

A. The results will display all traffic from 192.168.1.1 destined for port 80.

B. The results will display all HTTP traffic to 192.168.1.1.

C. The results will display all HTTP traffic from 192.168.1.1.

D. No results will display due to invalid syntax.

☑ **C.** Wireshark filters will be covered quite bit on your exam and, as stated before, these are easy questions for you. The preceding syntax designates the source IP and combines it with a source TCP port. This is effectively looking at all answers to port 80 requests by 192.168.1.1. As another important study tip, watch for the period (.) between "ip" and "src:" on the exam because they'll drop it or change it to a dash (-) to trick you.

    ☒ **A** is incorrect because port 80 is defined as the *source* port, not the destination. 192.168.1.1 is answering a request for an HTML page.

    ☒ **B** is incorrect because 192.168.1.1 is defined as the *source* address, not the destination.

    ☒ **D** is incorrect because the syntax is indeed correct.

22. You need to put the NIC into listening mode on your Linux box, capture packets, and write the results to a log file named my.log. How do you accomplish this with tcpdump?

    A. `tcpdump -i eth0 -w my.log`

    B. `tcpdump -l eth0 -c my.log.`

    C. `tcpdump/i eth0 /w my.log`

    D. `tcpdump/l eth0 /c my.log`

    ☑ **A.** Tcpdump syntax is simple: `tcpdump flag(s) interface`. The –i flag specifies the interface (in this example, eth0) for tcpdump to listen on, and the –w flag defines where you want your packet log to go. For your own study, be aware that many study references—including EC Council's official reference books—state that the i flag "puts the interface into listening mode." It doesn't actually modify the interface at all, so this is a little bit of a misnomer—it just identifies to tcpdump which interface to listen on for traffic. Lastly, be aware that the w flag dumps traffic in binary format. If you want it readable, you'll need to have it display onscreen. Better yet, you can dump it to a file using the "|" designator and a filename.

    ☒ **B** is incorrect because the –l flag does not put the interface in listening mode: It actually has to do with line buffering.

    ☒ **C and D** are incorrect for the same reason—flags are designated with a dash (-) not a slash (/).

23. Which of the following tools can assist with IDS evasion? (Choose all that apply.)

    A. Whisker

    B. Fragroute

    C. Capsa

    D. Wireshark

    E. ADMmutate

    F. Inundator

    ☑ **A, B, E, and F.** IDS evasion comes down to a few methods: encryption, flooding, and fragmentation (session splicing). Whisker is an HTTP scanning tool but also has the ability to craft session-splicing fragments.

Fragroute intercepts, modifies, and rewrites egress traffic destined for the specified host, and can be used to fragment an attack payload over multiple packets. ADMmutate can create multiple scripts that won't be easily recognizable by signature files, and Inundator is a flooding tool that can help you hide in the cover fire.

☒ C and D are incorrect because both Capsa (Colasoft) and Wireshark are sniffers.

24. Which command puts Snort into packet logger mode?

 A. `./snort -dev -l ./log`

 B. `./snort -v`

 C. `./snort -dev -l ./log -h 192.168.1.0/24 -c snort.conf`

 D. None of the above

☑ **A.** This is the proper syntax to start Snort in packet logger mode. Assuming you have the /log folder created, Snort will start happily logging packets as it captures them. Here are some other flags of note within this command:

 - -v puts SNORT in verbose mode, to look at all packets.

 - -d includes the application layer information, when used with the –v argument.

 - -e includes the data link layer information with the packet.

 When put altogether, the –dev arguments tell SNORT to display all packet data, including the headers.

☒ **B** is incorrect because this syntax starts Snort in sniffer mode—meaning packet headers will be displayed directly to the screen.

☒ **C** is incorrect because this syntax starts Snort in network intrusion detection mode. Yes, the –l switch logs files, but the bigger issue for you here is the addition of the –c switch, indicating the configuration file the NIDS needs.

☒ **D** is incorrect because the correct syntax is indeed displayed.

25. Examine the following hex dump of a packet capture:

```
0000  00 13 10 fece 6c 18 3d a2 5b 67 64 08 00 45 00   ....l.= .[gd..E.
0010  00 36 0b 48 40 00 80 06 fd 5e c0 a8 01 65 0f c0   .6.H@... .^...e..
0020  20 4e c2 73 00 15 0a 15 36 47 d9 0b 0b 4c 50 18   N.s21.. 6G...LP.
0030  0f 91 0a b2 00 00 55 53 45 52 20 75 73 65 72 5f   ......US ER user_
0040  31 33 0d 0a                                        13..
0000  00 13 10 fece 6c 18 3d a2 5b 67 64 08 00 45 00   ....l.= .[gd..E.
0010  00 37 0b 49 40 00 80 06 fd 5c c0 a8 01 65 0f c0   .7.I@... .\...e..
0020  20 4e c2 73 00 15 0a 15 36 55 d9 0b 0b 6f 50 18   N.s.... 6U...oP.
0030  0f 89 be 88 00 00 50 41 53 53 20 31 32 33 34 5f   ......PA SS 1234_
0040  35 36 37 0d 0a                                     567..
```

What does this packet capture show?

 A. An ARP spoofing attempt

 B. A Unicode IDS evasion attempt

C. An FTP session authentication

D. A ping sweep

☑ **C.** Admittedly, this one is a little tricky, but it's included here because you absolutely must know how to read simple packet capture dumps. If you had this capture in Wireshark, it would be easy—clicking TCP in the capture and then the port would point out the appropriate info in the hex dump. Without it, though, you need some observation skills. Note in line 0020 of the first packet that the source port is listed as 21 (telling you it's FTP). Additionally, if you're really paying attention, you can clearly see the user ID and password used for this authentication: The user ID "user_13" is found in lines 0030 and 0040 of the first packet, and the password "1234_567" is found in the same lines of packet 2. As an aside, if you learn how to convert ASCII to hex, you can do this without the ASCII conversion shown on the right side of the capture. Play with Wireshark and you'll quickly learn where to look in these captures.

☒ **A** is incorrect because ARP does not appear in either of these FTP packets.

☒ **B** is incorrect because this is not a Unicode attack. Unicode characters U+0020 (a space), U+0036 (the number 6), and U+0041 (a capital A) can be used instead of human-readable code to confuse signature-based IDS.

☒ **D** is incorrect because these two packets are clearly not part of a ping sweep (ICMP).

Attacking a System

CHAPTER 6

Attacking a System

This chapter includes questions from the following topics:

- Understand the different types of password, password attacks, and password-cracking techniques
- Understand Microsoft Authentication mechanisms
- Identify various password-cracking tools, keyloggers, and spyware technologies
- Understand privilege escalation
- Describe file-hiding methods, alternate data streams, and evidence erasure
- Identify rootkits
- Understand basic Linux file structure, directories, and commands
- Describe how to install, configure, and compile a Linux kernel, kernel patches, and LKM modules
- Understand GCC compilation commands
- List vulnerabilities and password-cracking techniques in Linux
- Understand password cracking in Linux
- Understand Linux-hardening methods

I think the people involved in remaking the movie *Total Recall* should be flogged. At the very least, they should be forced to provide an apology for what they've done to an American cinematic classic. If you haven't seen either movie, go rent the 1990 version with Arnold Schwarzenegger, alien artifacts, and that creepy little mutant guy that keeps saying, "Open your *mind* to me...." You need to see this movie because it's integral to what we're trying to accomplish in this chapter. Feel free to tell your mom, dad, or significant other that you have to watch it—the book guy says it's study material.

In the movie, Arnold's character (Douglas Quaid) is a 9-to-5, Joe-lunchbox average guy who one day discovers he's actually a secret agent spy-type person. He discovers this by taking out six armed spies in a confrontation after work. As he stands there looking at the bodies laid out in a circle all around him, he looks at his fists and asks, "How did I do that?"

Just as Douglas Quaid had no idea he was actually Hauser (the name of his alter-ego super-spy persona), you may be sitting there having no idea what kind of virtual damage you can do with the knowledge you've gained so far. Who knows if, put in the right

137

situation, you'd knock out virtual targets with ease? I can see you now, looking down at your keyboard in awe and answering the "How did you do that?" question with, "I don't know—the training just kicked in." Granted, we still have a lot of training to do, and I doubt you'll be punching any virtual targets outside an agreed-upon scope (after all, you are an ethical hacker, right?). However, this chapter will help hone your skills. Here, we'll talk all about system attacks and putting to use some of the training and knowledge you already have in place.

 STUDY TIPS Know your password rules, attacks, and tools very, very well. You will definitely see loads of questions about passwords. Use, storage, hashing of, and attacks against passwords will be covered ad nausea on your exam.

Pull some of these tools down and play with them, because you'll need to know what they look like, how they operate, and what capabilities they have.

Next, when it comes to this chapter, you really need to get to know Linux better. Questions regarding Linux will most likely revolve around kernel modules, file structure, storage locations, and the command-line interface. Again, the easiest way to learn all this is to go download a Linux distro and run it in a VM on your machine. Take advantage of the thousands of Linux how-to videos and articles you can find on the Internet: It's one thing to read it in a book, but you'll learn far more if you actually perform it yourself.

1. Examine the following password hashes obtained from a Windows XP machine using LM hashing:

   B757BF5C0D87772FAAD3B435B51404EE

   BA810DBA98995F1817306D272A9441BB

   E52CAC67419A9A224A3B108F3FA6CB6D

   0182BD0BD4444BF836077A718CCDF409

   CEC52EB9C8E3455DC2265B23734E0DAC

   Which of the following is true regarding the hashes listed?

   A. The hashes are protected using Syskey.

   B. The third hash listed is the local administrator's password.

   C. The first hash listed is from a password of seven characters or less.

   D. The hashes can be easily decrypted by reversing the hash algorithm.

2. Which of the following correctly describes brute-force password attacks?

   A. Feed a list of words into a cracking program.

   B. Compare the hash values to lists of pre-hashed values for a match.

   C. Attempt all possible combinations of letters, numbers, and special characters in succession.

   D. Threaten the user with physical violence unless they reveal their password.

3. Which password theft method is almost always successful, requires little technical knowledge, and is nearly impossible to detect?

   A. Install a hardware keylogger.

   B. Install a software keylogger.

   C. Sniff the network segment with Ettercap.

   D. Brute force using Cain and Abel.

4. Which of the following will extract an executable file from NTFS streaming?

   A. `c:\> cat file1.txt:hidden.exe > visible.exe`

   B. `c:\> more file1.txt | hidden.exe > visible.exe`

   C. `c:\> type notepad.exe > file1.txt:hidden.exe`

   D. `c:\> list file1.txt$hidden.exe > visible.exe`

5. Which command is used to allow all privileges to the user, read-only to the group and read-only for all others to a particular file, on a Linux machine?

    A. `chmod 411 file1`

    B. `chmod 114 file1`

    C. `chmod 117 file1`

    D. `chmod 711 file1`

    E. `chmod 744 file1`

6. Examine the following passwd file:

    ```
    root:x:0:0:root:/root:/bin/bash
    mwalk:x:500:500:Matt Walker,Room 2238,email:/home/mwalk:/bin/sh
    jboll:x:501:501:Jason Bollinger,Room 2239,email:/home/jboll:/bin/sh
    rbell:x:502:502:Rick Bell,Room 1017,email:/home/rbell:/bin/sh
    afrench:x:503:501:Alecia French,Room 1017,email:/home/afrench:/bin/sh
    ```

    Which of the following statements are true regarding this passwd file? (Choose all that apply.)

    A. None of the user accounts have passwords assigned.

    B. The system makes use of the shadow file.

    C. The root account password is root.

    D. The root account has a shadowed password.

    E. Files created by Alecia will initially be viewable by Jason.

7. You are attempting to hack a Windows machine and wish to gain a copy of the SAM file. Where can you find it? (Choose all that apply.)

    A. \etc\passwd

    B. \etc\shadow

    C. c:\windows\system32\config

    D. c:\winnt\config

    E. c:\windows\repair

8. Which of the following statements are true concerning Kerberos? (Choose all that apply.)

    A. Kerberos uses symmetric encryption.

    B. Kerberos uses asymmetric encryption.

    C. Clients ask for authentication tickets from the KDC in clear text.

    D. KDC responses to clients never include a password.

    E. Clients decrypt a TGT from the server.

9. What is the difference between a dictionary attack and a hybrid attack?

    A. Dictionary attacks are based solely on word lists, whereas hybrid attacks make use of both word lists and rainbow tables.

B. Dictionary attacks are based solely on whole word lists, whereas hybrid attacks can use a variety of letters, numbers, and special characters.

C. Dictionary attacks use predefined word lists, whereas hybrid attacks substitute numbers and symbols within those words.

D. Hybrid and dictionary attacks are the same.

10. Which of the following SIDs indicates the true administrator account?

A. S-1-5-21-1388762127-2960977290-773940301-1100

B. S-1-5-21-1388762127-2960977290-773940301-1101

C. S-1-5-21-1388762127-2960977290-773940301-500

D. S-1-5-21-1388762127-2960977290-773940301-501

11. You have obtained a password hash and wish to quickly determine the associated plaintext password. Which of the following is the best choice?

A. Use a rainbow table.

B. Reverse the hash algorithm.

C. Use User2SID.

D. Use SID2User.

E. Use the public key of the user.

12. You are monitoring traffic between two systems communicating over SSL. Which of the following techniques is your best bet in gaining access?

A. Sniff the traffic with Cain and Abel

B. Practice active sniffing

C. Sidejacking

D. ARP poisoning

13. Which password would be considered the most secure?

A. CEH123TEST

B. CEHisaHARDTEST

C. 638154849675

D. C3HisH@rd

14. Your client makes use of Sigverif on his servers. What functionality does this tool provide?

A. Verifies digital signatures in SSL certificates.

B. Displays a list of unsigned drivers.

C. Displays a list of corrupted (nonfunctioning) drivers.

D. Verifies SAM database integrity.

15. Which of the following are considered offline password attacks? (Choose all that apply.)

    A. Using a hardware keylogger

    B. Brute-force cracking with Cain and Abel on a stolen SAM file

    C. Using John the Ripper on a stolen passwd file

    D. Shoulder surfing

16. Examine the following portion of a log file, captured during a hacking attempt:

```
[matt@localhost]#rm -rf /tmp/mykit_headers
[matt@localhost]#rm -rf /var/log/messages
[matt@localhost]#rm -rf /root/.bash_history
```

    What was the attacker attempting to do?

    A. Copy files for later examination.

    B. Cover his tracks.

    C. Chang the shell to lock out other users.

    D. Upload a rootkit.

17. You suspect a hack has occurred against your Linux machine. Which command will display all running processes for you to review?

    A. ls -d

    B. ls -l

    C. su

    D. ps -ef

    E. ifconfig

18. Examine the following command output:

```
ANY_PC           <00>  UNIQUE      Registered
WORKGROUP        <00>  GROUP       Registered
ANY_PC           <20>  UNIQUE      Registered
WORKGROUP        <1E>  GROUP       Registered
WORKGROUP        <1D>  UNIQUE      Registered
.._MSBROWSE__.<01>  GROUP       Registered
MAC Address = 78-AC-C0-BA-E6-F2
```

    Which of the following are true regarding this output? (Choose all that apply.)

    A. This output is from net commands.

    B. This output is from nbtstat.

    C. This output is from netstat.

    D. This output is from nslookup.

19. Which rootkit type makes use of system-level calls to hide their existence?

    A. Application level

    B. Kernel level

C. Library level

D. System level

20. Which folder in Linux holds administrative commands and daemons?

   A. /sbin

   B. /bin

   C. /dev

   D. /mnt

   E. /usr

21. What are the three commands necessary to install an application in Linux?

   A. ./install

   B. make

   C. make install

   D. ./configure

22. You are examining files on a Windows machine and note one file's attributes include "h." What does this indicate?

   A. The file is flagged for backup.

   B. The file is part of the help function.

   C. The file is fragmented due to size.

   D. The file has been quarantined by an antivirus program.

   E. The file is hidden.

23. You have gained access to a SAM file from an older Windows machine and are preparing to run a Syskey cracker against it. How many bits are used for Syskey encryption?

   A. 128

   B. 256

   C. 512

   D. 1024

24. Which of the following tools can assist in discovering the use of NTFS file streams? (Choose all that apply.)

   A. LADS

   B. ADS Spy

   C. Sfind

   D. Snow

25. Which authentication method uses DES for encryption and forces 14-character passwords for hash storage?

   A. NTLMv1

   B. NTLMv2

   C. LAN Manager

   D. Kerberos

1. C
2. C
3. A
4. A
5. D
6. B, D, E
7. C, E
8. A, B, C, D, E
9. C
10. C
11. A
12. C
13. D
14. B
15. A, B, C
16. B
17. D
18. B
19. C
20. A
21. B, C, D
22. E
23. A
24. A, B, C
25. C

1. Examine the following password hashes obtained from a Windows XP machine using LM hashing:

   B757BF5C0D87772FAAD3B435B51404EE

   BA810DBA98995F1817306D272A9441BB

   E52CAC67419A9A224A3B108F3FA6CB6D

   0182BD0BD4444BF836077A718CCDF409

   CEC52EB9C8E3455DC2265B23734E0DAC

   Which of the following is true regarding the hashes listed?

   A. The hashes are protected using Syskey.

   B. The third hash listed is the local administrator's password.

   C. The first hash listed is from a password of seven characters or less.

   D. The hashes can be easily decrypted by reversing the hash algorithm.

   ☑ C. Windows 2000 and NT-type machines used something called LAN Manager, and then NT LAN Manager, to hash passwords. LM hashing is an older, outdated, and easily crackable method. It worked by converting all password characters to uppercase and, if necessary, appending blank spaces to reach 14 characters. Next, the password was split directly in the middle and both sides would then be hashed separately. The problem with this is the LM hash value of seven blank characters will always be the same (AAD3B435B51404EE). This greatly simplifies your cracking efforts, because running through only seven characters is much easier than 14.

   ☒ A is incorrect because Syskey is not in use here. Syskey is an older, optional utility added in Windows NT 4.0 SP3 that encrypted hashed password information in a SAM database using a 128-bit encryption key. It was meant to protect against offline password-cracking attacks; however, security problems were discovered that rendered it moot: Brute-force attacking worked even with Syskey in place.

   ☒ B is incorrect because there is no way to tell from a hash which password belongs with which user.

   ☒ D is incorrect because hashes cannot be reversed.

2. Which of the following correctly describes brute-force password attacks?

   A. Feed a list of words into a cracking program.

   B. Compare the hash values to lists of pre-hashed values for a match.

   C. Attempt all possible combinations of letters, numbers, and special characters in succession.

   D. Threaten the user with physical violence unless they reveal their password.

☑ **C.** A brute-force attack uses every possible combination of letters, numbers, and special characters against an authentication effort—whether in succession or (more commonly) at random. The drawbacks to its use are substantial: It takes the longest amount of time and a tremendous amount of processing resources. However, it is your best option on complex passwords, and there is no arguing its effectiveness—given enough time *every* password can be cracked using brute force. It may take years to try every combination, but if you keep at it long enough, it is successful 100 percent of the time.

☒ **A** is incorrect because this describes a dictionary attack. It is much easier and faster than a brute force, and uses far fewer resources. The attack works by using a list of passwords in a text file, which is then hashed by the same algorithm/process the original password was put through. The hashes are compared and, if a match is found, the password is cracked. Although this attack is supposed to (technically speaking) only use words you'd find in a dictionary, you can create your own word list to feed into the cracker. Using this method, you can crack "complex" passwords too; however, the word list you use must have the exact match in it—you can't get it close, it must be *exact*. Although it may be fun for you to spend hours of your day creating your own dictionary file, it's a lot easier to simply download one of the thousands already out on the Internet.

☒ **B** is incorrect because this describes the use of rainbow tables. A rainbow table crack effort can be faster than anything else, assuming you can pull the right one to look through. Rainbow tables are created when someone, with lots of time on their hands, feeds every conceivable password in creation through a hash. The hashes are then saved to a table, to which you can compare the password hashes off your target machine. It's simple and easy; however, keep in mind these tables are huge. Additionally, "salting" a password makes rainbow tables moot. One final note for the purists in the reading audience: The use of multi-GPU cracking systems (employing computing resources to cracking passwords that boggle the mind) may be faster than using rainbow tables. Just don't say that on your exam!

☒ **D** is incorrect because this refers to something defined by EC Council and the CEH exam as a *rubber hose attack*. No, I'm not making this up. And I'm not encouraging you to use this in your own pen testing—just know it for your exam.

3. Which password theft method is almost always successful, requires little technical knowledge, and is nearly impossible to detect?

   A. Install a hardware keylogger.

   B. Install a software keylogger.

   C. Sniff the network segment with Ettercap.

   D. Brute force using Cain and Abel.

☑ **A.** Questions on hardware keyloggers will almost always reference the fact that they're nearly impossible to detect. Unless the user notices them, or you have dedicated security staff watching for them, these are foolproof, easy to install, and great tools to use. These are usually small devices connected between the keyboard cable and the computer that simply capture all keystrokes going by. Install one day and just wait—when you pick it up it will be filled with all the access information you need.

☒ **B** is incorrect because although a software keylogger does the same thing as a hardware keylogger and will provide excellent results (I've used one on my kids before—it's fantastic), it's fairly easy to spot and requires a little configuration to get things just the way you want them.

☒ **C** is incorrect because sniffing a network tap with Ettercap isn't going to provide you with anything other than an open text protocol password (FTP and so on). Sniffing isn't guaranteed to provide anything password-wise. Yes, Ettercap is powerful, but it does require a fairly substantial amount of technical know-how to get the most out of it.

☒ **D** is incorrect because a brute-force attack—with any tool—is exceedingly easy to detect. Additionally, it's not just a point-and-shoot endeavor: You do have to have some technical ability to pull it off. Lastly, I know some of you are thinking that taking the passwords offline and pounding away at them is as quiet as you can get. Trust me, that's not the intent of this question, and don't let that fact trip you up.

4. Which of the following will extract an executable file from NTFS streaming?

   A. `c:\> cat file1.txt:hidden.exe > visible.exe`

   B. `c:\> more file1.txt | hidden.exe > visible.exe`

   C. `c:\> type notepad.exe > file1.txt:hidden.exe`

   D. `c:\> list file1.txt$hidden.exe > visible.exe`

   ☑ **A.** This is the correct syntax. The cat command will extract the executable directly into the folder you execute the command from. NTFS file steaming allows you to hide virtually any file behind any other file, rendering it invisible to directory searches. The file can be a text file, to remind you of steps to take when you return to the target, or even an executable file you can run at your leisure later on. Alternate Data Streams (ADS) in the form of NTFS file streaming is a feature of the Windows-native NTFS file systems to ensure compatibility with Apple file systems (called HFS). Be careful on the exam—you will see ADS and NTFS file streaming used interchangeably. As an aside, the cat command isn't available on Windows 7 machines—you'll need a Linux emulator or something like it to pull this off on a Windows 7 system.

☒ **B** is incorrect because this is not the correct syntax. There is no pipe (|) function in extracting a file, and the "more" command is used to display the contents of a text file, not extract an executable from ADS.

☒ **C** is incorrect because this is not the correct syntax. This option would display the contents of a hidden text file—maybe one you've stowed away instructions in for use later.

☒ **D** is incorrect because the syntax is not correct in any shape of the imagination. This is included as a distractor.

5. Which command is used to allow all privileges to the user, read-only to the group and read-only for all others to a particular file, on a Linux machine?

   A. `chmod 411 file1`

   B. `chmod 114 file1`

   C. `chmod 117 file1`

   D. `chmod 711 file1`

   E. `chmod 744 file1`

   ☑ **D.** You're going to need to know some basic Linux commands to survive this exam, and one command I can guarantee you'll see a question on is chmod. File permissions in Linux are assigned via the use of the binary equivalent for each rwx group: read is equivalent to 4, write to 2, and execute to 1. To accumulate permissions, you add the number: 4 is read-only, 6 is read and write, and adding execute to the bunch means a 7.

   ☒ **A, B, C,** and **E** are all incorrect syntax for what we're trying to accomplish here: 411 equates to read-only, execute, and execute (with 114 being the reverse of that), and 117 equates to execute, execute, full permissions, with 711 being the reverse.

6. Examine the following passwd file:

```
root:x:0:0:root:/root:/bin/bash
mwalk:x:500:500:Matt Walker,Room 2238,email:/home/mwalk:/bin/sh
jboll:x:501:501:Jason Bollinger,Room 2239,email:/home/jboll:/bin/sh
rbell:x:502:502:Rick Bell,Room 1017,email:/home/rbell:/bin/sh
afrench:x:503:501:Alecia French,Room 1017,email:/home/afrench:/bin/sh
```

   Which of the following statements are true regarding this passwd file? (Choose all that apply.)

   A. None of the user accounts have passwords assigned.

   B. The system makes use of the shadow file.

   C. The root account password is root.

   D. The root account has a shadowed password.

   E. Files created by Alecia will initially be viewable by Jason.

☑ **B, D, and E.** If there are not two to four questions on your exam regarding the Linux passwd file, I'll eat my hat. Every exam and practice exam I've ever taken references this file—a lot—and it's included here to ensure you pay attention. Fields in the passwd file, from left to right, are as follows:

- **User Name** This is what the user types in as the login name. Each of these must be unique.

- **Password** If a shadow file is being used, an x will be displayed here. If not, you'll see the password in clear text. As an aside, setting this to an asterisk (*) is a method to deactivate an account.

- **UID** The user identifier is used by the operating system for internal purposes. It is typically incremented by 1 for each new user added.

- **GID** The group identifier identifies the primary group of the user. All files that are created by this user will normally be accessible to this group, unless a chmod command prevents it.

- **Gecos** Descriptive field for the user, generally containing contact information separated by commas.

- **Home Directory** The location of the user's home directory.

- **Startup Program** This is the program that is started every time the user logs in. It's usually a shell for the user to interact with the system.

☒ **A** is incorrect because the x indicates a shadowed password, not the absence of one.

☒ **C** is incorrect because the x indicates that root does indeed have a password, but it is shadowed. Could it actually be root? Sure, but there's no way to tell that from this listing.

7. You are attempting to hack a Windows machine and wish to gain a copy of the SAM file. Where can you find it? (Choose all that apply.)

A. \etc\passwd

B. \etc\shadow

C. c:\windows\system32\config

D. c:\winnt\config

E. c:\windows\repair

☑ **C and E.** From Microsoft's definition, the Security Account Manager (SAM) is a database that stores user accounts and security descriptors for users on the local computer. The SAM file can be found in c:\windows\system32\ config. If you're having problems getting there, try pulling a copy from system restore (c:\windows\repair).

☒ **A and B** are both incorrect because the /etc is a dead giveaway this is a Linux folder (note the forward slash instead of the Windows backward slash). The etc folder contains all the administration files and passwords on a Linux system. Both the password and shadow file are found here.

☒ **D** is incorrect because this is not the correct location of the SAM. It's included as a distractor.

8. Which of the following statements are true concerning Kerberos? (Choose all that apply.)

   A. Kerberos uses symmetric encryption.

   B. Kerberos uses asymmetric encryption.

   C. Clients ask for authentication tickets from the KDC in clear text.

   D. KDC responses to clients never include a password.

   E. Clients decrypt a TGT from the server.

   ☑ **A, B, C, D,** and **E.** All answers are correct. Kerberos makes use of both symmetric and asymmetric encryption technologies to securely transmit passwords and keys across a network. The entire process is made up of a Key Distribution Center (KDC), an Authentication Service (AS), a Ticket Granting Service (TGS), and the Ticket Granting Ticket (TGT). A basic Kerberos exchange starts with a client asking the KDC, which holds the AS and TGS, for a ticket, which will be used to authenticate throughout the network. This request is in clear text. The server will respond with a secret key, which is hashed by the password copy kept on the server (password are never sent—only hashes and keys). This is known as the TGT. The client decrypts the message, since it knows the password, and the TGT is sent back to the server requesting a TGS service ticket. The server responds with the service ticket, and the client is allowed to logon and access network resources.

9. What is the difference between a dictionary attack and a hybrid attack?

   A. Dictionary attacks are based solely on word lists, whereas hybrid attacks make use of both word lists and rainbow tables.

   B. Dictionary attacks are based solely on whole word lists, whereas hybrid attacks can use a variety of letters, numbers, and special characters.

   C. Dictionary attacks use predefined word lists, whereas hybrid attacks substitute numbers and symbols within those words.

   D. Hybrid and dictionary attacks are the same.

   ☑ **C.** A hybrid attack is a variant on a dictionary attack. In this effort, you still have a word list, however the cracker is smart enough to replace letters and characters within those words. For example, both attacks might use a list containing the word Password. To have multiple variants on it, the dictionary attack would have to have each variant added to the list individually (P@ssword, Pa$$word, etc.). A Hybrid attack would only require the word list to include 'Password,' as it would swap out characters and letters to find different versions of the same word.

☒ **A** is incorrect because hybrid attacks don't use rainbow tables.

☒ **B** is incorrect because dictionary attacks can use all sorts of variants of a whole word, they just need to be listed separately in the list.

☒ **D** is incorrect because hybrid and dictionary attacks are most definitely different.

10. Which of the following SIDs indicates the true administrator account?

    A. S-1-5-21-1388762127-2960977290-773940301-1100

    B. S-1-5-21-1388762127-2960977290-773940301-1101

    C. S-1-5-21-1388762127-2960977290-773940301-500

    D. S-1-5-21-1388762127-2960977290-773940301-501

☑ **C.** The Security Identifier (commonly abbreviated SID) in Windows is used to identify a "security principle." It's unique to each account and service, and is good for the life of the principle. Everything else associated with the account is simply a property of the SID, allowing accounts to be renamed without affecting their security attributes. In a Windows system, the true administrator account always has an RID (relative identifier) of 500.

☒ **A and B** are incorrect because neither 1100 nor 1101 are the RID associated with the administrator account. RID values between 1000 and 1500 indicate a standard user account.

☒ **D** is incorrect because 501 is the RID for the guest account.

11. You have obtained a password hash and wish to quickly determine the associated plaintext password. Which of the following is the best choice?

    A. Use a rainbow table.

    B. Reverse the hash algorithm.

    C. Use User2SID.

    D. Use SID2User.

    E. Use the public key of the user.

☑ **A.** As discussed earlier, rainbow tables were created specifically for this purpose. If you have a password hash offline, running it against rainbow tables is a very quick way to obtain the password that created it. As an aside (and as mentioned earlier in this chapter), multi-GPU processing can beat rainbow table cracking in the modern world. A good write-up on how and why that can happen can be found at http://blog.ircmaxell.com/2011/08/rainbow-table-is-dead.html.

☒ **B** is incorrect because you cannot reverse a hash. By design, they are one-way algorithms.

☒ **C** is incorrect because User2SID is a program that can retrieve an SID from the SAM on a local or remote machine. It does not technically exploit anything—it just uses built-in functionality in Windows. For a remote machine, it does require a null session connection, though.

☒ **D** is incorrect because SID2User is used to retrieve the names of user accounts given an associated SID.

☒ **E** is incorrect because a public key has nothing to do with password cracking.

12. You are monitoring traffic between two systems communicating over SSL. Which of the following techniques is your best bet in gaining access?

    A. Sniff the traffic with Cain and Abel.

    B. Practice active sniffing.

    C. Sidejacking.

    D. ARP poisoning.

    ☑ **C.** Sidejacking is one of those neat little attacks you don't hear much about. The idea is to steal the cookies exchanged between two systems and determine which one to use as a replay-style attack. The attack monitors the victim's traffic using a sniffer and packet capture. For example, with a program called Ferret, a file called Hamster.txt is created. After the victim has logged in to a site or two, the attacker fires up the Hamster tool as a proxy, and the cookies and authentication streams from the captured .txt file will be displayed. Then, you simply click through them until one works. This can also be accomplished with other tools and methods—Ettercap and many other man-in-the-middle (MITM) tools can pull it off quite nicely.

    ☒ **A** is incorrect because sniffing an SSL connection won't reveal anything useful—it's encrypted, after all. Cain and Abel does provide some substantial password SSL cracking, but sniffing traffic isn't going to work here.

    ☒ **B** is incorrect for the same reason—sniffing an encrypted channel just won't work in this case.

    ☒ **D** is incorrect because ARP poisoning isn't used for this purpose. You could blow up traffic between the two, but you wouldn't gain any real access.

13. Which password would be considered the most secure?

    A. CEH123TEST

    B. CEHisaHARDTEST

    C. 638154849675

    D. C3HisH@rd

☑ **D.** According to EC Council and the CEH exam, D is the correct answer. On this exam, complexity trumps length no matter what. Sure, an argument can be made that a longer password is better than a shorter one (regardless of complexity and if used for a shorter amount of time), but just stick with complexity—using letters, numbers, and special characters—and you'll be fine. However, obviously, a longer complex password is more secure than a shorter one.

☒ **A** is incorrect because it only uses letters and numbers.

☒ **B** is incorrect for the same reason. It is much longer than the correct answer, but there's no complexity.

☒ **C** is incorrect because it only used numbers. It has no complexity and it's a fairly short length.

14. Your client makes use of Sigverif on his servers. What functionality does this tool provide?

   A. Verifies digital signatures in SSL certificates.

   B. Displays a list of unsigned drivers.

   C. Displays a list of corrupted (nonfunctioning) drivers.

   D. Verifies SAM database integrity.

   ☑ **B.** Drivers are, obviously, very important to a system. An unsigned driver can be an indicator of manipulated files on a system, indicating a malware infection or worse. For example, in 2010 a worm by the name of STUXNET (specifically targeting SCADA systems) used unsigned drivers in its trek across the Internet. Sigverif can find unsigned drivers and verify device drivers in Windows XP. Windows 7 makes using unsigned drivers much more difficult to pull off; however, just remember that in the real world, the bad guys know not to use unsigned drivers (they are a tipoff that something is amiss).

   ☒ **A** is incorrect because this tool has nothing to do with SSL certificates. This answer is included as a distractor.

   ☒ **C** is incorrect because Sigverif does not necessarily display corrupted or nonfunctioning drivers. It simply verifies *legitimate* drivers on your system.

   ☒ **D** is incorrect because this tool has nothing to do with the SAM on a machine. This answer is included as a distractor.

15. Which of the following are considered offline password attacks? (Choose all that apply.)

   A. Using a hardware keylogger

   B. Brute-force cracking with Cain and Abel on a stolen SAM file

   C. Using John the Ripper on a stolen passwd file

   D. Shoulder surfing

☑ **A, B, and C.** An offline password attack occurs when you take the password file (or the passwords themselves) offline for work. Common methods are stealing the SAM or passwd (shadow) files and then running dictionary, hybrid, or brute-force attacks against them (using a password-cracking tool such as Cain and Abel or John the Ripper). Keyloggers are also considered offline attacks because you examine the contents off network.

☒ **D** is incorrect because shoulder surfing is considered another form of attack altogether—a non-electronic attack. No, I'm not making this up— it's actually a term in CEH lingo, and refers to social engineering methods of obtaining a password. Shoulder surfing is basically standing behind someone and watching their keystrokes.

16. Examine the following portion of a log file, captured during a hacking attempt:

```
[matt@localhost]#rm -rf /tmp/mykit_headers
[matt@localhost]#rm -rf /var/log/messages
[matt@localhost]#rm -rf /root/.bash_history
```

What was the attacker attempting to do?

A. Copy files for later examination.

B. Cover his tracks.

C. Change the shell to lock out other users.

D. Upload a rootkit.

☑ **B.** You'll definitely see basic Linux commands on your test, and this is one example of how you'll be asked about them. In this example, the rm command is used to remove (delete) files on a Linux system. Looking at what the hacker is attempting to remove, it seems logical to assume—even without seeing the rest of the log—that the hacker is covering his tracks.

☒ **A** is incorrect because the command for copy in Linux is cp.

☒ **C** is incorrect because the shell is not being tampered with. This answer is included as a distractor.

☒ **D** is incorrect because there is no evidence in this capture that anything is being uploaded—all commands are for removal of files (using the rm command). Granted, it's highly likely something was uploaded before this portion, but we're not privy to that information here.

17. You suspect a hack has occurred against your Linux machine. Which command will display all running processes for you to review?

A. ls -d

B. ls -l

C. su

D. ps -ef

E. ifconfig

☑ **D.** The ps command is used in Linux to display processes. The –e switch selects all processes, running or not, and the –f switch provides a full listing. A couple of other options you might see include –r (restrict output to running processes), -u (select by effective user ID; supports names), and –p (select by process ID).

☒ **A and B** are incorrect because the ls command in Linux lists files inside a storage directory. A couple switches of note include –d (list directory entries instead of contents), -h (print sizes in human readable format), -l (use a long listing format) and –p (file type).

☒ **C** is incorrect because the su command in Linux is for "switch user." Assuming you have permission/authentication to do so, this allows you to change the effective user ID and group ID to whatever you want.

☒ **E** is incorrect because ifconfig is used to configure a network interface in Linux. It looks, and works, very much like the ipconfig command in Windows, which makes it an easy target for test question writers, so pay close attention to the OS when asked about configuring your NIC.

18. Examine the following command output:

```
ANY_PC          <00>  UNIQUE      Registered
WORKGROUP       <00>  GROUP       Registered
ANY_PC          <20>  UNIQUE      Registered
WORKGROUP       <1E>  GROUP       Registered
WORKGROUP       <1D>  UNIQUE      Registered
.._MSBROWSE__.<01>  GROUP       Registered
MAC Address = 78-AC-C0-BA-E6-F2
```

Which of the following are true regarding this output? (Choose all that apply.)

A. This output is from net commands.

B. This output is from nbtstat.

C. This output is from netstat.

D. This output is from nslookup.

☑ **B.** Nbtstat is a built-in tool Microsoft put into their operating systems to help troubleshoot NetBIOS name resolution issues. You have loads of options and switches you can use (this one came from the –r switch, displaying the count of all NetBIOS names resolved by broadcast and by querying a WINS server). This command is usually associated with the scanning and enumeration phases, but is often used once you've gained access to a machine, so it is included here. Additionally, CEH official documentation mentions this in the system hacking objectives, so there we are.

☒ **A** is incorrect because this is not output from the net commands. Common net commands you will see on the exam are the null session (`net use \\target\ipc$ "" /u:"`) and net view options (`net view / domain:domainname` to show all systems in the domain name provided and `net view \\systemname` to provide a list of open shares on the system named).

⊠ **C** is incorrect because this is not output from a netstat command. Netstat is another Microsoft goodie that displays active TCP connections, ports on which the computer is listening, network statistics, and the IP routing table. If you use it with no parameters defined, it will display active TCP connections.

⊠ **D** is incorrect because nslookup, as we covered previously, is used for DNS lookups and does not provide this type of output.

19. Which rootkit type makes use of system-level calls to hide their existence?

   A. Application level

   B. Kernel level

   C. Library level

   D. System level

   ☑ **C.** A rootkit is a collection of software put in place by an attacker that is designed to obscure system compromise. In other words, if a system has a properly introduced rootkit installed, neither the user nor security monitors will even know anything is wrong. Rootkits are designed to provide backdoors for the attacker to use later on, and they include measures to remove and hide evidence of any activity. A library-level rootkit will most commonly replace or alter system calls with versions that hide information so the rootkit is not visible by normal means.

   ⊠ **A** is incorrect because application-level rootkits, as the name implies, are directed toward replacing valid application files with Trojan binaries. These kits work inside an application and can use an assortment of means to change the application's behavior, user rights level, and actions.

   ⊠ **B** is incorrect because kernel-level rootkits attack the boot sectors and kernel level of the operating systems themselves, replacing kernel code with backdoor code. These are by far the most dangerous and are difficult to detect and remove. In fact, your recommended fix action on discovery of a kernel-level rootkit is a complete wipe and reload from clean software.

   ⊠ **D** is incorrect because this is not a rootkit type and is included as a distractor. A good one, but a distractor nonetheless.

20. Which folder in Linux holds administrative commands and daemons?

   A. /sbin

   B. /bin

   C. /dev

   D. /mnt

   E. /usr

☑ **A.** The system binaries folder holds most administrative commands (/etc holds others) and is the repository for most of the routines Linux runs (known as *daemons*).

☒ **B** is incorrect because this folder holds all sorts of basic Linux commands (a lot like the C:\Windows\System32 folder in Windows).

☒ **C** is incorrect because this folder contains the pointer locations to the various storage and input/output systems you will need to mount if you want to use them, such as optical drives and additional hard drives or partitions. By the way, *everything* in Linux is a file. Everything.

☒ **D** is incorrect because this folder holds the access locations you've actually mounted.

☒ **E** is incorrect because this folder holds most of the information, commands, and files unique to the users.

21. What are the three commands necessary to install an application in Linux?

    A. ./install

    B. make

    C. make install

    D. ./configure

☑ **B, C,** and **D.** Linux zealots are a funny group. Instead of enjoying the beauty of simply double-clicking an install file and watching it work on its own, they like to obtain software directly from the source code and install from there. Usually this involves three steps: configure, compile the code, and install the executable. A configure script accomplishes the first of these steps, and is what you'll be asked for on the exam. You won't actually be installing anything, just know the big three needs: ./configure, make and make install.

☒ **A** is incorrect because ./install isn't a part of this install process. It's a great distractor that probably fooled at least a couple of you. However, it isn't a correct answer.

22. You are examining files on a Windows machine and note one file's attributes include "h." What does this indicate?

    A. The file is flagged for backup.

    B. The file is part of the help function.

    C. The file is fragmented due to size.

    D. The file has been quarantined by an antivirus program.

    E. The file is hidden.

☑ **E.** The hidden attribute can be set on any file to hide it from standard directory searches. You can accomplish this with the `attrib +h` *filename* command line, or by right-clicking, choosing Properties, and checking the Hidden attribute check box at the bottom of the dialog.

☒ **A, B, C,** and **D** are all incorrect definitions of the hidden attribute.

23. You have gained access to a SAM file from an older Windows machine and are preparing to run a Syskey cracker against it. How many bits are used for Syskey encryption?

   A. 128

   B. 256

   C. 512

   D. 1024

   ☑ **A.** Okay, so Syskey is outdated, old, and you'll probably never see it again. However, it's still in your exam pool, so you have to know it. I could rehash the definition, but it appears in an earlier question and you should have it memorized by now anyway. Just know it provides additional security on older Windows NT boxes and uses 128 bits for encryption.

   ☒ **B, C,** and **D** are incorrect because Syskey only uses 128 bits for encryption.

24. Which of the following tools can assist in discovering the use of NTFS file streams? (Choose all that apply.)

   A. LADS

   B. ADS Spy

   C. Sfind

   D. Snow

   ☑ **A, B,** and **C.** NTFS streaming (alternate data streaming) isn't a huge security problem, but it is something many security administrators concern themselves with. If you want to know where it's going on, you can use any of these tools: LADS and Ads Spy are freeware tools that list all alternate data streams of an NTFS directory. Ads Spy can also remove Alternate Data Streams (ADS) from NTFS file systems. Sfind, probably the oldest one here, is a Foundstone forensic tool you can use for finding ADS.

   ☒ **D** is incorrect because snow is a steganography tool used to conceal messages in ASCII text by appending whitespace to the end of lines.

25. Which authentication method uses DES for encryption and forces 14-character passwords for hash storage?

   A. NTLMv1

   B. NTLMv2

   C. LAN Manager

   D. Kerberos

☑ **C.** LAN Manager is an older authentication model that burst onto the scene around the Windows 95 launch. It uses DES as an encryption standard (a 56-bit key DES, to be technical) and, as covered before, has a quirky habit of capitalizing passwords and splitting them into two seven-character halves. Believe it or not, this is still in use out there in the field.

☒ **A** is incorrect because NTLMv1 (NT LAN Manager) improved upon LM methods. It stopped crazy practices such as padding passwords to 14 characters and so on, and it supported stronger encryption.

☒ **B** is incorrect because NTLMv2 also did not follow the encryption methods used by LM. In addition to the improvements from version 1, NTLMv2 made use of 128-bit MD5 hashing.

☒ **D** is incorrect because Kerberos is a very strong and secure authentication method that does not work like LM. Kerberos makes use of a Key Distribution Center (KDC) and grants tickets to properly authenticated clients to access resources on the network.

Social Engineering and Physical Security

This chapter includes questions from the following topics:

- Define social engineering
- Describe the different types of social engineering attacks
- Describe insider attacks, reverse social engineering, dumpster diving, social networking, and URL obfuscation
- Describe phishing attacks and countermeasures
- List social engineering countermeasures
- Describe physical security measures

Did you hear the one about Proctor & Gamble, toothpaste, and one extraordinarily common-sense-laden guy? If not, I'll relate here. It seems that back in the 1950s, P&G was looking at different ways to increase sales—particularly in toothpaste. They tried different marketing techniques, radio ads, getting dentists involved to vouch for their products, and all sorts of things. None of it was effective, and vice presidents were getting chewed out on a regular basis.

Early on, while all this was going on, some little guy in the company booked a meeting with the upper management folks and told them he had the answer. His solution, he promised, would cost almost nothing to implement and would result in somewhere around a 40-percent increase in toothpaste sales. The only catch was he wanted $100,000 up front to hear the idea.

Obviously he was laughed out of the room. However, after all the efforts of the best minds the company had failed to deliver, they began to rethink their position and, after wasting thousands upon thousands in advertising and other efforts with no results, they set up a meeting to learn what this guy had to say. After the money was handed over, he slid a small piece of paper across the table. The leadership, marketing, and technical staff all gathered around to see what this guaranteed answer would be. On the paper, the guy had written, "Make the hole bigger."

Oftentimes people (including, and dare I say *especially*, technical people) overlook the obvious in favor of a harder, sexier solution. P&G had hundreds of marketing and technical people in their employment. These people were capable, smart, and knew what they were doing, and when given a task to increase sales, they went furiously to work designing a solution. However, they overlooked the obvious and the simple (a bigger hole at the end of the tube will result in more toothpaste being used), and the little guy walked out of the room a wealthy man.

Social engineering and physical security are those obvious and simple solutions you may accidentally overlook. Why spend all the effort to hack into a system and crack passwords offline when you can just call someone up and ask for them? Why bother with trying to steal sensitive business information from encrypted shares when you can walk into the building and sit in on a sales presentation? Sure, you occasionally almost get arrested shuffling around in a dumpster for good information (our esteemed technical editor can attest to this), but most of social engineering is easy, simple, and very effective.

 STUDY TIPS Thankfully, most questions you'll see about these topics are of the straight-forward, definition-based variety. Be careful with the wording in these questions, though, because they'll sometimes try to trick you up with petty minutia instead of actually testing your knowledge.

1. You are testing physical security measures as part of a pen test team. Upon entering the lobby of the building, you see the entrance has a guard posted at the lone entrance. A door leads into a smaller room with a second door heading into the interior of the building. Which physical security measure is in place?

   A. Guard shack

   B. Turnstile

   C. Man shack

   D. Man trap

2. In your social engineering efforts, you call the company help desk and pose as a user who has forgotten a password. You ask the technician to help you reset your password, which they happily comply with. Which social engineering attack is in use here?

   A. Piggybacking

   B. Reverse social engineering

   C. Technical support

   D. Halo effect

3. Your client is considering a biometric system for access to a controlled location. Which of the following is a true statement regarding his decision?

   A. The lower the CER, the better the biometric system.

   B. The higher the CER, the better the biometric system.

   C. The higher the FRR, the better the biometric system.

   D. The higher the FAR, the better the biometric system.

4. A pen tester sends an unsolicited e-mail to several users on the target organization. The e-mail is well crafted and appears to be from the company's help desk, advising users of potential network problems. The e-mail provides a contact number to call in the event they are adversely affected. The pen tester then performs a denial of service on several systems and receives phone calls from users asking for assistance. Which social engineering practice is in play here?

   A. Technical support

   B. Impersonation

   C. Phishing

   D. Reverse social engineering

5. A pen test member has gained access to a building and is observing activity as he wanders around. In one room of the building, he stands just outside a cubicle wall opening and watches the onscreen activity of a user. Which social engineering attack is in use here?

   A. Eavesdropping

   B. Tailgating

   C. Shoulder surfing

   D. Piggybacking

6. You are interviewing an incident response team member of an organization you're working with. He relates an incident where a user received an e-mail that appeared to be from the U.S. Postal Service, notifying her of a package headed her way and providing a link for tracking the package. The link provided took the user to what appeared to be the USPS site, where she input her user information to learn about the latest shipment headed her way. Which attack did the user fall victim to?

   A. Phishing

   B. Internet level

   C. Reverse social engineering

   D. Impersonation

7. Which type of social engineering attacks use phishing, pop-ups, and IRC channels?

   A. Technical

   B. Computer based

   C. Human based

   D. Physical

8. An e-mail sent from an attacker to a known hacking group contains a reference stating, "Rebecca works for the finance department at _business-name_ and is the administrative assistant to the chief. She can be reached at _phone-number_."
   What is most likely being communicated here?

   A. The name of an administrative assistant is being published to simplify later social engineering attacks.

   B. The administrative assistant for the chief of the finance department at this business is easily swayed by social engineering efforts.

   C. The finance department has a lax security policy in place.

   D. None of the above. There is not enough information to form a conclusion.

9. What are the three categories of measures taken to ensure physical security?

   A. Technical

   B. Computer based

   C. Physical

   D. Human based

   E. Operational

   F. Policy based

10. After observing a target organization for several days, you discover that finance and HR records are bagged up and placed in an outside storage bin for later shredding/recycling. One day you simply walk to the bin and place one of the bags in your vehicle, with plans to rifle through it later. Which social engineering attack was used here?

    A. Offline

    B. Physical

    C. Piggybacking

    D. Dumpster diving

11. An attacker waits outside the entry to a secured facility. After a few minutes an authorized user appears with an entry badge displayed. He swipes a key card and unlocks the door. The attacker, with no display badge, follows him inside. Which social engineering attack just occurred?

    A. Tailgating

    B. Piggybacking

    C. Identity theft

    D. Impersonation

12. Which threat presents the highest risk to an organization's resources?

    A. Government-sponsored hackers

    B. Social engineering

    C. Disgruntled employees

    D. Script kiddies

13. Which of the following may be effective countermeasures against social engineering? (Choose all that apply.)

    A. Security policies

    B. Operational guidelines

    C. Appropriately configured IDS

    D. User education and training

    E. Strong firewall configuration

14. Which of the following are indicators of a phishing e-mail? (Choose all that apply.)

    A. It does not reference you by name.

    B. It contains misspelled words or grammatical errors.

    C. It contains spoofed links.

    D. It comes from an unverified source.

15. You are discussing physical security measures and are covering background checks on employees and policies regarding key management and storage. Which type of physical security measures are being discussed?

    A. Physical

    B. Technical

    C. Operational

    D. Practical

16. Which of the following resources can assist in combating phishing in your organization? (Choose all that apply.)

    A. Phishkill

    B. Netcraft

    C. Phishtank

    D. IDA Pro

17. In order, what are the three steps in a reverse social engineering attack?

    A. Technical support, marketing, sabotage

    B. Sabotage, marketing, technical support

    C. Marketing, technical support, sabotage

    D. Marketing, sabotage, technical support

18. Which type of social engineering makes use of impersonation, dumpster diving, shoulder surfing, and tailgating?

    A. Physical

    B. Technical

    C. Human based

    D. Computer based

19. What is considered the best defense against social engineering?

    A. User education and training

    B. Strong security policy and procedure

    C. Clear operational guidelines

    D. Proper classification of information and individuals' access to that information

20. Which anti-phishing method makes use of a secret message or image referenced on the communication?

    A. Steganography

    B. Sign-in seal

    C. PKI

    D. Captcha

21. Which of the following should be in place to assist as a social engineering countermeasure? (Choose all that apply.)

    A. Classification of information

    B. Strong security policy

    C. User education

    D. Strong change management process

22. Joe uses a user ID and password to log into the system every day. Jill uses a PIV card and a pin number. Which of the following statements is true?

    A. Joe and Jill are using single-factor authentication.

    B. Joe and Jill are using two-factor authentication.

    C. Joe is using two-factor authentication.

    D. Jill is using two-factor authentication.

23. A system owner has implemented a retinal scanner at the entryway to the data floor. Which type of physical security measure is this?

    A. Technical

    B. Single factor

    C. Computer based

    D. Operational

24. Physical security also includes the maintenance of the environment and equipment for your data floor. Which of the following are true statements regarding this equipment? (Choose all that apply.)

    A. The higher the MTBF, the better.

    B. The lower the MTBF, the better.

    C. The higher the MTTR, the better.

    D. The lower the MTTR, the better.

25. Which fire extinguisher type is the best choice for an electrical system fire?

    A. An extinguisher marked "A"

    B. An extinguisher marked "B"

    C. An extinguisher marked "C"

    D. An extinguisher marked "D"

1. D
2. C
3. A
4. D
5. C
6. A
7. B
8. B
9. A, C, E
10. D
11. B
12. C
13. A, B, D
14. A, B, C, D
15. C
16. B, C
17. D
18. C
19. A
20. B
21. A, B, C, D
22. D
23. A
24. A, D
25. C

1. You are testing physical security measures as part of a pen test team. Upon entering the lobby of the building, you see the entrance has a guard posted at the lone entrance. A door leads into a smaller room with a second door heading into the interior of the building. Which physical security measure is in place?

   A. Guard shack

   B. Turnstile

   C. Man shack

   D. Man trap

   ☑ **D.** If you took a test on college football history, you know it would contain a question about Alabama. If you took one on trumpet players, there'd be one about Dizzy Gillespie. And if you take a test on physical security measures for Certified Ethical Hacker, you're going to be asked about the man trap. They love it that much.

   A *man trap* is nothing more than a locked space you can hold someone in while verifying their right to proceed into the secured area. It's usually a glass (or clear plastic) walled room that locks the exterior door as soon as you enter. Then there is some sort of authentication mechanism—such as a smart card with a PIN or a biometric system. Assuming the authentication is successful, the second door leading to the interior of the building will unlock and the person is allowed to proceed. If it's not successful, the doors will remain locked until the guard(s) can check things out. As an aside, in addition to authentication, some man traps add all sorts of extra fun—such as checking your weight to see if you've mysteriously gained or lost 20 pounds since Friday.

   A couple of other notes here may be of use to you: First, I've seen a man trap defined as either manual or automatic, where manual has a guard locking and unlocking the doors, and automatic has the locks tied to the authentication system, as described previously. Second, a man trap is also referred to in some definitions as an *air lock.* Should you see that term on the exam, know that they are referring to the man trap.

   ☒ **A** is incorrect because this question is not describing a small location at a gate where guards are stationed. Traditionally, these are positioned at gates to the exterior wall or the gate of the facility, where guards can verify identity and so on before allowing people through to the parking lot.

   ☒ **B** is incorrect because a turnstile is not described here and, frankly, does absolutely nothing for physical security. Anyone who has spent any time in subway systems knows this is true: Watching people jump the turnstiles is a great spectator sport.

☒ **C** is incorrect because, so far as I know, this term *man shack* is not a physical security term within CEH. Maybe the title of a 1970's disco hit, but not a physical security term you'll need to know for the exam.

2. In your social engineering efforts you call the company help desk and pose as a user who has forgotten a password. You ask the technician to help you reset your password, which they happily comply with. Which social engineering attack is in use here?

   A. Piggybacking

   B. Reverse social engineering

   C. Technical support

   D. Halo effect

   ☑ **C.** Although it may seem silly to label social engineering attacks (as many of them contain the same steps and bleed over into one another), you'll need to memorize them for your exam. A technical support attack is one in which the attacker calls the support desk in an effort to gain a password reset or other useful information. This is a very valuable method because if you get the right help desk person (that is, someone susceptible to a smooth-talking social engineer), you can get the keys to the kingdom.

   ☒ **A** is incorrect because *piggybacking* refers to a method to gain entrance to a facility—not to gain passwords or other information. Piggybacking is a tactic whereby the attacker follows authorized users through an open door without any visible authorization badge at all.

   ☒ **B** is incorrect because *reverse social engineering* refers to a method where an attacker convinces a target to call him with information. The method involves marketing services (providing the target with your phone number or e-mail address in the event of a problem), sabotaging the device, and then awaiting for a phone call from the user.

   ☒ **D** is incorrect because *halo effect* refers to a psychological principle that states a person's overall impression (appearance or pleasantness) can impact another person's judgement of them. For example, a good-looking, pleasant person will be judged as more competent and knowledgeable simply because of their appearance. The lesson here is to look good and act nice while you're trying to steal all the target's information.

3. Your client is considering a biometric system for access to a controlled location. Which of the following is a true statement regarding his decision?

   A. The lower the CER, the better the biometric system.

   B. The higher the CER, the better the biometric system.

   C. The higher the FRR, the better the biometric system.

   D. The higher the FAR, the better the biometric system.

☑ **A.** The crossover error rate (CER) is the point on a chart where the false acceptance rate (FAR) and false rejection rate (FRR) meet, and the lower the number the better the system. It's a means by which biometric systems are calibrated—getting the FAR and FRR the same. All that said, though, keep in mind that in certain circumstances a client may be more interested in a lower FAR than FRR, or vice versa, and therefore the CER isn't as much a concern. For example, a bank may be far more interested in preventing false acceptance than it is in preventing false rejection. In other words, so what if a user is upset they can't log on, so long as their money is safe from a false acceptance.

☒ **B** is incorrect because this is exactly the opposite of what you want. A high CER indicates a system that more commonly allows unauthorized users through and rejects truly authorized people from access.

☒ **C** is incorrect because the false rejection rate needs to be as low as possible. The FRR represents the amount of time a true, legitimate user is denied access by the biometric system.

☒ **D** is incorrect because false acceptance rate needs to be as low as possible. The FAR represents the amount of time an unauthorized user is allowed access to the system.

4. A pen tester sends an unsolicited e-mail to several users on the target organization. The e-mail is well crafted and appears to be from the company's help desk, advising users of potential network problems. The e-mail provides a contact number to call in the event they are adversely affected. The pen tester then performs a denial of service on several systems and receives phone calls from users asking for assistance. Which social engineering practice is in play here?

   A. Technical support

   B. Impersonation

   C. Phishing

   D. Reverse social engineering

☑ **D.** This may turn out to be a somewhat confusing question for some folks, but it's actually pretty easy. Reverse social engineering involves three steps. First, in the marketing phase, an attacker advertises himself as a technical point of contact for problems that may be occurring soon. As an aside, be sure to market to the appropriate audience: Attempting this against IT staff probably won't work as well as the "average" user, and may get you caught. Second, in the sabotage phase, the attacker performs a denial of service or other attack on the user. Third, in the tech support phase, the user calls the attacker and freely hands over information, thinking they are being assisted by company's technical support team.

☒ **A** is incorrect because a technical support attack involves the attacker calling a technical support help desk, not having the user calling back with information.

☒ **B** is incorrect because this is not *just* impersonation—the attack described in the question revolves around the user contacting the attacker, not the other way around. Impersonation can cover anybody, from a "normal" user to a company executive. And impersonating a technical support person can result in excellent results—just remember if you're going through steps to have the user call you back, you've moved into reverse social engineering.

☒ **C** is incorrect because a phishing attack is an e-mail crafted to appear legitimate, but in fact contains links to fake websites or to download malicious content. In this example, there is no link to click—just a phone number to call in case of trouble. Oddly enough, in my experience people will question a link in an e-mail far more than just a phone number.

5. A pen test member has gained access to a building and is observing activity as he wanders around. In one room of the building, he stands just outside a cubicle wall opening and watches the onscreen activity of a user. Which social engineering attack is in use here?

   A. Eavesdropping

   B. Tailgating

   C. Shoulder surfing

   D. Piggybacking

   ☑ **C.** This one is so easy I hope you maintain your composure and stifle the urge to whoop and yell in the test room. Shoulder surfing doesn't necessarily require you to actually be on the victim's shoulder—you just have to be able to watch their onscreen activity. I once shoulder surfed *in front of* someone (a mirror behind her showed her screen clear as day).

   ☒ **A** is incorrect because *eavesdropping* is a social engineering method where the attacker simply remains close enough to targets to overhear conversations. Although its doubtful users will stand around shouting passwords at each other, you'd be surprised how much useful information can be gleaned by just listening in on conversations.

   ☒ **B** is incorrect because *tailgating* is a method for gaining entrance to a facility by flashing a fake badge and following an authorized user through an open door.

   ☒ **D** is incorrect because *piggybacking* is another method to gain entrance to a facility. In this effort, though, you don't have a badge at all—you just follow people through the door.

6. You are interviewing an incident response team member of an organization you're working with. He relates an incident where a user received an e-mail that

CEH Certified Ethical Hacker Practice Exams

172

appeared to be from the U.S. Postal Service, notifying her of a package headed her way and providing a link for tracking the package. The link provided took the user to what appeared to be the USPS site, where she input her user information to learn about the latest shipment headed her way. Which attack did the user fall victim to?

A. Phishing

B. Internet level

C. Reverse social engineering

D. Impersonation

☑ **A.** Phishing is one of the most pervasive and effective social engineering attacks on the planet. It's successful because crafting a legitimate-looking e-mail that links a user to an illegitimate site or malware package is easy to do, easy to spread, and preys on our human nature to trust. If the source of the e-mail looks legitimate, or the layout looks legitimate, most people will click away without even thinking about it. Phishing e-mails can often include pictures lifted directly off the legitimate website and use creative means of spelling that aren't easy to spot: www.regions.com is a legitimate bank website that could be spelled in a phishing e-mail as www.regi0ns.

☒ **B** is incorrect because *Internet level* is not a recognized form of social engineering attacks by this exam. It's included here as a distractor.

☒ **C** is incorrect because reverse social engineering is an attack where the attacker cons the target into calling back with useful information.

☒ **D** is incorrect because this particular description does not cover impersonation. *Impersonation* is an attack where a social engineer pretends to be an employee, a valid user, or even an executive (or other V.I.P.). Generally speaking, when it comes to the exam, any impersonation question will revolve around an in-person visit or a telephone call.

7. Which type of social engineering attacks use phishing, pop-ups, and IRC?

A. Technical

B. Computer based

C. Human based

D. Physical

☑ **B.** All social engineering attacks fall into one of two categories: human based or computer based. Computer-based attacks are those carried out with the use of a computer or other data-processing device. Examples include, but are not limited to, fake pop-up windows, SMS texts, e-mails, and chat rooms or services. Social media sites (such as Facebook or LinkedIn) are consistent examples as well, and spoofing entire websites isn't out of the realm here either.

☒ **A** is incorrect because *technical* is not a social engineering attack type and is included here as a distractor.

☒ **C** is incorrect because *human-based* social engineering involves the art of human interaction for information gathering. Human-based social engineering uses interaction in conversation or other circumstances between people to gather useful information.

☒ **D** is incorrect because *physical* is not a social engineering attack type and is included here as a distractor.

8. An e-mail sent from an attacker to a known hacking group contains a reference stating, "Rebecca works for the finance department at _business-name_ and is the administrative assistant to the chief. She can be reached at _phone-number_." What is most likely being communicated here?

   A. The name of an administrative assistant is being published to simplify later social engineering attacks.

   B. The administrative assistant for the chief of the finance department at this business is easily swayed by social engineering efforts.

   C. The finance department has lax security policy in place.

   D. None of the above. There is not enough information to form a conclusion.

   ☑ **B.** Within the confines of this exam, you need to remember the names "Rebecca" and "Jessica" as potential targets of social engineering. According to CEH documentation, these names are used to refer to individuals who are easy targets for social engineering efforts. The reality of your day-to-day work in the field might be that you'll never hear this mentioned this way (I had never heard these names used this way before studying for this exam, myself); however, you need to memorize it for your exam. Jessica and Rebecca are easily swayed by social engineering and are targets for your efforts.

   ☒ **A** is incorrect because, frankly, there's a better answer here (B). Is it possible the person sending this e-mail knows the assistant's first name is Rebecca? Sure it is; however, it's unlikely to be shared in this manner and, more importantly here, this just is not the "most likely" answer.

   ☒ **C** is incorrect because the name Rebecca is not associated with security policy in any way. The company may very well have lax policy, but there's just nothing here to indicate that. As an aside (that is, it really has nothing to do with the question itself), whether the policy is weak or strong, an individual susceptible to social engineering *almost* makes the policy moot. Security policy is one of those things that has to be supported and enforced from the top down and made part of the very culture of the organization. If you have those things, it's a great countermeasure to a whole assortment of security issues. If you don't, it's a big waste of time.

☒ **D** is incorrect because there is a correct answer to the question. This answer is included as a distractor.

9. What are the three categories of measures taken to ensure physical security?

   A. Technical

   B. Computer based

   C. Physical

   D. Human based

   E. Operational

   F. Policy based

☑ **A, C, and E.** Physical security measures can be looked at through three major categories. Physical measures are all the things you can touch, taste, smell, or get shocked by. Examples include lighting, locks, fences, and guards. Technical measures are those using technology to protect explicitly at the physical level (an example might be a biometric system at the door to authenticate a visitor). Operational measures are the policies and procedures you set up to enforce a security-minded operation. Examples include background checks on employees, risk assessments on devices, and policies regarding key management and storage.

☒ **B and D** are incorrect because they refer to social engineering attack types.

☒ **F** is incorrect because *policy based* is not a physical security measure and is included here as a distractor.

10. After observing a target organization for several days, you discover that finance and HR records are bagged up and placed in an outside storage bin for later shredding/recycling. One day you simply walk to the bin and place one of the bags in your vehicle, with plans to rifle through it later. Which social engineering attack was used here?

   A. Offline

   B. Physical

   C. Piggybacking

   D. Dumpster diving

☑ **D.** Dumpster diving doesn't necessarily mean you're actually taking a header into a dumpster outside. It could be any waste canister, in any location, and you don't even have to place any more of your body in the canister than you need to extract the old paperwork with. And you'd be amazed what people just throw away without thinking about it: password lists, network diagrams, employee name and number listings, and financial documents are all examples.

☒ **A** is incorrect because *offline* is not a social engineering attack and is used here as a distractor.

☒ **B** is incorrect because *physical* is not a social engineering attack type.

☒ **C** is incorrect because *piggybacking* is a social engineering attack that allows entry into a facility and has nothing to do with digging through trash for information.

11. An attacker waits outside the entry to a secured facility. After a few minutes an authorized user appears with an entry badge displayed. He swipes a key card and unlocks the door. The attacker, with no display badge, follows him inside. Which social engineering attack just occurred?

  A. Tailgating

  B. Piggybacking

  C. Identity theft

  D. Impersonation

☑ **B.** This is one of those questions that just drives everyone batty—especially people who actually perform pen tests for a living. Does knowing that gaining entry without flashing a fake ID badge of any kind is called piggy-backing make it any easier or harder to pull off? I submit having two terms for what is essentially the same attack, separated by one small detail is unfair, in the least, but there's not a whole lot we can do about it. If it makes it easier to memorize, just keep in mind that pigs wouldn't wear a badge—they don't have any clothes to attach it to.

☒ **A** is incorrect because a tailgating attack requires the attacker to be holding a fake badge of some sort. I know it's silly, but that's the only differentiation between these two items: tailgaters have badges, piggybackers do not. If it makes it any easier, just keep in mind a lot of tailgaters at football games should have a badge on them—to prove they are of legal drinking age.

☒ **C** is incorrect because this attack has nothing to do with identity theft. Identity theft occurs when an attacker uses personal information gained on an individual to assume that person's identity. Although this is normally thought of in the criminal world (stealing credit cards, money, and so on), it has its uses elsewhere.

☒ **D** is incorrect because impersonation is not in play here. The attacker isn't pretending to be anyone else at all—he's just following someone through an open door.

12. Which threat presents the highest risk to an organization's resources?

  A. Government-sponsored hackers

  B. Social engineering

  C. Disgruntled employees

  D. Script kiddies

☑ **C.** I can almost guarantee you'll see this on your exam. EC Council made a big point of stressing this in the CEH version 7 documentation, so I in turn will stress it to you. Disgruntled employees can cause all sorts of havoc for a security team. The main reason is location: They're *already* inside the network. Inside attacks are generally easier to launch, are more successful, and are harder to prevent. When you add a human element of having an axe to grind, this can boil over quickly—whether the employee has the technical knowledge to pull it off or not.

☒ **A** is incorrect because most organizations won't have government-sponsored hackers knocking at their virtual front door and, even if they do, the attacks still generate from outside. Now I'm not saying a sponsored hacker group wouldn't seek out a disgruntled employee inside a government organization, but that proves the answer in itself.

☒ **B** is incorrect because social engineering as a whole is not the greatest threat. It is a major concern, though, because most people are susceptible to it and, frankly, users can't be trusted.

☒ **D** is incorrect because script kiddies by definition are relatively easy to find and squash. A *script kiddy* is someone who goes out and steals hack codes and techniques right off the Web, flinging them around wildly in an attempt to succeed. They don't really understand what the attack vector is, how the code works, or (usually) what to do if they actually find success, which make them very easy to spot.

13. Which of the following may be effective countermeasures against social engineering? (Choose all that apply.)

    A. Security policies

    B. Operational guidelines

    C. Appropriately configured IDS

    D. User education and training

    E. Strong firewall configuration

    ☑ **A, B,** and **D.** The problem with countermeasures against social engineering is they're almost totally out of your control. Sure you can draft strong policy requiring users to comply with security measures, implement guidelines on everything imaginable to reduce risks and streamline efficiency, and hold educational briefings and training sessions for each and every user in your organization, but when it comes down to it, it's the user who has to do the right thing. All countermeasures for social engineering have something to do with the user themselves because they are the weak link here.

    ☒ **C** and **E** are both incorrect for the same reason: A social engineering attack doesn't target the network or its defenses; it targets the users themselves.

Many a strongly defended network has been compromised because a user inside was charmed by a successful social engineer.

14. Which of the following are indicators of a phishing e-mail? (Choose all that apply.)

   A. It does not reference you by name.

   B. It contains misspelled words or grammatical errors.

   C. It contains spoofed links.

   D. It comes from an unverified source.

   ☑ **A, B, C,** and **D.** One of the objectives of CEHv7 is, and I quote, to "understand phishing attacks." Part of the official curriculum to study for the exam covers detecting phishing e-mail in depth, and all of these answers are indicators an e-mail may not be legitimate. First, most companies now sending e-mail to customers will reference you *by name* and sometimes by account number. An e-mail starting with "Dear Customer" or something to that effect may be an indicator something is amiss. Misspellings and grammatical errors from a business are usually dead giveaways, because companies do their best to proofread things before they are released. There are, occasionally, some slipups (Internet search some of these; they're truly funny), but those are definitely the exception and not the rule. Spoofed links can be found by hovering a mouse over them (or by looking at their properties). The link text may read www.yourbank.com, but the hyperlink properties will be sending you to some IP address you don't want to go to.

15. You are discussing physical security measures and are covering background checks on employees and policies regarding key management and storage. Which type of physical security measure is being discussed?

   A. Physical

   B. Technical

   C. Operational

   D. Practical

   ☑ **C.** Physical security has three major facets: physical measures, technical measures, and operational measures. Operational measures are the policies and procedures you put into place to assist with security. Background checks on employees and any kind of written policy for operational behaviors are prime examples.

   ☒ **A** is incorrect because physical measures can be seen or touched. Examples include guards (although you probably would want to be very careful touching one of them), fences, and locked doors.

   ☒ **B** is incorrect because technical measures include things such as authentication systems (biometrics anyone?) and specific permissions you assign to resources.

☒ **D** is incorrect because, although these may seem like practical measures to put into place, there is simply no category named such. It's included here as a distractor, nothing more.

16. Which of the following resources can assist in combating phishing in your organization? (Choose all that apply.)

    A. Phishkill

    B. Netcraft

    C. Phishtank

    D. IDA Pro

    ☑ **B and C.** For very obvious reasons, there are not a lot of questions from these objectives concerning tools—mainly because social engineering is all about the human side of things, not necessarily using technology or tools. However, you can put into place more than a few protective applications to help stem the tide. There are innumerable e-mail-filtering applications and appliances you can put on an e-mail network boundary to cut down on the vast amount of traffic (spam or otherwise) headed to your network. Additionally, Netcraft's phishing toolbar and Phishtank are two client-side, host-based options you can use (there are others, but these are pointed out specifically in EC Council's official courseware).

    Netcraft's (http://toolbar.netcraft.com/) and Phishtank's (www.phishtank .com/) toolbars are like neighborhood watches on virtual steroids, where eagle-eyed neighbors can see naughty traffic and alert everyone else. From the Netcraft site: "Once the first recipients of a phishing mail have reported the target URL, it is blocked for community members as they subsequently access the URL."

    These tools, although useful, are not designed to completely protect against phishing. Much like antivirus software, they will act on attempts that match a signature file. This, sometimes, makes it even easier on the attacker—because they know which phishing will *not* work right off the bat.

    ☒ **A** is incorrect because phishkill is not an anti-phishing application.

    ☒ **D** is incorrect because IDA Pro is a debugger tool you can use to analyze malware (viruses).

17. In order, what are the three steps in a reverse social engineering attack?

    A. Technical support, marketing, sabotage

    B. Sabotage, marketing, technical support

    C. Marketing, technical support, sabotage

    D. Marketing, sabotage, technical support

☑ **D.** Reverse engineering occurs when the attacker creates a circumstance or situation that makes users call him with information. This is carried out in three steps. First, the attacker will market his skills, position, and impending problem (for example, the attacker may send e-mails promoting himself as help desk personnel to call in the event of problems next Wednesday when the server is rebooted). Second, the attacker performs sabotage against the user or network segment (a denial of service attack to take users off network confirms with the user that the original e-mail must have been correct). Lastly, the attacker provides "technical support" to the users calling in for assistance (by stealing all their account information, which is gladly being handed over the phone by panicked users).

☒ **A, B,** and **C** are incorrect because the order presented is not correct.

18. Which type of social engineering makes use of impersonation, dumpster diving, shoulder surfing, and tailgating?

    A. Physical

    B. Technical

    C. Human based

    D. Computer based

    ☑ **C.** So once again, we're back to the two major forms of social engineering: human based and computer based. Human-based attacks include all the attacks mentioned here and a few more. Human-based social engineering uses interaction in conversation or other circumstances between people to gather useful information. This can be as blatant as simply asking someone for their password or pretending to be a known entity (authorized user, tech support, or company executive) in order to gain information.

    ☒ **A** is incorrect because social engineering attacks do not fall into a "physical" category.

    ☒ **B** is incorrect because social engineering attacks do not fall into a "technical" category.

    ☒ **D** is incorrect because computer-based social engineering attacks are carried out with the use of a computer or other data-processing device. These attacks can include everything from specially crafted pop-up windows, tricking the user into clicking through to a fake website, to SMS texts, which provide false technical support messages and dial-in information to a user.

19. What is considered the best defense against social engineering?

    A. User education and training

    B. Strong security policy and procedure

    C. Clear operational guidelines

    D. Proper classification of information and individuals' access to that information

☑ **A.** So anyone reading this book who has spent any time at all trying to educate users on a production, enterprise-level network is probably yelling right now, because results can sometimes be spotty. And, yes, I too can point out the multiple studies on the value, or lack thereof, of continuing user training. However, when you consider the options presented (and EC Council's training materials), this is the only answer that makes any sense. After all, the weak point in the chain is the users themselves. Therefore, we must do our best to educate them on what to look for and what to do as they see it. There simply is no better defense than a well-educated user.

☒ **B, C,** and **D** are all incorrect for the same reason—they do not address the root of the problem. It is absolutely essential to have good security policy, operational guidelines, and appropriate classification across the board. However, the user is at the heart of every social engineering attack and, therefore, requires our attention. A poorly educated user standing on strong policies still makes a very attractive target.

20. Which anti-phishing method makes use of a secret message or image referenced on the communication?

    A. Steganography

    B. Sign-in seal

    C. PKI

    D. Captcha

    ☑ **B.** Sign-in seal is an e-mail protection method in use at a variety of business locations. The practice is to use a secret message or image that can be referenced on any official communication with the site. If you receive an e-mail purportedly from the business but it does not include the image or message, you're aware it's probably a phishing attempt. This sign-in seal is kept locally on your computer, so the theory is that no one can copy or spoof it.

    ☒ **A** is incorrect because steganography is not used for this purpose. As we know, steganography is a method of hiding information inside another file—usually an image file.

    ☒ **C** is incorrect because PKI refers to an encryption system using public and private keys for security of information between members of an organization.

    ☒ **D** is incorrect because a captcha is an authentication test of sorts, which I am sure you've seen hundreds of times already. Captcha (actually an acronym meaning Completely Automated Public Turing test to tell Computers and Humans Apart) is a challenge-response-type method where an image is shown and the client is required to type the word from the image into a challenge box. An example is on a contest entry form—you type in your information at the top, then see an image with a word (or two) in crazy font at the bottom. If you type the correct word in, it's somewhat reasonable for the page to assume you're a human (as opposed to a script) and the request is sent forward.

21. Which of the following should be in place to assist as a social engineering countermeasure? (Choose all that apply.)

   A. Classification of information

   B. Strong security policy

   C. User education

   D. Strong change management process

   ☑ **A, B, C,** and **D.** All of the answers are correct. There's an argument to be made about these as being purely social engineering mitigations, but trust me, EC Council sees them this way, so you should, too. **A.** Classification of information is seen as a strong countermeasure because the information—and access to it—is stored and processed according to strict definitions of sensitivity. In the Government/DoD world, you'd see labels such as Confidential, Secret, and Top Secret. In the commercial world, you might see Public, Sensitive, and Confidential. I could write an entire chapter on the difference between DoD and commercial labels, and have all sorts of fun arguing the finer points of various access control methods, but we'll stick just to this chapter and what you need here. As a side note, classification of information won't do you a bit of good if the enforcement of access to that information, and the protection of it in storage or transit, is lax.

   ☑ **B.** Strong security policy has been covered earlier in the chapter, so I won't waste much print space here on it. You must have a good one in place to help prevent all sorts of security failures; however, you can't *rely* on it as a countermeasure on its own.

   ☑ **C.** User education is the number-one preventative measure you can take against social engineering. There's argument about just how successful it is, but try running an organization without any education and see how far that gets you.

   ☑ **D.** A change management process helps to organize change to a system or organization by providing a standardized, reviewable process to any major change. In other words, if you allow changes to your financial system, IT services, HR processes, or *fill-in-the-blank* without any review or control process, you're basically opening the door to Pandora's box. Change can be made on a whim (sometimes at the behest of a social engineer, maybe?) and there's no control or tracking of it.

22. Joe uses a user ID and password to log into the system every day. Jill uses a PIV card and a pin number. Which of the following are true?

   A. Joe and Jill are using single-factor authentication.

   B. Joe and Jill are using two-factor authentication.

   C. Joe is using two-factor authentication.

   D. Jill is using two-factor authentication.

☑ **D.** When it comes to authentication systems, you can use three factors to prove your identity to a system: something you *know*, something you *have*, and something you *are*. Items you know are, basically, a password or PIN number. Something you have is a physical token of some sort—usually a smart card—that is presented as part of the authentication process. Something you are relates to biometrics—a fingerprint or retinal scan, for instance. Generally speaking, the more factors you have in place, the better (more secure) the authentication system. In this example, Joe is using only something he knows, whereas Jill is using something she has (PIV card) *and* something she knows (PIN).

☒ **A** is incorrect because Jill is using two-factor authentication.

☒ **B** is incorrect because Joe is using single-factor authentication.

☒ **C** is incorrect because Joe is using single-factor authentication.

23. A system owner has implemented a retinal scanner at the entryway to the data floor. Which type of physical security measure is this?

    A. Technical

    B. Single factor

    C. Computer based

    D. Operational

☑ **A.** Physical security measures are characterized as *physical* (door locks, guards), *operational* (policies, procedures), and *technical* (authentications systems, permissions). This example falls into the technical security measure category. Sure, the door itself is physical, but the question centers on the biometric system itself—clearly technical in origin.

☒ **B** is incorrect because *single factor* refers to the method the authentication system uses, not the physical security measure itself. In this case, the authentication is using something you are—a biometric retina scan.

☒ **C** is incorrect because *computer based* refers to a social engineering attack type, not a physical security measure.

☒ **D** is incorrect because an operational physical security measure deals with policy and procedure.

24. Physical security also includes the maintenance of the environment and equipment for your data floor. Which of the following are true statements regarding this equipment? (Choose all that apply.)

    A. The higher the MTBF, the better.

    B. The lower the MTBF, the better.

    C. The higher the MTTR, the better.

    D. The lower the MTTR, the better.

☑ **A** and **D**. MTBF is an acronym translating to Mean Time Between Failure, and it references the amount of time a piece of equipment can be expected to last. It's a mathematical equation marking the average times between failures of the system. The higher this number, the longer the equipment is expected to perform. The MTTR is the Mean Time To Repair, which is an estimate of how long it will take to fix a potential problem with the equipment. Obviously, the lower the time it takes to repair, the better.

☒ **B** and **C** are incorrect because the MTBF is better when higher and the MTTR is better when lower.

25. Which fire extinguisher type is the best choice for an electrical system fire?

  A. An extinguisher marked "A"

  B. An extinguisher marked "B"

  C. An extinguisher marked "C"

  D. An extinguisher marked "D"

☑ **C**. Fire extinguishers are marked by the type of fire they are created to suppress, and usually have more than one marking (for example, the one I'm looking at right now across the hall from me is marked "BC"). A Class C fire is one involving electrical equipment. Generally speaking, you should first remove power and then try to extinguish the flames (although sometimes that's difficult to do). Any extinguishers marked for Class C uses CO_2 (carbon dioxide) or a dry chemical to extinguish the flames. Obviously, spraying water on an open electrical circuit could pose additional hazards, so these nonconductive methods are best.

☒ **A** is incorrect because Class A fires are ordinary combustibles, such as paper, wood, and most plastics. A pure Class A–marked extinguisher may use water.

☒ **B** is incorrect because Class B fires involve combustible liquids, such as gasoline.

☒ **D** is incorrect because Class D fires involve combustible chemicals, such as magnesium.

Web-Based Hacking: Servers and Applications

This chapter includes questions from the following topics:
- Identify features of common web server architecture
- Describe web server and web application attacks
- Identify web server and application vulnerabilities
- Identify web application hacking tools

In the Spring of 1863, a mismatch was shaping up on the battlefield. General Robert E. Lee and Stonewall Jackson had amassed a sizeable Confederate force of around 60,000 men in and around Chancellorsville, Virginia, after the recent victory in Fredericksburg. Major General Joseph Hooker, however, commanded a Union army of around 130,000 men and was under direct orders from President Lincoln to annihilate the Confederate army. He thus decided upon a plan of action, well based in current military strategy, to apply his vastly superior forces and march against the enemy. By any measure, this was shaping up as an easy victory for the North.

General Lee, however, wasn't well known for following strict rules of battle. While Hooker amassed forces for a front-on attack, Lee did something that, at the time, was considered either the dumbest move in history or brilliant strategy: He split his already outnumbered army into three groups. He left a paltry 10,000 men to meet the head-on charge, but sent the other 50,000 men in two groups to surround and flank the Union troops. Through a series of improbable victories on the Confederate side and utterly tentative and puzzling decision making by their Northern counterparts, the battle became a treatise on victory against all odds, and the power of mind and strategy on the battlefield.

And what is the relevance here for us, you may ask? By changing the focus of his attack, General Lee succeeded in pulling off one of the most unbelievable military victories in history. You can do the same in your pen testing by focusing your efforts on those areas the strong defenses of your target may overlook: their web applications and servers (yes, I know it's corny, just go with it). Businesses and corporations are like that Union army, with so many defenses arrayed against you they seem impenetrable. But most of them can be outflanked, via their public-facing web fronts (which may or may not have proper security included) and their customized, internal web applications. This chapter is all about web servers and applications and how you can exploit them. After all, if the target is going to trust them, why not have a look?

 STUDY TIPS Thankfully, most questions you'll see about these topics are of the straightforward, definition-based variety. Be careful with the wording in these questions, though, because they'll sometimes try to trick you up with petty minutia instead of actually testing your knowledge.

1. You are examining connection logs from a client machine and come across this entry:

    http://www.business123.com/../../../../../Windows/system.ini

    Which attack does this most likely indicate?

    A. Parameter manipulation

    B. XSS

    C. SQL injection

    D. Directory traversal

2. A hacker is looking at a publicly facing web front end. One of the pages provides an entry box with the heading "Forgot password? Enter your e-mail address." In the entry, he types **anything' OR '1'='1**.

    A message appears stating, "Your login information has been sent to a_username@emailaddress.target.com."

    Which of the following is true?

    A. The cross-site scripting attempt has succeeded.

    B. The SQL injection attempt has succeeded.

    C. The parameter tampering has succeeded.

    D. The buffer overflow attempt has succeeded.

3. A pen tester is examining a web front end on a target network. The page displays a "Search" text box form entry, allowing the user to search for items on the site. Instead of entering a search text string, the tester enters **<script>'It Worked'</ script>**. After the tester clicks the Search button beside the entry box, a pop up appears stating, "It Worked." Which of the following is true regarding this attempt?

    A. The site is vulnerable to XSS.

    B. Coding on the site is poor, and a buffer overflow attack may result in a DoS.

    C. The attacker's next entry in the Search box should be **' OR '1'='1**.

    D. This is expected behavior on properly configured sites

4. Which of the following is representative of a parameter-tampering attack?

    A. http://www.anybiz.com/../../../../../windows\system32\cmd.exe

    B. http://www.anybiz.com/search.asp?lname=walker%27%update%20 usertable%20%20set%3d%23hAxor%27

    C. http://anybiz.com/add.asp?ItemID=513&Qty=1&Price=15

    D. http://www.anybiz.com/?login='OR 1=1

5. A security administrator is called for advice. The sales staff has noticed a large amount of orders being filled at prices far below those posted on the site. After some research, it does not appear that the web server or the underlying SQL database have been directly compromised. Next, the security administrator reviews IDS logs and finds nothing unusual. Additionally, the local logs on the server itself do not show anything indicating a problem. Which of the following is the most likely explanation for the false orders?

   A. The website uses hidden fields for price values, which have been altered by the attacker.

   B. SQL injection has been used to update pricing in the database. After the order was placed, pricing was reset to normal, to cover tracks.

   C. Server-side scripting was used to alter the price.

   D. A tool such as Metasploit was used to carry out the attack.

6. A tool named StackGuard is put in place to assist in preventing buffer overflow attacks. Which of the following is used by StackGuard to accomplish this?

   A. Cookies

   B. Input validation

   C. Canary words

   D. CGI manipulation

7. The source code of software used by your client seems to have a large number of gets() alongside sparsely used fgets().What kind of attack is this software potentially susceptible to?

   A. SQL injection

   B. Buffer overflow

   C. Parameter tampering

   D. Cookie manipulation

8. Which code entry will stop input at 100 characters?

   A. `if (I > 100) then exit (1)`

   B. `if (I >= 100) then exit (1)`

   C. `if (I <= 100) then exit (1)`

   D. `if (I < 100) then exit (1)`

9. You are examining cookies provided from a target website and come across this sample:

```
LCID=1033&WTT=GlsWe34_KTUu1w9OBHpQUH*CvPAtzDGAfzwSAY&UR=32768&UREXP=
1/30/2012 12:26:14
30203596*MEMBERTID=33818317&MRVUID=004b0cdf-0006-0000-0000-000000000
=Adam+Adams;ADMIN=NO;Y=1;TIME=02:15GMT
AM&MSAV=0&MSFNF=DEFAULT&MSLNF=DEFAULT&NEWSFLAGS=5242881&USID=
1B81F9E4-033A-4790-9B7E-DE5ADC372A05anybiz.com/15363832422144
```

Which of the following statements is true regarding this site?

A. Cookie tampering may provide additional access to information on or through the site.

B. Cookie tampering is prevented.

C. An underlying SQL database is in use on this site.

D. This is a zombie cookie.

10. Which of the following tools can be used to clone a copy of a website to your machine, to be scrutinized later?

A. BurpSuite

B. NetCraft

C. HttpRecon

D. BlackWidow

11. Which character is your best option in testing for SQL injection vulnerability?

A. The @ symbol

B. A double dash

C. The + sign

D. A single quote

12. A web administrator asks you for a recommendation on a vulnerability scanner for his server. Which of the following are appropriate choices? (Choose all that apply.)

A. NetCat

B. Nessus

C. Nikto

D. Nmap

13. Efforts to gain information from a target website have produced the following error message:

```
Microsoft OLE DB Provider for ODBC Drivers error '80040e08'
[Microsoft]{OBDC SQL Server Driver}
```

Which of the following best describes the error message?

A. The site is may be vulnerable to XSS.

B. The site may be vulnerable to buffer overflow.

C. The site may be vulnerable to SQL injection.

D. The site may be vulnerable to a malware injection.

14. Which buffer overflow attack is designed to make use of memory that remains in use while a program is running?

   A. Stack

   B. Heap

   C. Active

   D. Permanent

15. Which of the following is a standard method for web servers to pass a user's request to an application program and receive data back to forward to the user?

   A. SSI

   B. SSL

   C. CGI

   D. CSI

16. Which of the following are true given the following URL? (Choose all that apply.)

   http://www.anybiz.com/%c0%af%c0%af%c0%af%c0%af%c0%af%c0%af%c0%af/windows\system32\cmd.exe

   A. The attacker is attempting a buffer overflow.

   B. The attacker is attempting directory traversal.

   C. The attacker is using SQL code.

   D. The attacker is using Unicode.

17. Which of the following can be used for remote password cracking of web servers? (Choose all that apply.)

   A. Brutus

   B. Nikto

   C. THC-Hydra

   D. Nessus

18. An attacker is attempting to elevate privileges on a machine by using Java or other functions, through nonvalidated input, to cause the server to execute a malicious piece of code and provide command-line access. Which of the following best describes this action?

   A. Shell injection

   B. File injection

   C. SQL injection

   D. URL injection

19. Which Windows-based web security scanner is known for its fuzzy logic code checking?

    A. Nessus

    B. Nikto

    C. Wikto

    D. Sandcat

20. HTML forms include several methods for transferring data back and forth. Inside a form, which of the following encodes the input into the Uniform Resource Identifier (URI)?

    A. HEAD

    B. PUT

    C. GET

    D. POST

21. An attacker is looking at a target website and is viewing an account from the store on URL http://www.anybiz.com/store.php?id=2. He next enters the following URL:

    http://www.anybiz.com/store.php?id=2 and 1=1

    The web page loads normally. He then enters the following URL:

    http://www.anybiz.com/store.php?id=2 and 1=2

    A generic page noting "An error has occurred" appears.

    Which of the following is a correct statement concerning these actions?

    A. The site is vulnerable to cross-site scripting.

    B. The site is vulnerable to blind SQL injection.

    C. The site is vulnerable to buffer overflows.

    D. The site is not vulnerable to SQL injection.

22. Which of the following are valid methods to harden a web server? (Choose all that apply.)

    A. Ensure patching is kept up to date.

    B. Remove nonessential applications.

    C. Remove or disable nonessential ports and protocols.

    D. Allow remote access via Telnet.

    E. Keep web applications and scripts on the same partition as the operating system.

    F. Use secure coding techniques.

23. An attacker is viewing a blog entry showing a news story and asking for comments. In the comment field, the attacker enters the following:

```
Nice post and a fun read
<script>onload=window.location='http://www.badsite.com'</script>
```

What is the attacker attempting to perform?

A. A SQL injection attack against the blog's underlying database

B. A cross-site scripting attack

C. A buffer overflow DoS attack

D. A file injection DoS attack.

24. An attacker attempts to manipulate an application by advancing the instruction pointer with a long run of instructions containing no action. What is this attack called?

A. File injection

B. Stack flipping

C. NOP sled

D. Heap based

25. You are examining website files and find the following text file:

```
# robots.txt for http://www.anybiz.com/
User-agent: Googlebot
Disallow: /tmp/
User-agent: *
Disallow: /
Disallow: /private.php
Disallow: /listing.html
```

Which of the following is a true statement concerning this file?

A. All web crawlers are prevented from indexing the listing.html page.

B. All web crawlers are prevented from indexing all pages on the site.

C. The Googlebot crawler is allowed to index pages starting with /tmp/.

D. The Googlebot crawler can access and index everything on the site except for pages starting with /tmp/.

1. D
2. B
3. A
4. C
5. A
6. C
7. B
8. B
9. A
10. D
11. D
12. B, C
13. C
14. B
15. C
16. B, D
17. A, C
18. A
19. C
20. C
21. B
22. A, B, C, F
23. B
24. C
25. D

1. You are examining connection logs from a client machine and come across this entry:

   http://www.business123.com/../../../../Windows/system.ini.

   Which attack does this most likely indicate?

   A. Parameter manipulation

   B. XSS

   C. SQL injection

   D. Directory traversal

   ☑ **D.** Sure directory traversal is an older attack (working mainly on now-outdated servers), but it's still worth a shot and, more importantly to you dear reader, it's going to be on your test. In this attack, the hacker attempts to access restricted directories and execute commands outside intended web server directories. Also known as the known as the *dot-dot-slash* attack, *directory climbing,* and *backtracking,* this attack basically sends HTTP requests asking the server to drop back to the root directory and give access to other folders. Assuming you know the folder directory structure, and the location where you want to run commands and so on, this one is easy enough to pull off.

   ☒ **A** is incorrect because parameter manipulation (also known as parameter tampering) deals with changing portions of the URL string in hopes of modifying data or eliciting a response. An example might be changing the "orderID" portion of a URL string to see if you can peruse other users' information.

   ☒ **B** is incorrect because cross-site scripting (XSS) isn't being discussed in this question. XSS is all about website design and dynamic content, passing client-side scripts into a web page viewed by a different person. In addition to simply bringing it down in a good old DoS attack, XSS can also be used to steal users' cookies, upload malicious code to users connected to the server, and send pop-up messages to users.

   ☒ **C** is incorrect because SQL injection is not being performed here. SQL injection involves passing SQL queries through a web front end to manipulate, display, replace, or destroy records in the underlying database.

2. A hacker is looking at a publicly facing web front end. One of the pages provides an entry box with the heading "Forgot password? Enter your email address." In the entry, he types **anything' OR '1'='1**.

   A message appears stating, "Your login information has been sent to a_username@ emailaddress.target.com."

Which of the following is true?

A. The cross-site scripting attempt has succeeded.

B. The SQL injection attempt has succeeded.

C. The parameter tampering has succeeded.

D. The buffer overflow attempt has succeeded.

☑ **B.** Any time you see *' or 1=1*, I can promise you it's a SQL injection question. Because the hacker got a response, this site is susceptible to SQL injection. As an aside, it's just as likely an attempt like this may fail to return an actual record, but if it does you may wind up getting valuable information anyway in the form of an error message from the underlying SQL database. Remember with SQL you're simply trying to pass SQL queries through an entry point never made to take them (at least, not *designed* or *thought of* to do so anyway). What's going on here, as much as we can tell from the question, is a result has been returned from the site from input designed as a SQL query, and not the designed user input (username or e-mail address).

☒ **A** is incorrect because this is not an XSS attempt. Cross-site scripting would involve something like JavaScript inserting data into the page—usually to manipulate web content.

☒ **C** is incorrect because parameter tampering is not in use here. Parameter tampering is inside the URL itself, manipulating parameters to change the response to something you're looking for (changing *order=13752+user=500* to *order =13752+user=1* inside the URL, or something like that).

☒ **D** is incorrect because buffer overflow is not in play here. Buffer overflow is an attempt to write more data into an application's prebuilt buffer area in order to overwrite adjacent memory, execute code, or crash a system (application).

3. A pen tester is examining a web front end on a target network. The page displays a "Search" text box form entry, allowing the user to search for items on the site. Instead of entering a search text string, the tester enters **<script>'It Worked'</ script>**. After the tester clicks the Search button beside the entry box, a pop-up appears stating, "It Worked." Which of the following is true regarding this attempt?

A. The site is vulnerable to XSS.

B. Coding on the site is poor, and a buffer overflow attack may result in a DoS.

C. The attacker's next entry in the Search box should be **' OR '1'='1**.

D. This is expected behavior on properly configured sites.

☑ **A.** A somewhat simplistic but undeniably classic example of cross-site scripting. A common cross-site scripting attempt is to insert malicious script into an input field on a site. If the site is not configured properly, it'll become confused and execute the script instead of erroring out and telling you you're naughty. By manipulating input fields, you can accomplish all sorts of things, such as redirecting users to an alternate site, stealing cookies or other data from users, and performing a plain-old DoS against the site/server.

☒ **B** is incorrect because, although the site is undeniably configured poorly, there is no indication here a buffer overflow will work at all. It might, later, but we just can't tell from this.

☒ **C** is incorrect because there is no indication here of a SQL injection vulnerability. As before, it may very well be vulnerable, but this question doesn't provide that information.

☒ **D** is incorrect because the site is configured poorly to even allow XSS in the first place.

4. Which of the following is representative of a parameter-tampering attack?

   A. http://www.anybiz.com/../../../../../windows\system32\cmd.exe

   B. http://www.anybiz.com/search.asp?lname=walker%27%update%20 usertable%20%20set%3d%23hAxor%27

   C. http://anybiz.com/add.asp?ItemID=513&Qty=1&Price=15

   D. http://www.anybiz.com/?login='OR 1=1

   ☑ **C.** Parameter tampering (a.k.a. URL tampering) is an attack where the hacker searches a URL string for parameters that can be adjusted. These entries are then manipulated within the URL string in hopes of modifying data, such as permissions and elevation of privilege, prices and quantities of goods, and credentials. In this example, you can clearly see the "price" parameter as part of the URL. Why not change price to 1 and see if you can't get the product on the cheap? Other tampering scenarios you'll probably see on your exam will have admin=0 or admin=no in the URL.

   ☒ **A** is incorrect because this is a directory traversal example. Note the "../" entries, attempting to follow the directory tree back to execute a command.

   ☒ **B and D** are incorrect, but only because of a slight delineation applicable to your test taking. It can be argued that these two are also examples of parameter manipulation, because the URL is being adjusted for a purpose. However, your exam will count these as examples of SQL injection attempts. Yes, this is normally done in a form on the page, passing commands into an entry box, but there's no reason why you can't try the same thing from the URL. In answer B, the attacker is attempting to update a table, whereas in answer C the standard *'OR 1=1* has been entered to elicit a SQL response.

5. A security administrator is called for advice. The sales staff has noticed a large amount of orders being filled at prices far below those posted on the site. After some research, it does not appear that the web server or the underlying SQL database have been directly compromised. Next, the security administrator reviews IDS logs and finds nothing unusual. Additionally, the local logs on the server itself do not show anything indicating a problem. Which of the following is the most likely explanation for the false orders?

   A. The website uses hidden fields for price values, which have been altered by the attacker.

   B. SQL injection has been used to update pricing in the database. After the order was placed, pricing was reset to normal, to cover tracks.

   C. Server-side scripting was used to alter the price.

   D. A tool such as Metasploit was used to carry out the attack.

   ☑ **A.** This is actually more common than you might think. No, I'm not advising you to go do your Christmas shopping early—that could get you in serious trouble—I'm just stating an outright fact that many websites simply don't have their collective stuff together. If you view the source code for a site offering products for sale, many times you can find the pricing secreted away in a "hidden" field (just do a search for "hidden" on the form). If you copy that source to your computer, alter the value in the hidden field, save and launch in the browser, you can order at whatever price you set.

   ☒ **B and C** are both incorrect for the same reason. This level of interaction would most certainly be easy to spot between the IDS and server logs. SQL injection involves passing SQL queries and commands through the interface and would be evident in the logs. SSIs (Server Side Includes) are directives placed in HTML pages and evaluated on the server while the pages are being served.

   ☒ **D** is incorrect because there is simply no evidence any tool has been used here. Of course, this might have been a super-talented, ace hacker who jumped in and out of the site leaving absolutely no crumbs to track him down with, but it's *very* unlikely.

6. A tool named StackGuard is put in place to assist in preventing buffer overflow attacks. Which of the following is used by StackGuard to accomplish this?

   A. Cookies

   B. Input validation

   C. Canary words

   D. CGI manipulation

   ☑ **C.** *Canaries* or *canary words* are known values placed between the buffer and control data. If a buffer overflow occurs, the canary word will be altered first, triggering a halt to the system. StackGuard was released way back in 1997 as an extension for the GNU Compiler Collection (GCC), a compiler produced by the GNU Project. When it comes to buffer overflow protection and this exam, you need to know canaries, input validation, and StackGuard.

☒ **A** is incorrect because cookies are not used for buffer overflow prevention. A *cookie* is a small, text-based file that is stored on your system for use by the web server the next time you log in, in an effort to provide a continuous, stable web view for customers, and to make things easier for return surfers. Cookies are sent in the header of an HTTP response from a web server and may or may not have an expiration date.

☒ **B** is incorrect because StackGuard does not perform input validation. This is not to say that input validation is not a preventative measure against buffer overflow—it is. You just need to know that the design of StackGuard is to make use of canaries in prevention.

☒ **D** is incorrect because CGI manipulation plays no role here and is included as a distractor. CGI (Common Gateway Interface) is a standard method for web servers to pass a user's request to an application program and receive data back to forward to the user.

7. The source code of software used by your client seems to have a large number of gets() alongside sparsely used fgets().What kind of attack is this software potentially susceptible to?

   A. SQL injection

   B. Buffer overflow

   C. Parameter tampering

   D. Cookie manipulation

   ☑ **B.** A buffer overflow is an attempt to write more data into an application's pre-built buffer area in order to overwrite adjacent memory, execute code, or crash a system (application). By inputting more data than the buffer is allocated to hold, you may be able to crash the application or machine or alter the application's data pointers. gets() is a common source of buffer overflow vulnerabilities because it reads a line from standard input into a buffer until a terminating EOF is found. It performs no check for buffer overrun and is largely replaced by fgets().

   ☒ **A** is incorrect because SQL injection has nothing to do with this scenario. No evidence is presented that this software even interacts with a database.

   ☒ **C** is incorrect because parameter tampering deals with manipulating a URL.

   ☒ **D** is incorrect because cookie manipulation has nothing to do with this software. As covered earlier, a cookie is a small file used to provide a more consistent web experience for a web visitor. Because it holds all sorts of information, though, it can be manipulated for nefarious purposes (using the Firefox add-on Cookie Editor, for instance).

8. Which code entry will stop input at 100 characters?

   A. `if (I > 100) then exit (1)`

   B. `if (I >= 100) then exit (1)`

   C. `if (I <= 100) then exit (1)`

   D. `if (I < 100) then exit (1)`

   ☑ **B.** There won't be very many pure coding type questions on the exam, and when they do appear they're pretty clear cut. Because 0 (zero) is used in counting in most computer programming code (many indeed start at 1, but the examples in your exam don't), any value from 0 to 99 would suffice. Thus, an entry of 100 would represent the 101st character. Therefore, you can accept anything less than 100 as a character count: "I" must be less than 100 to be accepted, and if it's 100 or above, exit and quit. So, if the character value count is equal to 100, or greater, exit the program (I >= 100).

   ☒ **A, C,** and **D** are all incorrect expressions. (I > 100) indicates any entry greater than 100, which *does* work; however, it leaves the extra 101st entry (that is, 100) as acceptable. (I < 100) would exit on any character entry less than 100 (meaning the only acceptable entries would be 101 characters or more—the exact opposite of what we're trying to accomplish). Finally, (I <= 100) is just as bad, for obvious reasons.

9. You are examining cookies provided from a target website and come across this sample:

   ```
   LCID=1033&WTT=GlsWe34_KTUu1w9OBHpQUH*CvPAtzDGAfzwSAY&UR=32768&UREXP=
   1/30/2012 12:26:14
   30203596*MEMBERTID=33818317&MRVUID=004b0cdf-0006-0000-0000-000000000
   =Adam+Adams;ADMIN=NO;Y=1;TIME=02:15GMT
   AM&MSAV=0&MSFNF=DEFAULT&MSLNF=DEFAULT&NEWSFLAGS=5242881&USID=
   1B81F9E4-033A-4790-9B7E-DE5ADC372A05anybiz.com/15363832422144
   ```

   Which of the following statements is true regarding this site?

   A. Cookie tampering may provide additional access to information on or through the site.

   B. Cookie tampering is prevented.

   C. An underlying SQL database is in use on this site.

   D. This is a zombie cookie.

   ☑ **A.** Although it may fail miserably, altering a cookie might lead to additional access to information on or through the site. In the example provided, we can clearly see a portion that reads "ADMIN=NO." Well, what would happen if you changed it to "ADMIN=YES"? Again, it may seem simplistic and may not change a thing, but editing this cookie and going back to the site may very well easily open a door for you. Cookie Editor is an add-on in Firefox for doing just this (be careful of versioning with this, though, because the original Cookie Editor add-on stopped working on Firefox 15.0).

☒ **B** is incorrect because nothing in this sample indicates any sort of tamper prevention. As a matter of fact, the cookie itself is merely a text file, so there wouldn't be any indication of tamper prevention in the first place.

☒ **C** is incorrect because nothing in this cookie points to anything SQL- or database-related at all. Does the site use a backend SQL database? Maybe, but we can't tell that from a cookie.

☒ **D** is incorrect because there is no way to tell from this output whether or not the cookie is a zombie. Zombie cookies are re-created after deletion from backups stored outside your browsers' normal cookie storage area. They are very difficult to remove, and may even install on a browser that does not receive cookies (due to where they are stored).

10. Which of the following tools can be used to clone a copy of a website to your machine, to be scrutinized later?

   A. BurpSuite

   B. NetCraft

   C. HttpRecon

   D. BlackWidow

   ☑ **D. BlackWidow** is an easy-to-use application that can perform all sorts of things—mainly, to this question, downloading a clone of a website for scanning and vulnerability discovery at your leisure. The following is from the developer's website (sbl.net): "Black Widow is a state-of-the-art website scanner for both experts and beginners. It can download an entire website, or download portions of a site, and can build a site structure first, then download later; you select what to download. The integrated scripting engine is an easy to learn and use programing language to facilitate scanning 'hard to scan' sites. It allows you to control the scan by trapping the scanner event so you can process the request yourself."

   ☒ **A** is incorrect because BurpSuite isn't designed to pull an entire copy of a website externally and run through tests. The following is from the website (http://www.portswigger.net/burp/): "BurpSuite is an integrated platform for performing security testing of web applications. Its various tools work seamlessly together to support the entire testing process, from initial mapping and analysis of an application's attack surface, through to finding and exploiting security vulnerabilities."

   ☒ **B** is incorrect because NetCraft isn't a tool to be used for this purpose. NetCraft is actually a security corporation in England that provides all sorts of security tools aimed at the web sector. They're currently well known for their anti-phishing toolbar, which was hailed by Microsoft as being "among the most effective tools to combat phishing on the Internet." This probably explains why Microsoft purchased licensing for NetCraft and added that functionality in Internet Explorer 7 as Microsoft Phishing Filter (also known as SmartScreen Filter in IE8).

   ☒ **C** is incorrect because HttpRecon isn't used in this manner. HttpRecon is known as a web server fingerprinting tool, providing "highly accurate identification of given httpd implementations" (http://www.computec.ch/ projekte/httprecon/). HttpRecon uses traditional approaches, such as banner-grabbing, status code enumeration, and header ordering analysis, but also adds other analytical techniques to increase accuracy.

11. Which character is your best option in testing for SQL injection vulnerability?

   A. The @ symbol

   B. A double dash

   C. The + sign

   D. A single quote

   ☑ **D.** SQL injection is all about entering queries and commands into a form field (or URL) to elicit a response, gain information, or manipulate data. On a web page, many times entries into a form field are inserted into a SQL command: When you enter your username and information into the fields and click the button, the SQL command in the background might read something like this:

```
SELECT OrderID, FirstName, Lastname FROM Orders
```

In SQL, a single quote is used to indicate an upcoming character string. Once SQL sees that open quote, it starts parsing everything behind it as string input. If there's no close quote, an error occurs because SQL doesn't know what to do with it. If the web page is configured poorly, that error will return to you and let you know it's time to start injecting SQL commands.

   ☒ **A, B,** and **C** are incorrect characters to use as part of a SQL injection test. The @ symbol is used to designate a variable in SQL (you'll need to define the variable, of course). The + sign is used to combine strings together (as in Matt+Walker). A double dash indicates an upcoming comment in the line.

12. A web administrator asks you for a recommendation on a vulnerability scanner for his server. Which of the following are appropriate choices? (Choose all that apply.)

   A. NetCat

   B. Nessus

   C. Nikto

   D. Nmap

☑ **B and C.** Both Nessus and Nikto are well-known vulnerability scanners. Nessus has been around seemingly forever, and is a de facto choice for many folks in the security field. The following is from the Tenable Network Security site: "Nessus® is the world's most widely-deployed vulnerability and configuration assessment product with more than five million downloads to date. Nessus 5 features high-speed discovery, configuration auditing, asset profiling, sensitive data discovery, patch management integration, and vulnerability analysis of your security posture with features that enhance usability, effectiveness, efficiency, and communication with all parts of your organization." Nikto is an open source scanner that's more web server centric in its vulnerability assessment efforts. From the Nikto site (http://cirt.net/nikto2): "Nikto is an Open Source (GPL) web server scanner which performs comprehensive tests against web servers for multiple items, including over 6500 potentially dangerous files/CGIs, checks for outdated versions of over 1250 servers, and version specific problems on over 270 servers. It also checks for server configuration items such as the presence of multiple index files, HTTP server options, and will attempt to identify installed web servers and software." Keep in mind that neither tool is designed for stealth. These are security tools designed for security professionals to discover problems before the bad guys do. If you aim these tools at a site, you will be noticed.

☒ **A is incorrect** because Netcat is not a vulnerability assessment tool. Sometimes referred to as a Swiss Army Knife for TCP/IP hacking, it is a utility that reads and writes data across network connections. The following is from the GNU Netcat project home page (http://netcat.sourceforge.net/): "It is designed to be a reliable back-end tool that can be used directly or easily driven by other programs and scripts. At the same time, it is a feature-rich network debugging and exploration tool, since it can create almost any kind of connection you would need and has several interesting built-in capabilities."

☒ **D is incorrect** because nmap is not a vulnerability scanning tool. It is an open source utility for network discovery and security auditing. Per the website (http://nmap.org/): "Many systems and network administrators also find it useful for tasks such as network inventory, managing service upgrade schedules, and monitoring host or service uptime."

13. Efforts to gain information from a target website have produced the following error message:

```
Microsoft OLE DB Provider for ODBC Drivers error '80040e08'
[Microsoft]{OBDC SQL Server Driver}
```

Which of the following best describes the error message?

A. The site is may be vulnerable to XSS.

B. The site may be vulnerable to buffer overflow.

C. The site may be vulnerable to SQL injection.

D. The site may be vulnerable to a malware injection.

☑ **C.** Once again, you will get a few "gimme" questions on the exam. The error message clearly displays a SQL error, telling us (1) there's an underlying SQL database to contend with and (2) it's most likely not configured correctly (or we wouldn't be getting an error message like this—through a web interface and telling us exactly what's there—in the first place).

☒ **A, B** and **D** are all incorrect for the same reason: The error message simply doesn't provide enough information to make those leaps. There is nothing here indicating cross-site scripting or buffer overflow on either side of the ledger. Although it's true the error may be an indication as to which kinds of malware may increase your odds of success, there's nothing there to indicate, by itself, that the site is vulnerable.

14. Which buffer overflow attack is designed to make use of memory that remains in use while a program is running?

A. Stack

B. Heap

C. Active

D. Permanent

☑ **B.** Granted, this is a little bit of a picky question, but you'll definitely see something like this on your exam. Buffer overflows are all about the same thing: inputting more information into a buffer area that was designed for one action, in order to write code to a different area of memory so it can be executed. At best, the code will execute and you can do all sorts of good things. At worse, the program will reject the code and crash. A 'heap' buffer attack takes advantage of the memory space set aside for the program itself. Heap is the memory area immediately "on top" of the program and is not temporary (it's supposed to remain in use as long as the application is running). Pages in the heap can be read from and written to, which is what the attacker will be trying to exploit.

☒ **A** is incorrect only because of the actual buffer area being exploited. Whereas heap is memory set aside in the application and is not "temporary," the stack is *designed* that way: Each task is added on top of the previous tasks and is executed in order. Overflow the buffer, and you can affect which area executes.

☒ **C** and **D** are incorrect because neither is a buffer overflow attack type. These are added as distractors.

15. Which of the following is a standard method for web servers to pass a user's request to an application program and receive data back to forward to the user?

A. SSI

B. SSL

C. CGI

D. CSI

☑ **C.** Common Gateway Interface (CGI) is a standardized method for transferring information between a web server and an executable (a CGI script designed to perform some task with the data). CGI is considered a server-side solution because processing is done on the web server and not the client. Because CGI scripts can run essentially arbitrary commands on your system with the permissions of the web server user, and because they are almost always wrapped so that a script will execute as the owner of the script, they can be extremely dangerous if not carefully checked. Additionally, all CGI scripts on the server will run as the same user, so they have the potential to conflict (accidentally or deliberately) with other scripts (an attacker could, for example, write a CGI script to destroy all other CGI databases).

☒ **A** is incorrect because SSIs (Server Side Includes) are directives placed in HTML pages and evaluated on the server while the pages are being served. They let you add dynamically generated content to an existing HTML page, without having to serve the entire page via a CGI program or other dynamic technology.

☒ **B and D** are incorrect because both are included as distractors. By now you're certainly familiar with Secure Sockets Layer (SSL) and its value as an encryption method. CSI? Well, that's just good television. Or used to be, anyway.

16. Which of the following are true given the following URL? (Choose all that apply.)

    http://www.anybiz.com/%c0%af%c0%af%c0%af%c0%af%c0%af%c0%af%c0%af/windows\system32\cmd.exe

    A. The attacker is attempting a buffer overflow.

    B. The attacker is attempting directory traversal.

    C. The attacker is using SQL code.

    D. The attacker is using Unicode.

    ☑ **B and D.** Directory traversal is easy enough to spot when it's spelled out in readable format. The "dot-dot-slash" attack is designed to have older servers climb up and back down their directory tree to execute commands. One way to obfuscate this attempt is to make use of Unicode characters. Per the Unicode.org website, it "provides a unique number for every character, no matter what the platform, no matter what the program, no matter what the language." Unicode was invented because no single encoding method could contain enough characters (the example from the site included the European Union alone requiring several different encodings to cover all its languages).

Unicode provided the standard for ensuring consistent encoding and text representation, and also succeeded in providing one more avenue for attackers to use.

☒ **A** is incorrect because this is not a buffer overflow attempt.

☒ **C** is incorrect because no SQL code is shown in the URL.

17. Which of the following can be used for remote password cracking of web servers? (Choose all that apply.)

   A. Brutus

   B. Nikto

   C. THC-Hydra

   D. Nessus

   ☑ **A and C.** Brutus is a fast, flexible remote password cracker. According to the tool's website (www.hoobie.net/brutus/), it was originally invented to help its creator check routers and network devices for default and common passwords. It has since grown and evolved to much more and is among the more popular security tools available for remote password cracking. THC-Hydra (www.thc.org/thc-hydra/) is another remote password cracker. It's a "parallelized login cracker" that provides the ability to attack over multiple protocols.

   ☒ **B** is incorrect because Nikto is not a remote password cracker. It's an open source web-server-centric vulnerability scanner that performs comprehensive tests against web servers for multiple items.

   ☒ **D** is incorrect because Nessus is not a remote password cracker—it's a vulnerability assessment tool.

18. An attacker is attempting to elevate privileges on a machine by using Java or other functions, through nonvalidated input, to cause the server to execute a malicious piece of code and provide command-line access. Which of the following best describes this action?

   A. Shell injection

   B. File injection

   C. SQL injection

   D. URL injection

   ☑ **A.** When it comes to web application attacks, there are many vectors and avenues to take. One of the more common is injecting something into an input string to exploit poor code. The EC Council defines these attacks in many ways. Shell injection is defined as an attempt to gain shell access using Java or other functions. In short, the attacker will pass commands through a form input (or other avenue) in order to elevate privileges and open a shell for further naughtiness. Also known as *command injection,* this occurs when commands are entered into form fields instead of the expected entry.

☒ **B** is incorrect because the EC Council defines a file injection attack as one where the attacker injects a pointer in the web form input to an exploit hosted on a remote site. Sure, this may accomplish the same thing, but it's not the best choice in this case.

☒ **C** is incorrect because SQL injection attacks involve using SQL queries and commands to elicit a response or action.

☒ **D** is incorrect because URL injection is not an attack type, and is included here as a distractor.

19. Which Windows-based web security scanner is known for its fuzzy logic code checking?

   A. Nessus

   B. Nikto

   C. Wikto

   D. Sandcat

   ☑ **C.** I've read the following on several sites about the tool, so I feel confident in repeating it here: Wikto is Nikto for Windows, with a little more added. The development website notes that in addition to everything Nikto offers, Wikto adds extra features such as fuzzy logic error code checking, a backend miner, Google-assisted directory mining, and real-time HTTP request/response monitoring (http://www.sensepost.com/labs/tools/pentest/wikto).

   ☒ **A** is incorrect because Nessus isn't a "fuzzy logic" scanner and isn't designed solely for web server efforts. It *is* one of the most popular vulnerability assessment scanners available and will work well in defining vulnerabilities that may have been overlooked, however.

   ☒ **B** is incorrect because Nikto is a Linux/Unix-based web security scanning tool, and doesn't hold the "fuzzy logic" features of Wikto.

   ☒ **D** is incorrect because the Sandcat is a pen-test-oriented web browser that's part of Syhunt's tool collection (http://www.syhunt.com/). Sandcat Browser includes the following pen-test-oriented features: Live HTTP Headers, Request Editor extension, Fuzzer extension with multiple modes and support for filters, JavaScript Executor extension, Lua Executor extension, SyhuntGelo, PageInfo extension (for viewing page headers and JavaScript objects), Tor extension (for Anonymity), HTTP Brute Force, CGI Scanner scripts, Encoders/Decoders, and more. It's also freeware and portable, so feel free to play!

20. HTML forms include several methods for transferring data back and forth. Inside a form, which of the following encodes the input into the Uniform Resource Identifier (URI)?

A. HEAD

B. PUT

C. GET

D. POST

☑ **C.** An HTTP GET is a method for returning data from a form that "encodes" the form data to the end of the URI (a character string that identifies a resource on the Web, such as a page of text, a video clip, an image, or an application). Generally speaking, a POST is "more secure" than a GET, although they both have their uses. If you're wondering when a GET should be used as opposed to a POST, the answer has to do with a vocabulary lesson: defining the term *idempotent*. Thrown about with HTTP GET, idempotent is a mathematical concept about an operation property: If the operation can be performed without changing results, even if it is run multiple times, it's considered idempotent. So, if the input return is assured of having no lasting effect on the state of the form in total, then using a GET is perfectly reasonable. Also, a GET can usually only transfer up to 8Kb, whereas a POST can usually handle up to 2GB. However, keep in mind it may wind up including sensitive information in that URI. Suppose your form returns a credit card number and a bad guy is logging URIs: If HTTP GET is in place, the attacker may be able to derive the information.

☒ **A** is incorrect because although HEAD and GET are similar, HEAD is not used in forms. It's usually used to pull header information from a web server (remember your banner grabbing from earlier?) and to test links.

☒ **B** is incorrect because HTTP PUT is not used in forms. It's used to transfer files to a web server.

☒ **D** is incorrect because POST does not include the form data in the URI request. According to the World Wide Web Consortium (http://www.w3.org/), HTML specifications define the difference between GET and POST so that GET means that form data will be encoded by a browser into a URL, whereas POST means the form data is to appear within the message body. In short, a GET can be used for basic, simple retrieval of data, and a POST should be used for most everything else (such as sending an e-mail, updating data on a database, and ordering an item).

21. An attacker is looking at a target website and is viewing an account from the store on URL http://www.anybiz.com/store.php?id=2. He next enters the following URL:

http://www.anybiz.com/store.php?id=2 and 1=1

The web page loads normally. He then enters the following URL:

http://www.anybiz.com/store.php?id=2 and 1=2

A generic page noting "An error has occurred" appears.

Which of the following is a correct statement concerning these actions?

A. The site is vulnerable to cross site scripting.

B. The site is vulnerable to blind SQL injection.

C. The site is vulnerable to buffer overflows.

D. The site is not vulnerable to SQL injection.

☑ **B.** The URLs shown here are attempting to pass a SQL query through to see what may be going on in the background. Notice the first URL entered added **and 1=1**. Because this was a true statement, the page loaded without problem. However, changing that to a false statement—**and 1=2**—caused the database to return an error. This would now be considered "blind" SQL injection because the actual error was not returned to the attacker (instead, he got a generic page most likely configured by the dB administrator). As an aside, sometimes the attacker won't receive the error message or error page at all, but the site will be displayed differently—images out of place, text messed up, and so on—which also indicates blind SQL may be in order.

☒ **A and C** are incorrect because neither this attack nor the results has anything to do with cross-site scripting or buffer overflows.

☒ **D** is incorrect because the results indicate SQL injection is possible. Granted, it will take longer, because we can't see error messaging, and will require lots of guesswork and trial and error, but it is susceptible.

22. Which of the following are valid methods to harden a web server? (Choose all that apply.)

A. Ensure patching is kept up to date.

B. Remove nonessential applications.

C. Remove or disable nonessential ports and protocols.

D. Allow remote access via Telnet.

E. Keep web applications and scripts on the same partition as the operating system.

F. Use secure coding techniques.

☑ **A, B, C, and F.** "Hardening" anything—whether a server, end-client machine, network device, or even a printer—is usually a matter of common sense. Keeping patching, hotfixes, and service packs up to date is a no-brainer (being sure to appropriately test before installing, of course). Removing unused applications and disabling ports and protocols clearly reduces your vulnerability footprint. Some items to look at deleting include but are not limited to unnecessary services, files (header files, archives, old text documents), directories, ISAPI filters, user accounts, and protocols.

☒ **D** is incorrect because Telnet passes everything in the clear, so if you're going to allow remote access at all, SSH is a better, more secure method.

☒ **E** is incorrect because keeping these in the same location as the operating system makes no sense at all. The opposite is true—don't allow a problem or vulnerability with a script or application to corrupt your OS.

23. An attacker is viewing a blog entry showing a news story and asking for comments. In the comment field, the attacker enters the following:

```
Nice post and a fun read
<script>onload=window.location='http://www.badsite.com'</script>
```

What is the attacker attempting to perform?

A. A SQL injection attack against the blog's underlying database

B. A cross-site scripting attack

C. A buffer overflow DoS attack

D. A file injection DoS attack

☑ **B.** This is a classic (an overly simplified, but classic nonetheless) example of cross-site scripting. In a blog, the post entry field is intended to take text entry from a visitor and copy it to a database in the background. What's being attempted here is to have more than just the text copied—the <script> indicator is adding a nice little pointer to a naughty website. If it works, the next visitor to the site who clicks that news story will see the bad site pop up.

☒ **A, C,** and **D** are all incorrect because this example contains nothing to indicate a SQL injection or a buffer overflow. Additionally, the idea here is not to perform a denial of service. Actually, it's quite the opposite: The attacker wants the site up and operational so more and more users can be sent to badsite.com.

24. An attacker attempts to manipulate an application by advancing the instruction pointer with a long run of instructions containing no action. What is this attack called?

A. File injection

B. Stack flipping

C. NOP sled

D. Heap based

☑ **C.** Computer languages usually contain a command most CPUs will recognize as "do nothing." This No Operation (NOP) instruction serves to advance an instruction pointer to a known memory area. The idea behind it is to provide time for unknown activities to occur until it's time to execute the main code (avoiding an exception code and a halt to the system or application). For a ridiculously over-simplified example, if you were "coding" a human's morning routine and wanted them to brush their teeth, you might provide a whole bunch of "do nothing's" in front and behind the "pick up toothbrush, put toothpaste on brush, and so on" steps—to provide space for things you may not be aware of.

When it comes to attacks, hackers will send tons of NOP instructions in an effort to move the pointer to an area they control—and to execute the naughty payload there. This "NOP sled" is relatively easy to see in action, and all IDSs will pick it up.

☒ **A** is incorrect because file injection occurs when the attacker injects a pointer in a web form input to an exploit hosted on a remote site. There is no file injection occurring in this example.

☒ **B** is incorrect because the term *stack flipping* is not a recognized term on the CEH exam and is included here as a distractor.

☒ **D** is incorrect because a heap-based buffer overflow deals with a buffer overflow specifically aimed at the lower part of the heap, to overwrite dynamic content there.

25. You are examining website files and find the following text file:

```
# robots.txt for http://www.anybiz.com/
User-agent: Googlebot
Disallow: /tmp/
User-agent: *
Disallow: /
Disallow: /private.php
Disallow: /listing.html
```

Which of the following is a true statement concerning this file?

A. All web crawlers are prevented from indexing the listing.html page.

B. All web crawlers are prevented from indexing all pages on the site.

C. The Googlebot crawler is allowed to index pages starting with /tmp/.

D. The Googlebot crawler can access and index everything on the site except for pages starting with /tmp/.

☑ **D.** The robots.txt file was created to allow web designers to control index access to their sites. There are a couple of things you need to know about this file—for your exam and the real world. The first is, no matter what the robots.txt file says, attackers using a crawler to index your site are going to ignore it anyway: It's only valid for "good-guy" crawlers. After that, the rest is easy: robots.txt is stored on the root, is available to anyone (by design), and is read in order from top to bottom, much like an ACL on a router. The format is simple: Define the crawler (User-agent :*name_of_crawler*), then define what it does not have access to. Most robot.txt files will make use of the "*" variable to signify all crawlers, but you can certainly get specific with who is allowed in and what they can see.

In this example, from top to bottom, the Googlebot crawler is defined and restricted from seeing /tmp/ pages—no other restrictions are listed. After that, all other crawlers (User-agent: *) are restricted from seeing any page (Disallow: /). The last two lines are truly irrelevant because the condition to ignore all pages has been read.

For additional information here, if you think about what a robots.txt file does, you could consider it a pointer to pages you, as an attacker, *really* want to see. After all, if the security person on the site didn't want Google indexing it, useful information probably resides there. On the flip side, a security-minded person may get a little snippy with it and have a little fun, sending you to some truly terrible Internet locations should you try to access one of the pages listed there.

☒ **A** and **B** are incorrect because the Googlebot crawler is allowed to crawl the site.

☒ **C** is incorrect because Googlebot is instructed to ignore all /tmp/ pages.

Wireless Network Hacking

This chapter includes questions from the following topics:

- Identify wireless network architecture and terminology
- Identify wireless network types and forms of authentication
- Describe WEP and WPA wireless encryption
- Identify wireless hacking methods and tools
- Define Bluetooth hacking methods

I went to high school in the 80s and lived virtually every stereotype from the age you're picturing in your head right now. I had parachute pants, a Members-Only jacket, listened to big-hair rock music, and thought Eddie Murphy was *original* (and even funny). It's hard to imagine, now, how wrong we were about so much of that. Not to mention kids nowadays dress for Halloween like I did for school.

One day I was sitting in Mr. Rockwell's math class and was listening to two girls talk about their Friday night dates. It wasn't like I was sitting around a corner eavesdropping or anything like that—I was just sitting at my desk and they were talking loud enough to be overheard. They didn't seem to care, though, because they were using a crazy fad that started back in the 80s to communicate: speaking gibberish (it's not as well known, mainly because it's annoying and startlingly dumb, but it was a fad for a long while). Gibberish consisted of injecting the sound *otha-ga* between the syllables of a word (for example, *fishing* would be pronounced *fish-otha-ga-ing-otha-ga*) so that only another gibberish speaker could understand you. Some of these girls were really quick with it, too, so it did indeed sound like gibberish.

As inane and dumb as this sounds, it was pretty popular when I was in school: for the girls anyway (we dudes were just way too cool for that). The problem with it was, once you knew the setup, their communication wasn't secret anymore. There they sat, broadcasting information over the air believing it to be secure, when all the while I sat there listening in and understanding everything that was said (not to mention finding out some really juicy information about Brian, Ashley, and an after-game late night around the Burger King parking lot). And the opportunity was abundant: Literally every class had girls speaking gibberish—sometimes right in the middle of a conversation with guys they'd turn to each other and gibber away—and those of us who knew the score had a leg up on information in the school. For a guy like me, information has always, *always* been valuable.

Wireless networks are much the same today as those gibbering girls from my high school. They're literally everywhere, and they're broadcasting information across the air that anyone can pick up. Sure, most of it is gibberish, but if you can crack that code (if you can find the "otha-ga" in the wireless transmission), you sure can find some juicy information of your own. Maybe not as much fun as a friend's Friday night escapades, but useful to your job as a pen tester.

 STUDY TIPS Depending on the pool of test questions the system pulls for your exam, you'll either grow to love the test you're taking or hate it with a fiery passion. Questions on wireless are fairly easy and shouldn't bother you too much, except for the ones that aren't. Questions on war chalking, for instance, can sometimes be maddeningly obtuse. Others that will drive you bonkers will be on the encoding methods used, channel interference, and things of that nature. The vast majority of the questions, as you can read in this chapter, shouldn't pose much of a problem for you.

1. Which of the following is *not* true regarding SSIDs?

    A. The SSID is broadcast by APs in the network, unless otherwise configured.

    B. If the SSID changes, all clients must update to the new SSID to communicate.

    C. Turning off the SSID broadcast ensures only authorized clients, who know the SSID, can connect.

    D. The SSID serves to identify wireless networks.

    E. SSIDs are case sensitive.

2. Which of the following correctly describe the war chalk shown here? (Choose all that apply.)

    Guest_AnyBiz

    A. The nearby access point is secured via WPA2.

    B. The nearby access point uses MAC filtering.

    C. The non-broadcasted SSID is Guest_AnyBiz.

    D. The network access only provides guest-level resource access.

3. Which wireless technology provides NIST FIPS 140-2 compliant encryption?

    A. WPA

    B. WPA2

    C. WAP

    D. WEP

4. Which of the following uses a 48-bit Initialization Vector? (Choose all that apply.)

    A. WEP

    B. WPA

    C. WPA2

    D. WEP2

5. Which of the following are true statements? (Choose all that apply.)

    A. WEP uses shared key encryption with TKIP.

    B. WEP uses shared key encryption with RC4.

    C. WPA2 uses shared key encryption with RC4.

    D. WPA2 uses TKIP and AES encryption.

6. Which of the following best describes the "evil twin" wireless hacking attack?

   A. An attacker sets up a client machine using the same MAC as an authorized user.

   B. An attacker connects using the same username and password as an authorized user.

   C. An attacker sets up an access point inside the network range for clients to connect to.

   D. An attacker sets up an authentication server on the wireless network.

7. During an outbrief of a pen test, you share successes your team has had against the target's wireless network. The client asks for an explanation of the results, stating directional antennas for the access points were strategically placed to provide coverage for the building instead of omnidirectional antennas. Which of the following statements provides the correct response?

   A. Positioning and types of antennas are irrelevant.

   B. Directional antennas only provide for weak encryption of signal.

   C. Positioning of the antennas is irrelevant unless 802.11n is the standard chosen.

   D. Wireless signals can be detected from miles away; therefore, this step alone will not secure the network.

8. An attacker is attempting to crack a WEP code to gain access to the network. After enabling monitor mode on wlan0 and creating a monitoring interface (mon 0), she types this command:

   ```
   aireplay -ng -0 0 -a 0A:00:2B:40:70:80 -c mon0
   ```

   What is she trying to accomplish?

   A. Gain access to the WEP access code by examining the response to deauthentication packets, which contain the WEP code.

   B. Use deauthentication packets to generate lots of network traffic.

   C. Determine the BSSID of the access point.

   D. Discover the cloaked SSID of the network.

9. Which wireless standard works at 54 Mbps on a frequency range of 2.4GHz?

   A. 802.11a

   B. 802.11b

   C. 802.11g

   D. 802.11n

10. Which of the following describes sending unsolicited messages to a Bluetooth device?

   A. BlueSmacking

   B. Bluejacking

C. BlueSniffing

D. BlueSnarfing

11. Which of the tools listed here is a passive discovery tool?

    A. Aircrack

    B. Kismet

    C. NetStumbler

    D. Netsniff

12. You have discovered an access point using WEP for encryption purposes. Which of the following is the best choice for uncovering the network key?

    A. NetStumbler

    B. Aircrack

    C. John the Ripper

    D. Kismet

13. Which of the following statements are true regarding TKIP? (Choose all that apply.)

    A. Temporal Key Integrity Protocol forces a key change every 10,000 packets.

    B. Temporal Key Integrity Protocol ensures keys do not change during a session.

    C. Temporal Key Integrity Protocol is an integral part of WEP.

    D. Temporal Key Integrity Protocol is an integral part of WPA.

14. Regarding SSIDs, which of the following are true statements? (Choose all that apply.)

    A. SSIDs are always 32 characters in length.

    B. SSIDs can be up to 32 characters in length.

    C. Turning off broadcasting prevents discovery of the SSID.

    D. SSIDs are a part of every packet header from the AP.

    E. SSIDs provide important security for the network.

    F. Multiple SSIDs are needed to move between APs within an ESS.

15. You are discussing WEP cracking with a junior pen test team member. Which of the following are true statements regarding the Initialization Vectors? (Choose all that apply.)

    A. IVs are 32 bits in length.

    B. IVs are 24 bits in length.

    C. IVs get reused frequently.

    D. IVs are sent in clear text.

    E. IVs are encrypted during transmission.

    F. IVs are used once per encryption session.

16. A pen test member has configured a wireless access point with the same SSID as the target organization's SSID and has set it up inside a closet in the building. After some time, clients begin connecting to his access point. Which of the following statements are true regarding this attack? (Choose all that apply.)

    A. The rogue access point may be discovered by security personnel using NetStumbler.

    B. The rogue access point may be discovered by security personnel using NetSurveyor.

    C. The rogue access point may be discovered by security personnel using Kismet.

    D. The rogue access point may be discovered by security personnel using Aircrack.

    E. The rogue access point may be discovered by security personnel using ToneLoc.

17. A pen test member is running the airsnarf tool from a Linux laptop. What is she attempting to do?

    A. MAC flooding against an AP on the network

    B. Denial of service attacks against APs on the network

    C. Cracking network encryption codes from the WEP AP

    D. Stealing usernames and passwords from an AP

18. What frequency does Bluetooth operate in?

    A. 2.4–2.48 GHz

    B. 2.5 GHz

    C. 2.5–5 GHz

    D. 5 GHz

19. Which of the following is true regarding wireless network architecture?

    A. The service area provided by a single AP is known as an ESS.

    B. The service area provided by a single AP is known as a BSSID.

    C. The service area provided by multiple APs acting within the same network is known as an ESS.

    D. The service area provided by multiple APs acting within the same network is known as an ESSID.

20. A pen tester boosts the signal reception capabilities of a laptop. She then drives from building to building in the target organization's campus searching for wireless access points. What attack is she performing?

    A. War chalking

    B. War walking

C. War driving

D. War moving

21. You are examining the physical configuration of a target's wireless network. You notice on the site survey that omnidirectional antenna access points are located in the corners of the building. Which of the following statements are true regarding this configuration? (Choose all that apply.)

A. The site may be vulnerable to sniffing from locations outside the building.

B. The site is not vulnerable to sniffing from locations outside the building.

C. The use of dipole antennas may improve the security of the site.

D. The use of directional antennas may improve the security of the site.

22. Which of the following is a true statement regarding wireless security?

A. WPA2 is a better encryption choice than WEP.

B. WEP is a better encryption choice than WPA2.

C. Cloaking the SSID and implementing MAC filtering eliminates the need for encryption.

D. Increasing the length of the SSID to its maximum increases security for the system.

23. A pen test colleague is attempting to use a wireless connection inside the target's building. On his Linux laptop he types the following commands:

```
ifconfig wlan0 down
ifconfig wlan0 hw ether 0A:0B:0C:1A:1B:1C
ifconfig wlan0 up
```

What is the most likely reason for this action?

A. Port security is enabled on the access point.

B. The SSID is cloaked from the access point.

C. MAC filtering is enabled on the access point.

D. Weak signaling is frustrating connectivity to the access point.

24. An individual attempts to make a call using his cell phone; however, it seems unresponsive. After a few minutes effort, he turns it off and turns it on again. During his next phone call, the phone disconnects and becomes unresponsive again. Which Bluetooth attack is underway?

A. BlueSmacking

B. Bluejacking

C. BlueSniffing

D. BlueSnarfing

25. Which wireless standard achieves high data rate speeds by implementing MIMO antenna technology?

    A. 802.11b

    B. 802.11g

    C. 802.11n

    D. 802.16

1. C

2. A, B, C

3. B

4. B, C

5. B, D

6. C

7. D

8. B

9. C

10. B

11. B

12. B

13. A, D

14. B, D

15. B, C, D

16. A, B, C

17. D

18. A

19. C

20. C

21. A, D

22. A

23. C

24. A

25. C

1. Which of the following is *not* true regarding SSIDs?

   A. The SSID is broadcast by APs in the network, unless otherwise configured.

   B. If the SSID changes, all clients must update to the new SSID to communicate.

   C. Turning off the SSID broadcast ensures only authorized clients, who know the SSID, can connect.

   D. The SSID serves to identify wireless networks.

   E. SSIDs are case sensitive.

   ☑ C. The intent of a Service Set Identifier (SSID) is solely to identify one wireless network from another. It is not designed, nor should it be relied on, as a security feature. Although you can turn off broadcasting of the SSID, just remember that it is sent in the header of every single packet the AP sends anyway—not to mention by every single device on the network as well. So, while you did make it a little harder to find (using a packet sniffer instead of just looking at "available networks" in wireless properties), and will frustrate the most lazy among us pen testers (or your pesky neighbors looking for free Internet access), it doesn't really keep anyone out.

   ☒ A, B, D, and E are incorrect choices because these are true statements. SSIDs are case-sensitive, 32-character strings that are *designed* to be broadcast. They're identifiers for networks, with their entire purpose on the planet being to provide a means for clients to differentiate between wireless networks they are capable of connecting to. So, unless you tell the access point (AP) not to, it will gladly broadcast the SSID for easy network discovery by potential clients. The SSID will also need to be updated on all clients if you change it on the AP, which should make perfect sense: If you change it on an AP and don't tell your clients, they will consistently send packets out with bad headers, pointing to a network that no longer exists.

2. Which of the following correctly describe the war chalk shown here? (Choose all that apply.)

   Guest_AnyBiz

   A. The nearby access point is secured via WPA2.

   B. The nearby access point uses MAC filtering.

   C. The non-broadcasted SSID is Guest_AnyBiz.

   D. The network access only provides guest-level resource access.

☑ **A, B,** and **C.** War chalking is one of those items you'll probably never come across in the real world, but you'll definitely see on your exam. A war chalk is a symbol drawn somewhere in a public place indicating the presence of a wireless network. They indicate free networks, hidden SSIDs, pay-for-use hotspots, and which encryption technique is in use. A basic war chalk involves two parentheses back to back with other variables added to tell the whole story. A key through the middle indicates a restricted Wi-Fi spot, and the lock icon indicates MAC filtering. Any wording around the symbol indicates the SSID, encryption password, or even the administrative password for the access point.

☒ **D** is incorrect because there is no indication in this war chalk of resource access levels. You may see questions on your exam with all sorts of stuff written around the symbol. If the answer you're reading isn't readily apparent in the wording around the symbol (that is, clearly spelled out), then don't select it. More often than not, wording will indicate an SSID or password. Every so often it will indicate other things—such as resource access or the actual make/model of the access point, but those should be easy to spot.

3. Which wireless technology provides NIST FIPS 140-2 compliant encryption?

   A. WPA

   B. WPA2

   C. WAP

   D. WEP

☑ **B.** Wi-Fi Protected Access, version 2, provides encryption using AES, complying with National Institute of Standards and Technology (NIST) FIPS 140-2 requirements. It's an improvement over WPA by using AES instead of RC4, CRC, and "Michael algorithm" (an integrity check procedure). Another item you may get quizzed on concerning WPA2 is different use cases: WPA2 Personal and WPA2 Enterprise. The major difference between the two is authentication. Personal uses a pre-shared key, whereas Enterprise makes use of a centralized client authentication method (assigning login credentials to users and using a RADIUS server).

☒ **A** is incorrect because WPA does not use AES for encryption. Instead, it uses CRC, RC4, and Michael algorithm.

☒ **C** is incorrect because the acronym WAP stands for *wireless access point* and is, therefore, not a valid encryption method.

☒ **D** is incorrect because Wireless Equivalent Protocol (WEP) isn't technically designed for encryption at all. It was intended to provide the same amount of protection one might have plugging directly into a network—in short, nothing at all.

4. Which of the following uses a 48-bit Initialization Vector? (Choose all that apply.)

    A. WEP

    B. WPA

    C. WPA2

    D. WEP2

    ☑ **B and C.** One of the improvements from WEP to WPA involved extending the Initialization Vector (IV) to 48 bits from 24 bits. An Initialization Vector (IV) provides for confidentiality and integrity. Wireless encryption algorithms use it to calculate an integrity check value (ICV), appending it to the end of the data payload. The IV is then combined with a key to be input into an algorithm (RC4 for WEP, AES for WPA2). Therefore, because the length of an IV determines the total number of potential random values that can possibly be created for encryption purposes, doubling to 48 bits increased overall security. By itself, this didn't answer *all* security problems—it only meant it took a little longer to capture enough IV packets to crack the code—however, combined with other steps it did provide for better security.

    ☒ **A** is incorrect because WEP uses a 24-bit IV. In WEP, this meant there were approximately 16 million unique IV values. Although this may seem like a large number, it's really not—a determined hacker can capture enough IVs in a brute-force attack in a matter of hours to crack the key.

    ☒ **D** is incorrect because there is no such thing as WEP2.

5. Which of the following are true statements? (Choose all that apply.)

    A. WEP uses shared key encryption with TKIP.

    B. WEP uses shared key encryption with RC4.

    C. WPA2 uses shared key encryption with RC4.

    D. WPA2 uses TKIP and AES encryption.

    ☑ **B and D.** WEP uses a 24-bit Initialization Vector and RC4 to "encrypt" data transmissions, although saying that makes me shake in disgust as it's really a misnomer. WEP was designed as *basic* encryption merely to simulate the "security" of being on a wired network—hence, the "equivalent" part in Wired Equivalent Privacy. It was never intended as true encryption protection. WPA was an improvement on two fronts. First, the shared key portion of encryption was greatly enhanced by the use of Temporal Key Integrity Protocol (TKIP). In short, the key used to encrypt data was made temporary in nature, and is swapped out every 10,000 packets or so. Additionally, WPA2 uses NIST-approved encryption with AES as the algorithm of choice.

⊠ **A** is incorrect because WEP does not use TKIP. Along with the same key being used to encrypt and decrypt (shared key), it's not changed and remains throughout the communication process—which is part of the reason it's so easy to crack.

⊠ **C** is incorrect because WPA2 does not use RC4 as an encryption algorithm.

6. Which of the following best describes the "evil twin" wireless hacking attack?

    A. An attacker sets up a client machine using the same MAC as an authorized user.

    B. An attacker connects using the same username and password as an authorized user.

    C. An attacker sets up an access point inside the network range for clients to connect to.

    D. An attacker sets up an authentication server on the wireless network.

    ☑ **C.** The "evil twin" attack is one involving a rogue access point. The idea is pretty simple: Set up your own access point (AP) somewhere—even outside the building if you want, so long as it's within range for clients—and have users connect to your AP instead of the legitimate target's network. If a user looks at available wireless networks and connects to yours (because the signal strength is better, yours is free whereas the other is not, and so on), you effectively have control over all their network traffic. For example, you could configure completely new DNS servers and have your AP configure those addresses within the DHCP address offering, routing users to fake websites you've created to steal authentication information. Not to mention you could funnel everything through a packet capture, or shut off access to anyone you felt like virtually neutering for the day. In real-world use, these are set up mostly for sniffing purposes—waiting for some juicy bit of authentication traffic to steal.

    Keep in mind, though, the real drawback in this attack is it's fairly easy to spot, and you may run a substantial risk of discovery if the security staff is doing its job. Tools such as NetStumbler, NetSurveyor, Kismet, and a host of others can help ferret out these rogue APs.

    ⊠ **A, B,** and **D** are all incorrect because they do not reflect an evil twin attack. MAC spoofing is not defined as evil twin (it may work as a way into APs that are using MAC filtering, but it's not called evil twin). User accounts and authentication, although definitely important throughout the network, even on the wireless side, have nothing to do with evil twin.

7. During an outbrief of a pen test, you share successes your team has had against the target's wireless network. The client asks for an explanation of the results, stating directional antennas for the access points were strategically placed to provide coverage for the building instead of omnidirectional antennas. Which of the following statements provides the correct response?

A. Positioning and types of antennas are irrelevant.

B. Directional antennas only provide for weak encryption of signal.

C. Positioning of the antennas is irrelevant unless 802.11n is the standard chosen.

D. Wireless signals can be detected from miles away; therefore, this step alone will not secure the network.

☑ **D.** Also sometimes called a *yagi antenna* (all yagi antennas are directional, but not all directional antennas are yagi, so don't get confused), a directional antenna focuses the signal in a specific direction, which greatly increases signal strength *and* distance. The benefit in using them should be fairly obvious (controlling the signal's direction as opposed to using an omnidirectional antenna); however, it interjects its own problems. Because the signal is now greatly increased in strength and distance, you may find attackers actually have an easier time gaining network access. Sure they will need a way to boost their own sending strength, but they'll be able to pick up your signal for *miles*. Wireless network design needs to take into account not only the type of antenna used, but where it is placed and what is set up to contain or corral the signal. Additionally, don't forget that the narrower the beam, the less space is available for clients to connect. Show me a highly directional parabolic antenna, and I'll show you a lot of users who can't connect to the network.

☒ **A** is incorrect because antenna positioning is of great importance to your overall network security. The placement of antennas will dictate signal strength and direction for your clients. Not paying attention to signal spill—into parking lots or across to buildings you don't own—is a recipe for disaster because you're providing an easy means for an attacker to access your network.

☒ **B** is incorrect because antennas don't provide encryption by themselves. They are connected to devices that implement security, but the type of antenna used doesn't dictate your encryption method (WEP or WAP2).

☒ **C** is incorrect because the encoding method used—whether 802.11n or otherwise (for example, 802.11a)—has relatively nothing to do with keeping attackers out of your network.

8. An attacker is attempting to crack a WEP code to gain access to the network. After enabling monitor mode on wlan0 and creating a monitoring interface (mon 0), she types this command:

```
aireplay -ng -0 0 -a 0A:00:2B:40:70:80 -c mon0
```

What is she trying to accomplish?

A. Gain access to the WEP access code by examining the response to deauthentication packets, which contain the WEP code.

B. Use deauthentication packets to generate lots of network traffic.

C. Determine the BSSID of the access point.

D. Discover the cloaked SSID of the network.

☑ **B.** Within 802.11 standards, there are several different management-type frames in use: everything from a beacon and association request to something called (and I'm not making this up) a "probe request." One of these management frames is a deauthentication packet, which basically shuts off a client from the network. The client then has to reconnect—and will do so quickly. The idea behind this kind of activity is to generate lots of traffic to capture in order to discern the WEP access code (from clients trying to re-associate to all the new ARP packets that will come flying around, since many machines will dump their ARP cache after being shut off the network). Remember the Initialization Vectors within WEP are relatively short (24 bits) and are reused frequently, so any attempt to crack the code requires, in general, around 15,000 or so packets. You can certainly gather these over time, but generating traffic can accomplish it much faster. One final note on this must be brought up: This type of attack can just as easily result in a denial of service against hosts and the AP in question, so be careful.

☒ **A** is incorrect because the response to a deauth packet does not contain the WEP access code in the clear. If it did, we wouldn't need to bother with all this traffic generation in the first place—one simple packet would do to crack all security.

☒ **C** is incorrect because the BSSID (Basic Service Set Identifier) is the MAC address of the AP. It's usually easy enough to gain from any number of methods (using airodump, for instance) and isn't a reason for sending multiple deauth packets. There are networks where the BSSID is hidden (referred to as *cloaking*), but other tools (airmon and airodump) can help with that.

☒ **D** is incorrect because even if an SSID is "cloaked," that doesn't mean it's actually hidden: All it means is that it is not *broadcast*. The SSID is still contained in every single packet sent from the AP, and discovering it is easy enough.

9. Which wireless standard is designed to work at 54 Mbps on a frequency range of 2.4GHz?

   A. 802.11a

   B. 802.11b

   C. 802.11g

   D. 802.11n

   ☑ **C.** The 802.11 series of standards identifies all sorts of wireless goodies, such as the order imposed on how clients communicate, rules for authentication, data transfer, size of packets, how the messages are encoded into the signal, and so on. 802.11g combines the advantages of both the "a" and "b" standards without as many of the drawbacks. It's fast (at 54 Mbps), backward compatible with 802.11b clients, and doesn't suffer from the coverage area restrictions 802.11a has to contend with. Considering it operates in the 2.4GHz range, however, there may be some interference issues to deal with. Not only are a plethora of competing networks blasting their signals (sometimes on the same channel) near and around your network, but you've also got to take into account Bluetooth devices, cordless phones, and even baby monitors that may cause disruption (due to interference) of wireless signals. And microwave ovens happen to run at 2.45 GHz—right smack dab in the middle of the range.

☒ **A** is incorrect because 802.11a operates at 54 Mbps, but uses the 5 GHz frequency range. The big drawback to 802.11a was the frequency range itself—due to the higher frequency, network range was limited. Whereas 802.11b clients could be spread cross a relative large distance, 802.11a clients could communicate much faster, but had to be closer together. Combined with the increased cost of equipment, this contributed to 802.11a not being fully accepted as a de facto standard. That said, for security purposes it may not be a bad choice: Not as many people use it, or even look for it, and its smaller range may work to assist you in preventing spillage outside your building.

☒ **B** is incorrect because 802.11b operates at 11 Mbps on the 2.4GHz frequency range. It's slower than "a" or "g," but soon after its release it became the de facto standard for wireless. Price and network range contributed to this.

☒ **D** is incorrect because 802.11n works at 100 Mbps (+) in frequency ranges from 2.4GHz to 5 GHz. It achieves this rate using MIMO (multiple in, multiple out) antennas.

10. Which of the following describes sending unsolicited messages to a Bluetooth device?

    A. BlueSmacking

    B. Bluejacking

    C. BlueSniffing

    D. BlueSnarfing

    ☑ **B.** Bluejacking is a relatively simple attack—even if it usually just annoys the person it's aimed at. In Bluejacking, the attacker gets close enough that the Bluetooth device being targeted in is range (usually around 30 feet) and just sends messages to the target. In many cases this is just an annoyance—much like spam in your e-mail box. However, it can be used to trick a target (almost like a social engineering attack) into performing actions that do put security at risk.

☒ **A** is incorrect because BlueSmacking is a denial of service attack on a Bluetooth device. It has been described as a "ping of death for Bluetooth" and makes use of the same echo response time type of features ICMP provides within a wired network. The Linux Bluez packages (www.bluez.org) can carry this attack out.

☒ **C** is incorrect because BlueSniffing is, amazingly enough, and attack where the device's transmissions are sniffed for useful information.

☒ **D** is incorrect because BlueSnarfing refers to the actual theft of data directly from the device. This takes advantage of the "pairing" feature of most Bluetooth devices, willingly seeking out other devices to link up with.

11. Which of the tools listed here is a passive discovery tool?

    A. Aircrack

    B. Kismet

    C. NetStumbler

    D. Netsniff

    ☑ **B.** A question like this one can be a little tricky, depending on its wording; however, per the EC Council, Kismet works as a true passive network discovery tool, with no packet interjection whatsoever. The following is from www.kismetwireless.net: "Kismet is an 802.11 layer 2 wireless network detector, sniffer, and intrusion detection system. Kismet will work with any wireless card which supports raw monitoring (rfmon) mode, and (with appropriate hardware) can sniff 802.11b, 802.11a, 802.11g, and 802.11n traffic. Kismet also supports plugins which allow sniffing other media." You might also see two other interesting notables about Kismet on your exam: First, it works by "channel hopping," to discover as many networks as possible. Second, it has the ability to sniff packets and save them to a log file, readable by Wireshark or TCPDump.

    ☒ **A** is incorrect because aircrack is "an 802.11 WEP and WPA-PSK keys cracking program that can recover keys once enough data packets have been captured. It implements the standard FMS attack along with some optimizations like KoreK attacks, as well as the all-new PTW attack" (www.aircrack-ng.org).

    ☒ **C** is incorrect because NetStumbler is considered an active network discovery application. NetStumbler is among the most popular wireless tools you might see in anyone's arsenal.

    ☒ **D** is incorrect because Netsniff is included as a distractor and is not a valid tool.

12. You have discovered an access point using WEP for encryption purposes. Which of the following is the best choice for uncovering the network key?

    A. NetStumbler

    B. Aircrack

C. John the Ripper

D. Kismet

☑ **B.** Aircrack is a very fast tool for cracking WEP. You'll need to gather a lot of packets (assuming you've collected at least 50,000 packets or so, it'll work swimmingly fast) using another toolset, but once you have them together aircrack does a wonderful job cracking the key. One method aircrack uses that you may see referenced on the exam is *KoreK implementation*, which basically involves slicing bits out of packets and replacing them with guesses—the more this is done, the better the guessing and, eventually, the faster the key is recovered. Other tools for cracking WEP include Cain (which can also use KoreK), KisMac, WEPCrack, and Elcomsoft's Wireless Security Auditor tool.

☒ **A** is incorrect because NetStumbler is a network discovery tool. It can also be used to identify rogue access points and interference, and is also useful in measuring signal strength (for aiming antennas and such).

☒ **C** is incorrect because John the Ripper is a Linux-based password-cracking tool, not a wireless key discovery one.

☒ **D** is incorrect because Kismet is a passive network discovery (and other auditing) tool, but does not perform key cracking.

13. Which of the following statements are true regarding TKIP? (Choose all that apply.)

    A. Temporal Key Integrity Protocol forces a key change every 10,000 packets.

    B. Temporal Key Integrity Protocol ensures keys do not change during a session.

    C. Temporal Key Integrity Protocol is an integral part of WEP.

    D. Temporal Key Integrity Protocol is an integral part of WPA.

    ☑ **A and D.** TKIP is a significant step forward in wireless security. Instead of sticking with one key throughout a session with a client and reusing it, as occurred in WEP, *Temporal* Key Integrity Protocol changes the key out every 10,000 packets or so. Additionally, the keys are transferred back and forth during an EAP (Extensible Authentication Protocol) authentication session, which makes use of a four-step handshake process in proving the client belongs to the AP, and vice versa. TKIP came about in WPA.

    ☒ **B and C** are simply incorrect statements. TKIP does not maintain a single key, it changes it frequently, and it is part of WPA (and WPA2), not WEP.

14. Regarding SSIDs, which of the following are true statements? (Choose all that apply.)

    A. SSIDs are always 32 characters in length.

    B. SSIDs can be up to 32 characters in length.

C. Turning off broadcasting prevents discovery of the SSID.

D. SSIDs are a part of every packet header from the AP.

E. SSIDs provide important security for the network.

F. Multiple SSIDs are needed to move between APs within an ESS.

☑ **B and D.** Service Set Identifiers only have one real function in life, so far as you're concerned on this exam: identification. They are not a security feature in any way, shape, or form, and are designed solely to identify one access point's network from another's. SSIDs can be up to 32 characters in length, but don't have to be that long (in fact, you'll probably discover most of them are not).

☒ **A** is incorrect because SSIDs do not *have* to be 32 characters in length. They *can* be, but they do not have to fill 32 characters of space.

☒ **C** is incorrect because "cloaking" the SSID really doesn't do much at all. It's still a part of every packet header, so discovery is relatively easy.

☒ **E** is incorrect because SSIDs are not considered a security feature for wireless networks.

☒ **F** is incorrect because an Extended Service Set (ESS, an enterprise-wide wireless network consisting of multiple APs) only requires a single SSID that all APs work with.

15. You are discussing WEP cracking with a junior pen test team member. Which of the following are true statements regarding the Initialization Vectors? (Choose all that apply.)

A. IVs are 32 bits in length.

B. IVs are 24 bits in length.

C. IVs get reused frequently.

D. IVs are sent in clear text.

E. IVs are encrypted during transmission.

F. IVs are used once per encryption session.

☑ **B, C, and D.** Weak Initialization Vectors and poor encryption are part of the reason WEP implementation is not encouraged as a true security measure on wireless networks. And, let's be fair here, it was never truly designed to be: hence it being named Wired Equivalent Privacy instead of Wireless Encryption Protocol (as some have erroneously tried to name it). IVs are 24 bits in length, are sent in clear text and are reused a lot. Capture enough packets, and you can easily crack the code.

☒ **A, E, and F** are incorrect statements. IVs are not 32 bits in length, are not encrypted themselves, and are definitely not used once per session (that would be even worse than being reused).

16. A pen test member has configured a wireless access point with the same SSID as the target organization's SSID and has set it up inside a closet in the building. After some time, clients begin connecting to his access point. Which of the following statements are true regarding this attack? (Choose all that apply.)

A. The rogue access point may be discovered by security personnel using NetStumbler.

B. The rogue access point may be discovered by security personnel using NetSurveyor.

C. The rogue access point may be discovered by security personnel using Kismet.

D. The rogue access point may be discovered by security personnel using aircrack.

E. The rogue access point may be discovered by security personnel using ToneLoc.

☑ **A, B,** and **C.** Rogue access points (sometimes called evil twin attacks) can provide a very easy way to gain useful information from clueless users on a target network. However, be forewarned, security personnel can use multiple tools and techniques to discover rogue APs. NetStumbler is one of the more popular, and useful, tools available. It's a great network discovery tool that can also be used to identify rogue access points, network interference, and signal strength. Kismet, another very popular tool, provides many of the same features and is noted as a "passive" network discovery tool. NetSurveyor is a free, easy-to-use Windows-based tool that provides many of the same features as NetStumbler and Kismet, and works with virtually every wireless NIC in modern existence. A "professional" version of NetSurveyor is now available (you get 10 uses of it before you're required to buy a license). Lastly, identification of a rogue access point requires the security staff to have knowledge of every access point owned—and its MAC. If it's known there are 10 APs in the network and suddenly an 11th appears, that alone won't help find and disable the bad one. It takes some level of organization to find these things, and that plays into your hands as an ethical hacker. The longer your evil twin is left sitting there, the better chance it will be found, so keep it short and sweet.

☒ **D** is incorrect because aircrack is used to crack network encryption codes, not to identify rogue access points.

☒ **E** is incorrect because ToneLoc is a tool used for war dialing (identifying open modems within a block of phone numbers). As an aside, this was also the moniker for a 90s one-hit-wonder "rap" artist, although I can promise that won't be on your exam.

17. A pen test member is running the airsnarf tool from a Linux laptop. What is she attempting to do?

A. MAC flooding against an AP on the network

B. Denial of service attacks against APs on the network

C. Cracking network encryption codes from the WEP AP

D. Stealing usernames and passwords from an AP

☑ **D.** Identifying tools and what they do is a big part of the exam—which is easy enough because it's pure memorization, and this is a prime example. Per the website (http://airsnarf.shmoo.com/), "Airsnarf is a simple rogue wireless access point setup utility designed to demonstrate how a rogue AP can steal usernames and passwords from public wireless hotspots. Airsnarf was developed and released to demonstrate an inherent vulnerability of public 802.11b hotspots—snarfing usernames and passwords by confusing users with DNS and HTTP redirects from a competing AP." It basically turns your laptop into a competing AP in the local area and confuses client requests to send your way.

☒ **A** is incorrect because airsnarf does not provide MAC flooding. You may want to MAC flood a network switch for easier sniffing, but that doesn't work the same way for an access point on a wireless network.

☒ **B** is incorrect because airsnarf is not a DoS tool. You can make an argument the clients themselves are denied service while they're erroneously communicating with the airsnarf laptop, but it's not the intent of the application to DoS the network. Quite the opposite: The longer things stay up and running, the more usernames and passwords that can be gathered.

☒ **C** is incorrect because airsnarf is not an encryption-cracking tool. It reads a lot like "air*crack*," so don't get confused (these will be used as distractors against one another on your exam).

18. What frequency does Bluetooth operate in?

   A. 2.4–2.48 Ghz

   B. 2.5 GHz

   C. 2.5–5 GHz

   D. 5 GHz

☑ **A.** Yes, you may actually get a question this "down in the weeds" regarding Bluetooth. As an additional study note, you will commonly see a reference to Bluetooth working at 2.45 GHz (it's in the range). Bluetooth is designed to work at around 10 meters of range and can attach up to eight devices simultaneously. It makes use of something call *spread-spectrum frequency hopping,* which significantly reduces the chance that more than one device will use the same frequency in communicating.

☒ **B, C,** and **D** are incorrect frequency ranges for Bluetooth.

19. Which of the following is true regarding wireless network architecture?

   A. The service area provided by a single AP is known as an ESS.

   B. The service area provided by a single AP is known as a BSSID.

C. The service area provided by multiple APs acting within the same network is known as an ESS.

D. The service area provided by multiple APs acting within the same network is known as an ESSID.

☑ **C.** An Extended Service Set (ESS) is created by having multiple access points work within the same network SSID and encryption standard to provide extended, uninterrupted coverage for clients. So long as you have everything configured correctly (SSID, channels, and so on), as a client moves from one AP in your network to another they'll disassociate from one AP and (re)associate with another seamlessly. This movement across multiple APs within a single ESS is known as *roaming*.

☒ **A** is incorrect because a single AP's coverage area is referred to as a Basic Service Set (BSS).

☒ **B** is incorrect because the Basic Service Set Identification (BSSID) is the MAC address of the access point within the BSS.

☒ **D** is incorrect because the Extended Service Set Identification (ESSID) is the SSID for an ESS (the up-to-32-bit code that identifies the network you're on as you roam from AP to AP in the organization's wireless network).

20. A pen tester boosts the signal reception capabilities of a laptop. She then drives from building to building in the target organization's campus searching for wireless access points. What attack is she performing?

A. War chalking

B. War walking

C. War driving

D. War moving

☑ **C.** This is one of those easy questions on the exam, because the term *war driving* is fairly well known. In war driving, an attacker boosts the reception capability of a laptop as best as possible and installs NetStumbler, Kismet, OmniPeek, NetSurveyor, or any of hundreds of network discovery tools. She then simply drives around, identifying which networks are available and where their signal is the strongest.

☒ **A** is incorrect because *war chalking* is the act of drawing a symbol to indicate wireless hotspot locations. A *war chalk* is a symbol drawn somewhere in a public place indicating the presence of a wireless network. These can indicate free networks, hidden SSIDs, pay-for-use hotspots, and which encryption technique is in use.

☒ **B** is incorrect because *war walking*, sometimes referred to as *war jogging*, is done on foot. In practice, it's no different than war driving—only that the attacker is walking or jogging as opposed to driving a vehicle.

   ☒ **D** is incorrect because *war moving,* to my knowledge, is not a wireless network discovery term, and is included purely as a distractor.

21. You are examining the physical configuration of a target's wireless network. You notice on the site survey that omnidirectional antenna access points are located in the corners of the building. Which of the following statements are true regarding this configuration? (Choose all that apply.)

   A. The site may be vulnerable to sniffing from locations outside the building.

   B. The site is not vulnerable to sniffing from locations outside the building.

   C. The use of dipole antennas may improve the security of the site.

   D. The use of directional antennas may improve the security of the site.

   ☑ **A and D.** There are a couple of problems with an omnidirectional (dipole) antenna. The first is coverage area itself. Because it's *omni*directional, it's sending (and looking for) signals in all directions. Therefore, if the AP is placed in the corner of the building, roughly three-quarters of the coverage space is wasted. Unless, of course, you're an attacker sitting in a car outside, drinking coffee and happily surfing away on the free wireless the company has so carelessly provided to the parking lot. The second problem is the power consumption needed for this coverage. Because it's designed to send in all directions, the coverage area is reduced, and users on the edges will definitely notice it. Think about it—if your AP is in the corner and three-quarters of its coverage is outside the building, that's three-quarters of the power of the device wasted. If you were to concentrate that power—by focusing the signal with a directional antenna—just think of the range and speed of access you could provide your clients.

   Allow me to make one last thought here and I promise I'll stop talking about antennas: It is a far greater use of time and resources for an organization to securely implement networking in the first place than it is to worry about antenna types and placement. Your security staff isn't saving money by following some ridiculous bean-counting analysis that results in buying a $100 antenna versus paying for a $200-an-hour security analyst—especially if you wind up getting hacked by some guy in a van using a +40db dish to sniff traffic you failed to protect.

   ☒ **B and C** are incorrect statements regarding this architecture. Because the antenna is omnidirectional, the signals will spill out around the building if the AP is put in the corner. Therefore, the site is susceptible to unauthorized clients accessing the signal from outside. Additionally, a dipole antenna is, by its very design and nature, omnidirectional.

22. Which of the following is a true statement regarding wireless security?

   A. WPA2 is a better encryption choice than WEP.

   B. WEP is a better encryption choice than WPA2.

C. Cloaking the SSID and implementing MAC filtering eliminates the need for encryption.

D. Increasing the length of the SSID to its maximum increases security for the system.

☑ **A.** WPA2 is, by far, a better security choice for your system. It makes use of TKIP, to change out the keys every 10,000 packets instead of using one for the entire session (as in WEP). Additionally, WPA2 uses AES for encryption and a 128-bit encryption key, as opposed to RC4 and 24-bit IVs in WEP.

☒ **B** is incorrect because WEP only provides the equivalent privacy of being on a wired network. Its "encryption" is ridiculously easy to crack and is not considered a valid security measure. It's perfectly reasonable to use it if your goal is just to frustrate causal surfers from connecting to your network (such as your neighbors), but it's not a valid encryption method.

☒ **C** is incorrect because these two options do nothing to protect the actual data being transmitted. SSID cloaking is somewhat pointless, given that SSIDs are included in every header of every packet (not to mention that SSIDs aren't designed for security). MAC filtering will frustrate casual observers; however, spoofing a MAC address on the network is relatively easy and eliminates this as a foolproof security method.

☒ **D** is incorrect because the length of an SSID has nothing whatsoever to do with security and encryption. Increasing the length of the SSID does not increase network security.

23. A pen test colleague is attempting to use a wireless connection inside the target's building. On his Linux laptop he types the following commands:

```
ifconfig wlan0 down
ifconfig wlan0 hw ether 0A:0B:0C:1A:1B:1C
ifconfig wlan0 up
```

What is the most likely reason for this action?

A. Port security is enabled on the access point.

B. The SSID is cloaked from the access point.

C. MAC filtering is enabled on the access point.

D. Weak signaling is frustrating connectivity to the access point.

☑ **C.** The sequence of the preceding commands has the attacker bringing the wireless interface down, changing its hardware address, then bringing it back up. The most likely reason for this is MAC filtering is enabled on the AP, which is restricting access to only those machines the administrator wants connecting to the wireless network. The easy way around this is to watch traffic and copy one of the MAC addresses. A quick spoof on your own hardware and—*voilà*—you're connected.

☒ **A** is incorrect because port security isn't an option on wireless access points. Were this attacker connecting to a switch, this might be valid, but not on a wireless connection.

☒ **B** is incorrect because SSID cloaking has nothing to do with this scenario. The commands are adjusting a MAC address.

☒ **D** is incorrect because weak signal strength has nothing to do with this scenario. The commands are adjusting a MAC address.

24. An individual attempts to make a call using his cell phone; however, it seems unresponsive. After a few minutes effort, he turns it off and turns it on again. During his next phone call, the phone disconnects and becomes unresponsive again. Which Bluetooth attack is underway?

   A. BlueSmacking

   B. Bluejacking

   C. BlueSniffing

   D. BlueSnarfing

☑ **A.** From the description, it appears the phone is either defective or—since it's spelled out so nicely in the question for you—there is a denial of service attack against the phone. As stated earlier, BlueSmacking is a denial of service attack on a Bluetooth device. An attacker somewhere nearby (within 10 meters or, for the real bad guys, farther away using a big enough transmitter, amplifier, and antenna) is using something like the Linux Bluez packages (www.bluez.org) to carry out a DoS against the phone.

☒ **B** is incorrect because Bluejacking involves sending unsolicited messages—much like SPAM—to a Bluetooth device.

☒ **C** is incorrect because BlueSniffing is a basic sniffing attempt, where the device's transmissions are sniffed for useful information.

☒ **D** is incorrect because BlueSnarfing refers to the actual theft of data directly from the device. This takes advantage of the "pairing" feature of most Bluetooth devices, willingly seeking out other devices to link up with.

25. Which wireless standard achieves high data rate speeds by implementing MIMO antenna technology?

   A. 802.11b

   B. 802.11g

   C. 802.11n

   D. 802.16

☑ **C.** 802.11n boasts speeds of over 100 Mbps, operating in a frequency range from 2.4 to 5 GHz. One method it uses to achieve this is known as MIMO (multiple in, multiple out). MIMO, not unlike other technologies you're supposed to learn about, has tons of mind-numbing technical minutia to explore concerning how it works, but basically the thought behind it is to use multiple antennas, in somewhat of an array, to send and receive simultaneously. Also known as *smart antennas,* these greatly speed up wireless communications. Once the technology dropped to a more affordable range, it became more and more prevalent. Another note you may see referenced on this standard has to do with multiplexing used within the transmission: 802.11n uses something called Spatial Division Multiplexing (SDM).

☒ **A** and **B** are incorrect because neither standard uses MIMO antennas.

☒ **D** is incorrect because 802.16 is a set of IEEE standards for wireless within a metropolitan area network. Referred to as *WiMax* (Worldwide Interoperability for Microwave Access), 802.16 was written for the global development of broadband wireless metropolitan area networks. It provides speeds up to 40 Mbps and is moving toward Gb speed.

Trojans and Other Attacks

This chapter includes questions from the following topics:

- Define Trojans and their purpose
- Identify common Trojan ports
- Identify Trojan deployment methods
- Identify Trojan countermeasures
- Define viruses and worms
- Identify virus countermeasures
- Describe DoS attacks
- Define common DoS attack types
- Describe session hijacking and sequence prediction

I don't have anything against tattoos, per se, but I do have some very strong negative opinions of pain. I'm not saying I cry like a three-year-old when I get a boo-boo or anything, but I am sitting here in my living room tattoo-less. Were I to inebriate myself sufficiently enough to forget my aversion to pain, there are only two inks I'd be willing to scar my arm with: the script "A" for the University of Alabama and the bat signal from Batman. As a huge fan of the Crimson Tide, the "A" is easy enough to understand—not to mention it just looks awesome. But, you may be wondering, why the bat signal? The answer, dear reader, is very simple: I love Batman.

Batman is, without a doubt, the single coolest hero of all time. You comic-book-reading Sheldon Cooper zealots can drop the Superman claim because it's really not a fair comparison to put a freaked-out, super-strong, invulnerable alien against a man who bleeds like the rest of us. Batman is a normal guy with no super powers whatsoever; he just happens to have an unending supply of wealth at his disposal, a mansion built on top of a giant super-hero lair built by Mother Nature, and a highly intelligent mind bordering just on the edge of insanity. Batman appeals to me as a fan because he's committed to ensuring justice and right with the world, while simultaneously being dark, brooding, and angry, and not that far removed from being a bad guy himself. He's just as likely to beat a villain to an absolute pulp and throw him off the side of a fire escape as he is to drop a guy off at the police station for the authorities to handle things appropriately.

It's the dark side of Batman that is apropos to this chapter. Much like the end goal of bright shining justice can come in the form of a Dark Knight wielding acts of violence and vigilantism to accomplish the greater good, your pen test efforts can be assisted by visiting the dark side yourself, wielding tools and actions that may seem a bit unsavory to you. Although you may not think of malware and viruses as pen test methods, they're definitely tools in the arsenal, and something you really need to know about—or your job and especially this exam.

 STUDY TIPS Most of the questions from the malware sections—especially those designed to trip you up—will be of the pure memorization stripe. Stick with key words for each definition (it'll help you in separating good answers from bad ones), especially for the virus types. Don't miss an easy point on the exam because your forgot the difference between polymorphic and multipartite. Tool identification should also be relatively straightforward (assuming you commit all those port numbers to memory, like I told you to).

Finally, as always, get rid of the answers you know to be wrong in the first place. It's actually easier sometime to identify the ones you downright know aren't relevant to the question. Then, from the remainder, you can scratch your gray matter for the key word that will shed light on the answer.

1. Examine the Wireshark TCP flow capture here:

```
Host A      --- SYN --- >              Host B Seq = 0 Ack = 13425675
Host A      < --- SYN, ACK ---         Host B Seq = 0 Ack = 1
Host A      --- ACK --- >              Host B Seq = 1 Ack = 1
Host A      --- PSH, ACK Len:700 --- > Host B Seq = 1 Ack = 1
Host A      < --- ACK ---              Host B Seq = 1 Ack = 701
Host A      < --- ACK Len:1341 ---     Host B Seq = 1 Ack = 701
Host A      --- ACK --- >              Host B Seq = 701 Ack = 1342
Host A      < --- ACK Len : 1322 ---   Host B Seq = 1342 Ack = 701
Host A      --- ACK --- >              Host B Seq = 701 Ack = 2664
Host A      < --- ACK Len : 1322 ---   Host B Seq = 2664 Ack = 701
```

   Which of the following represents the next appropriate acknowledgement from Host A?

   A. Sequence Number 701, Acknowledgement Number 3986.

   B. Sequence Number 701, Acknowledgement Number 2664.

   C. Sequence Number 2664, Acknowledgement Number 2023.

   D. Sequence Number 2664, Acknowledgement Number 701.

2. You have established a netcat connection to a target machine. Which flag can be used to launch a program?

   A. -p

   B. -a

   C. -l

   D. -e

3. Which virus type will rewrite itself after each new infection?

   A. Multipartite

   B. Metamorphic

   C. Cavity

   D. Macro

4. A pen test colleague is carrying out attacks. In one attack, she attempts to guess the ISN for a TCP session. Which attack is she most likely carrying out?

   A. XSS

   B. Session splicing

   C. Session hijacking

   D. Multipartite attack

5. Malware takes many forms and is activated on a machine in a variety of ways. Which of the following malware types does not require user intervention to spread?

    A. Trojan

    B. Virus

    C. Worm

    D. Polymorphic

6. An attacker is attempting a DoS against a machine. She first spoofs the target's IP address and then begins sending large amounts of ICMP packets containing the MAC address FF:FF:FF:FF:FF:FF. What attack is underway?

    A. ICMP flood

    B. Ping of Death

    C. SYN flood

    D. Smurf

    E. Fraggle

7. Tripwire is one of the most popular tools to protect against Trojans. Which of the following statements best describes Tripwire?

    A. Tripwire is a signature-based antivirus tool.

    B. Tripwire is a vulnerability assessment tool used for port scanning.

    C. Tripwire is a file integrity program.

    D. Tripwire is a session-splicing tool.

8. Which of the following tools are good choices for session hijack attempts? (Choose all that apply.)

    A. Ettercap

    B. Netcat

    C. Hunt

    D. Nessus

9. In regard to Trojans, which of the following best describes a "wrapper"?

    A. The legitimate file the Trojan is attached to.

    B. A program used to bind the Trojan to a legitimate file.

    C. Encryption methods used for a Trojan.

    D. Polymorphic code used to avoid detection by antivirus programs.

10. What is the default port used by RAT?

   A. 31337

   B. 1095

   C. 1524

   D. 7777

   E. 666

11. Which of the following is a legitimate communication path for the transfer of data?

   A. Overt

   B. Covert

   C. Authentic

   D. Imitation

   E. Actual

12. Which Trojan is well known for attempting to steal banking information from infected machines?

   A. Apocalypse

   B. HTTP RAT

   C. Zeus

   D. BioDox

13. A pen test team member types the following command:

   ```
   nc222.15.66.78 -p 8765
   ```

   Which of the following is true regarding this attempt?

   A. The attacker is attempting to connect to an established listening port on a remote computer.

   B. The attacker is establishing a listening port on his machine for later use.

   C. The attacker is attempting a DoS against a remote computer.

   D. The attacker is attempting to kill a service on a remote machine.

14. Examine the partial command line output listed here:

```
Active Connections
Proto   Local Address           Foreign Address         State
  TCP   0.0.0.0:912             COMPUTER11:0            LISTENING
  TCP   0.0.0.0:3460            COMPUTER11:0            LISTENING
  TCP   0.0.0.0:3465            COMPUTER11:0            LISTENING
  TCP   0.0.0.0:8288            COMPUTER11:0            LISTENING
  TCP   0.0.0.0:16386           COMPUTER11:0            LISTENING
  TCP   192.168.1.100:139       COMPUTER11:0            LISTENING
  TCP   192.168.1.100:58191     173.194.44.81:https     ESTABLISHED
  TCP   192.168.1.100:58192     173.194.44.81:https     TIME_WAIT
  TCP   192.168.1.100:58193     173.194.44.81:https     TIME_WAIT
  TCP   192.168.1.100:58194     173.194.44.81:https     ESTABLISHED
  TCP   192.168.1.100:58200     bk-in-f138:http         TIME_WAIT
```

Which of the following is a true statement regarding the output?

A. This is output from a netstat –an command.

B. This is output from a netstat –b command.

C. This is output from a netstat –e command.

D. This is output from a netstat –r command.

15. You are discussing malware with a new pen test member who asks about restarting executables. Which registry keys within Windows automatically run executables and instructions? (Choose all that apply.)

A. HKEY_LOCAL_MACHINE\Software\Microsoft\Windows\CurrentVersion\RunServicesOnce

B. HKEY_LOCAL_MACHINE\Software\Microsoft\Windows\CurrentVersion\RunServices

C. HKEY_LOCAL_MACHINE\Software\Microsoft\Windows\CurrentVersion\RunOnce

D. HKEY_LOCAL_MACHINE\Software\Microsoft\Windows\CurrentVersion\Run

16. Which of the following best describes a sheepdip computer?

A. A system used to confuse malware developers, attracting them away from real network systems.

B. A system that has multiple malware infections.

C. A system used to screen physical media for malware.

D. A system infected with botnet malware.

17. Which denial of service attack involves sending SYN packets to a target machine, but never responding to any of the SYN/ACK replies?

A. SYN flood

B. SYN attack

C. Smurf

D. LOIC

18. A user sees the following pop-up window appear:

Which of the following best describes the pop-up?

A. A hardware corrupted USB drive is inserted into the machine.

B. The pop-up is purely informational.

C. The pop-up indicates a Conficker worm propagation attempt.

D. None of the above.

19. IPSec is an effective preventative measure against session hijacking. Which IPSec mode encrypts only the data payload?

A. Transport

B. Tunnel

C. Protected

D. Spoofed

20. Which of the following are MITM session hijacking tools? (Choose all that apply.)

A. Netcat

B. LOIC

C. Hunt

D. Paros

E. T-sight

F. Nmap

21. Which of the following best describes the comparison between spoofing and session hijacking?

    A. Spoofing and session hijacking are the same thing.

    B. Spoofing interrupts a client's communication whereas hijacking does not.

    C. Hijacking interrupts a client's communication whereas spoofing does not.

    D. Hijacking emulates a foreign IP address whereas spoofing refers to MAC addresses.

22. Which of the following is an effective deterrent against session hijacking?

    A. Install and use an HIDS on the system.

    B. Install and use Tripwire on the system.

    C. Enforce good password policy.

    D. Use unpredictable sequence numbers.

23. A pen test team member types the following command:

```
ettercap -T -q -M ARP /200.70.55.12
```

    Which of the following are true regarding this command? (Choose all that apply.)

    A. Ettercap is being configured for a GUI interface.

    B. Ettercap is being configured as a sniffer.

    C. Ettercap is being configured for text mode.

    D. Ettercap is being configured for manual mode.

    E. Ettercap is being configured for a man-in-the-middle attack.

24. Within a TCP packet dump, a packet is noted with the SYN flag set and a sequence number set at A13F. What should the acknowledgement number in the return SYN/ACK packet be?

    A. A131

    B. A130

    C. A140

    D. A14F

25. When is session hijacking performed?

    A. Before the three-step handshake

    B. During the three-step handshake

    C. After the three-step handshake

    D. After a FIN packet

1. B

2. D

3. B

4. C

5. C

6. D

7. C

8. A, C

9. B

10. B

11. A

12. C

13. A

14. A

15. A, B, C, D

16. C

17. A

18. C

19. A

20. C, D, E

21. C

22. D

23. C, E

24. C

25. C

ANSWERS

1. Examine the Wireshark TCP Flow capture here:

```
Host A       --- SYN --- >                  Host B Seq = 0 Ack = 13425675
Host A       < --- SYN, ACK ---             Host B Seq = 0 Ack = 1
Host A       --- ACK --- >                  Host B Seq = 1 Ack = 1
Host A       --- PSH, ACK Len:700 --- >     Host B Seq = 1 Ack = 1
Host A       < --- ACK ---                  Host B Seq = 1 Ack = 701
Host A       < --- ACK Len:1341 ---         Host B Seq = 1 Ack = 701
Host A       --- ACK --- >                  Host B Seq = 701 Ack = 1342
Host A       < --- ACK Len : 1322 ---       Host B Seq = 1342 Ack = 701
Host A       --- ACK --- >                  Host B Seq = 701 Ack = 2664
Host A       < --- ACK Len : 1322 ---       Host B Seq = 2664 Ack = 701
```

Which of the following represents the next appropriate acknowledgement from Host A?

A. Sequence Number 701, Acknowledgement Number 2664.

B. Sequence Number 701, Acknowledgement Number 3986.

C. Sequence Number 2664, Acknowledgement Number 2023.

D. Sequence Number 2664, Acknowledgement Number 701.

☑ **B.** Sequence and acknowledgement number prediction can get really, really confusing when you take all the options into account—acknowledgement numbers, window sizes, and so on—but thankfully it'll be pretty easy on your exam. An acknowledgement packet will recognize the agreed-upon sequence number (in this case, 701) and then acknowledge receipt of the previous packet by incrementing the acknowledgement number with the packet size of the receipt. In this example, the agreed-upon sequence number is 701 and the receipt of the previous packet is acknowledged by adding the previous sequence number (2664) to the packet length (1322): 2664 + 1322 = 3986.

☒ **A, C,** and **D** are incorrect choices because the sequence and acknowledgement numbers do not add up. You can follow the preceding TCP stream and watch the acknowledgement number increment by the packet length. You can also see this at home: Open a Wireshark session and capture a TCP session; then choose Statistics, Flow Graph, and TCP Flow.

2. You have established a netcat connection to a target machine. Which flag can be used to launch a program?

A. -p

B. -a

C. -l

D. -e

☑ **D.** Netcat is often referred to as the "Swiss army knife" of hacking efforts. You can use it to set up a listening port on target machines that you can then revisit to wreak all sorts of havoc. The flag associated with launching a program is –e. For example, issuing the command

```
nc -L -p 12657 -t -e cmd.exe
```

will open a Windows command shell on the target machine; the –t flag sets up a telnet connection over the port you defined with the –p flag (12657).

☒ **A** is incorrect because the –p flag indicates the protocol port you wish to use for your session.

☒ **B** is incorrect because –a is not a recognized netcat flag.

☒ **C** is incorrect because the –l flag indicates netcat should open the port for listening. As an aside, the –L flag does the same thing; however, it restarts listening after the inbound session completes.

3. Which virus type will rewrite itself after each new infection?

   A. Multipartite

   B. Metamorphic

   C. Cavity

   D. Macro

   ☑ **B.** EC Council defines several different virus types, depending on what the virus does, how it acts, and how it is written. In the case of a metamorphic virus, it will rewrite itself each time it infects a new file. Metamorphic viruses write versions of themselves in machine code, so they may even be able to infect machines of different operating systems.

   ☒ **A** is incorrect because multipartite viruses do not rewrite themselves. They attempt to infect and spread in multiple ways and try to infect files and the boot sector at the same time. They can spread very quickly and are notoriously hard to clean.

   ☒ **C** is incorrect because a cavity virus writes itself into unused space within a file. The idea is to maintain the file's size.

   ☒ **D** is incorrect because macro viruses do not rewrite themselves. Macro viruses usually attack Microsoft Office files, executing as a macro within the file itself (anyone who's ever been stuck in Excel purgatory should be very familiar with macros within a spreadsheet). "Melissa" (a famous virus attacking Microsoft Word 1997) is a classic example of a macro virus.

4. A pen test colleague is carrying out attacks. In one attack, she attempts to guess the ISN for a TCP session. Which attack is she most likely carrying out?

   A. XSS

   B. Session splicing

   C. Session hijacking

   D. Multipartite attack

☑ **C.** The idea behind session hijacking is fairly simple: The attacker waits for a session to begin and, after all the pesky authentication gets done, jumps in to steal the session for herself. In practice, it's a little harder and more complicated than that, but the key to the whole attack is in determining the Initial Sequence Number (ISN) used for the session. The ISN is sent by the initiator of the session in the first step (SYN). This is acknowledged in the second handshake (SYN/ACK) by incrementing that ISN by 1, and then another ISN is generated by the recipient. This second number is acknowledged by the initiator in the third step (ACK) and from there on out communication can occur. Per EC Council, the following steps describe the session hijack:

1. Sniff the traffic between the client and the server.

2. Monitor the traffic and predict the sequence numbering.

3. Desynchronize the session with the client.

4. Predict the session token and take over the session.

5. Inject packets to the target server.

For what it's worth, pulling this attack off correctly requires you to do some fairly significant traffic sniffing. And if you're already positioned to sniff the traffic in the first place, this whole scenario may be a moot point. You need to know it for the exam, but real-world application may be small and rare.

☒ **A** is incorrect because cross-site scripting is a web application attack.

☒ **B** is incorrect because session splicing is an IDS evasion method. The attacker delivers a payload that the IDS would have otherwise seen by "slicing" it over multiple packets. The payload can be spread out over a long period of time.

☒ **D** is incorrect because *multipartite* refers to a virus type, not an attack that requires ISN determination.

5. Malware takes many forms and is activated on a machine in a variety of ways. Which of the following malware types does not require user intervention to spread?

A. Trojan

B. Virus

C. Worm

D. Polymorphic

☑ **C.** A *worm* is a self-replicating malware computer program that uses a computer network to send copies of itself to other systems without human intervention. Usually it doesn't necessarily alter files, but it resides in active memory and duplicates itself, eating up resources and wreaking havoc along the way. The most common use for a worm in the hacking world is the creation of botnets. A classic worm example you will no doubt see on your exam is Conficker. It targeted Windows machines starting back in 2008, infecting millions of computers worldwide, making it the largest computer worm infection in history.

☒ **A** is incorrect because Trojans need human interaction to spread. A *Trojan* is software that appears to perform a desirable function for the user prior to run or install, but instead performs a function, usually without the user's knowledge, that steals information or otherwise harms the system (or data). Much like the horse used to fool Troy, Trojan malware is usually hidden inside something that appears totally harmless or even beneficial.

☒ **B** is incorrect because viruses do not spread without user intervention. By definition, viruses are attached to other files and are activated when those files are executed. Viruses are spread when users copy infected files from one machine to another.

☒ **D** is incorrect because viruses need human interaction to spread. A polymorphic piece of malware (a type of virus) still requires interaction, it just morphs its code along the way.

6. An attacker is attempting a DoS against a machine. She first spoofs the target's IP address and then begins sending large amounts of ICMP packets containing the MAC address FF:FF:FF:FF:FF:FF. What attack is underway?

   A. ICMP flood

   B. Ping of Death

   C. SYN flood

   D. Smurf

   E. Fraggle

   ☑ **D.** A Smurf attack is a generic denial of service (DoS) attack against a target machine. The idea is simple: have so many ICMP requests going to the target that all its resources are taken up. To accomplish this, the attacker spoofs the target's IP address and then sends thousands of ping requests from that spoofed IP to the subnet's broadcast address. This, in effect, pings every machine on the subnet. Assuming they're configured to do so, each and every machine will respond to the request, effectively crushing the target's network resources.

   ☒ **A** is incorrect because an ICMP flood does not act this way. In this attack, the hacker sends ICMP Echo packets to the target with a spoofed (fake) source address. The target continues to respond to an address that doesn't exist and eventually reaches a limit of packets per second sent.

   ☒ **B** is incorrect because a Ping of Death does not act this way. Not a valid attack with modern systems due to preventative measures in the OS, in the Ping of Death, an attacker fragments an ICMP message to send to a target.

When the fragments are reassembled, the resulting ICMP packet is larger than the maximum size and crashes the system. As an aside, each OS has its own method of dealing with network protocols, and the implementation of dealing with particular protocols opens up things like this.

☒ **C** is incorrect because a SYN flood takes place when an attacker sends multiple SYN packets to a target without provided an acknowledgement to the returned SYN/ACK. This is another attack that does not necessarily work on modern systems.

☒ **E** is incorrect because in a Fraggle attack, UDP packets are used. The same principle applies—spoofed IP and echo requests sent to the broadcast address—it's just with UDP.

7. Tripwire is one of the most popular tools to protect against malware. Which of the following statements best describes Tripwire?

   A. Tripwire is a signature-based antivirus tool.

   B. Tripwire is a vulnerability assessment tool used for port scanning.

   C. Tripwire is a file integrity program.

   D. Tripwire is a session-splicing tool.

   ☑ **C.** Although it has grown substantially from its very early days as nothing more than a file integrity checker, Tripwire is a very well respected integrity verifier that can act as a host-based intrusion detection system (HIDS) in protection against Trojans. Simply put, Tripwire runs a file integrity check against critical files on your system. If they change—due to malware or any other circumstance—Tripwire can alert you and prevent the Trojan from being activated.

   ☒ **A** and **B** are incorrect because these are not functions Tripwire performs. Per the Tripwire website (www.tripwire.com), "Tripwire offerings solve the security configuration management, continuous monitoring, and incident detection problems facing organizations of all sizes, as stand-alone solutions or in concert with other IT security controls." Antivirus and vulnerability assessment are not functions this particular tool is designed for.

   ☒ **D** is incorrect because session splicing is an IDS evasion technique, not a function of Tripwire—not to mention session splicing does absolutely nothing to prevent Trojans.

8. Which of the following tools are good choices for session hijack attempts? (Choose all that apply.)

   A. Ettercap

   B. Netcat

   C. Hunt

   D. Nessus

☑ **A and C.** Both Ettercap and Hunt are good tools for session hijacking. Ettercap is an excellent man-in-the-middle tool and can be run from a variety of platforms (although it is Linux native). Per the Ettercap home page (http://ettercap.sourceforge.net/), "Ettercap is a comprehensive suite for man in the middle attacks. It features sniffing of live connections, content filtering on the fly and many other interesting tricks. It supports active and passive dissection of many protocols and includes many features for network and host analysis." Hunt is probably one of the best known session-hijacking tools. Hunt can sniff, hijack, and reset connections at will.

☒ **B** is incorrect because netcat is not a session hijack application. It *is* valuable for setting up listening ports and executing commands on target machines, but it's not designed for session hijacking.

☒ **D** is incorrect because Nessus is a vulnerability assessment tool.

9. In regard to Trojans, which of the following best describes a "wrapper"?

    A. The legitimate file the Trojan is attached to.

    B. A program used to bind the Trojan to a legitimate file.

    C. Encryption methods used for a Trojan.

    D. Polymorphic code used to avoid detection by antivirus programs.

    ☑ **B.** *Wrappers* are programs that allow you to bind an executable of your choice (Trojan) to an innocent file your target won't mind opening. For example, you might use a program such as EliteWrap to embed a backdoor application with a game file (.exe). A user on your target machine then opens the latest game file (maybe to play a hand of cards against the computer, or to fling a bird at pyramids built by pigs) while your backdoor is installing and sits there waiting for your use later. As an aside, many wrappers themselves are considered malicious and will show up on any up-to-date virus signature list.

    ☒ **A, C, and D** are all incorrect definitions of a wrapper in regard to Trojans. The wrapper is used to bind the Trojan to the legitimate file, and has nothing to do with encryption of the Trojan itself. Polymorphic code deals with a type of virus that changes its code to avoid detection by signature-based antivirus programs.

10. What is the default port used by RAT?

    A. 31337

    B. 1095

    C. 1524

    D. 7777

    E. 666

☑ **B.** Believe it or not, you will be asked to define port numbers for some Trojans—at least a couple of times on your exam. RAT (Remote Access Tool) is one of hundreds of remote access control Trojans attackers can use on a system. RAT provides a user on a remote computer near total control over another. Installed, usually, as a Trojan without the user's knowledge, RAT allows for things such as screen captures, file downloading from the target, file execution on the target, and command shell(s) on the target. By default, RAT uses port 1095 (1097–1098 are also used sometimes).

☒ **A** is incorrect because 31337 is the default port used by BackOrifice. BackOrifice is an older remote control Trojan program that was used on Windows machines.

☒ **C** is incorrect because 1524 is the default port used by Trinoo. Trinoo is a distributed denial of service Trojan.

☒ **D** is incorrect because 7777 is the default port for Tini. Per the website http://ntsecurity.nu/toolbox/tini/, "Tini is a simple and very small (3Kb) backdoor for Windows, coded in assembler. It listens at TCP port 7777 and gives anybody who connects a remote Command Prompt." Interestingly, the developers didn't intend this as a Trojan at all, and did not create it to actually install on a machine (rebooting kills it).

☒ **E** is incorrect because 666 is the default port for several different malware applications. Doom, Cain and Abel, NokNok, and Attack FTP are all examples.

11. Which of the following is a legitimate communication path for the transfer of data?

   A. Overt

   B. Covert

   C. Authentic

   D. Imitation

   E. Actual

☑ **A.** This is another one of those easy, pure definition questions you simply can't miss on your exam. Whether the channel is inside a computer, between systems, or across the Internet, any legitimate channel used for communications and data exchange is known as an *overt channel*. And don't let the inherit risk with any channel itself make the decision for you—even if the channel itself is a risky endeavor, if it is being used for its intended purpose, it's still overt. For example, an IRC or a gaming link is still an overt channel, so long as the application(s) making use of it are legitimate. Overt channels are legitimate communication channels used by programs across a system or a network, whereas covert channels are used to transport data in ways they were not intended for.

☒ **B** is incorrect because an overt channel, per EC Council's own definition, is "a channel that transfers information within a computer system or network in a way that violates security policy." For example, a Trojan might create a channel for stealing passwords or downloading sensitive data from the machine.

☒ **C, D,** and **E** are incorrect because none of these are terms for the communications channel and are included here as distractors.

12. Which Trojan is well known for attempting to steal banking information from infected machines?

    A. Apocalypse

    B. HTTP RAT

    C. Zeus

    D. BioDox

    ☑ **C.** There are many "well-known" Trojans out there, and you'll definitely get quizzed on a couple. Zeus is one of the better-known, still-rampaging Trojans making its way around the Internet world. First hitting the scene in 2007, Zeus spread via phishing e-mails (usually) and drive-by installations (exploiting older Java installations). Zeus even made use of Facebook to propagate.

    ☒ **A** and **B** are incorrect because both Apocalypse and HTTP RAT are remote access Trojans. Other remote access Trojans you may want to know include Poison Ivy, Dark Comet, and CCTT (Covert Channel Trojan).

    ☒ **D** is incorrect because BioDox is referred to as a "GUI Trojan" by EC Council and is used for all sorts of badness—from remote control to password sniffing.

13. A pen test team member types the following command:

    ```
    nc222.15.66.78 -p 8765
    ```

    Which of the following is true regarding this attempt?

    A. The attacker is attempting to connect to an established listening port on a remote computer.

    B. The attacker is establishing a listening port on his machine for later use.

    C. The attacker is attempting a DoS against a remote computer.

    D. The attacker is attempting to kill a service on a remote machine.

    ☑ **A.** As covered earlier, netcat is a wonderful tool that allows all sorts of remote access wizardry on a machine, and you'll need to be able to recognize the basics of the syntax. In the command example, netcat is being told, "Please attempt a connection to the machine with the IP address of 222.15.66.78 on port 8765: I believe you'll find the port in a listening state, waiting for our arrival." Obviously at some point previous to issuing this command on his local machine, the pen tester planted the netcat Trojan on the remote system (222.15.66.78) and set it up in a listening state. He may have set it up with a command shell access (allowing a Telnet-like connection to issue commands at will) using the following command:

```
nc -L -p 8765 -t -e cmd.exe
```

☒ **B** is incorrect because this command is issued on the client side of the setup, not the server side. At some point previously, the port was set to a listening state, and this netcat command will access it.

☒ **C** is incorrect because this command is not attempting a denial of service against the target machine. It's included here as a distractor.

☒ **D** is incorrect because this command is not attempting to kill a process or service on the remote machine. It's included here as a distractor.

14. Examine the partial command line output listed here:

```
Active Connections
Proto   Local Address            Foreign Address          State
  TCP     0.0.0.0:912              COMPUTER11:0             LISTENING
  TCP     0.0.0.0:3460             COMPUTER11:0             LISTENING
  TCP     0.0.0.0:3465             COMPUTER11:0             LISTENING
  TCP     0.0.0.0:8288             COMPUTER11:0             LISTENING
  TCP     0.0.0.0:16386            COMPUTER11:0             LISTENING
  TCP     192.168.1.100:139        COMPUTER11:0             LISTENING
  TCP     192.168.1.100:58191      173.194.44.81:https      ESTABLISHED
  TCP     192.168.1.100:58192      173.194.44.81:https      TIME_WAIT
  TCP     192.168.1.100:58193      173.194.44.81:https      TIME_WAIT
  TCP     192.168.1.100:58194      173.194.44.81:https      ESTABLISHED
  TCP     192.168.1.100:58200      bk-in-f138:http          TIME_WAIT
```

Which of the following is a true statement regarding the output?

A. This is output from a netstat –an command.

B. This is output from a netstat –b command.

C. This is output from a netstat –e command.

D. This is output from a netstat –r command.

☑ **A.** You'll need to get to know netstat before your exam. It's not a huge thing, and you won't get bogged down in minutia, but you do need to know the basics. Netstat is a great command-line tool built into every Microsoft operating system. From Microsoft's own description, netstat "displays active TCP connections, ports on which the computer is listening, Ethernet statistics, the IP routing table, IPv4 statistics (for the IP, ICMP, TCP, and UDP protocols), and IPv6 statistics (for the IPv6, ICMPv6, TCP over IPv6, and UDP over IPv6 protocols)." It's a great, easy way to see which ports you have open on your system, helping you to identify any naughty Trojans that may be hanging around. A netstat –an command will show all connections and listening ports in numerical form.

☒ **B** is incorrect because the –b option displays the executable involved in creating each connection or listening port. Its output appears something like this:

```
Proto  Local Address      Foreign Address  State
  TCP    127.0.0.1:5354     COMPUTER11:49155 ESTABLISHED
[mDNSResponder.exe]
  TCP    127.0.0.1:27015   COMPUTER11:49175 ESTABLISHED
[AppleMobileDeviceService.exe]
  TCP    127.0.0.1:49155   COMPUTER11:5354   ESTABLISHED
[AppleMobileDeviceService.exe]
  TCP    127.0.0.1:49175   COMPUTER11:27015 ESTABLISHED
[iTunesHelper.exe]
```

☒ **C** is incorrect because the –e flag displays Ethernet statistics for the system. Output appears something like this:

```
                         Received          Sent
Bytes                    125454856       33551337
Unicast packets             164910         167156
Non-unicast packets            570          15624
Discards                         0              0
Errors                           0            268
Unknown protocols                0
```

☒ **D** is incorrect because the –r flag displays the route table for the system. A sampling of the output looks like this:

```
IPv4 Route Table
===================================================================
Active Routes:
Network Destination   Netmask       Gateway      Interface    Metric
      0.0.0.0      0.0.0.0     192.168.1.1 192.168.1.100    25
      15.0.0.0    255.0.0.0     On-link      16.213.104.24    26
15.195.201.216 255.255.255.255 192.168.1.1 192.168.1.100    26
15.255.255.255 255.255.255.255 On-link      16.213.104.24   281.
```

15. You are discussing malware with a new pen test member who asks about restarting executables. Which registry keys within Windows automatically run executables and instructions? (Choose all that apply.)

   A. HKEY_LOCAL_MACHINE\Software\Microsoft\Windows\CurrentVersion\ RunServicesOnce

   B. HKEY_LOCAL_MACHINE\Software\Microsoft\Windows\CurrentVersion\ RunServices

   C. HKEY_LOCAL_MACHINE\Software\Microsoft\Windows\CurrentVersion\ RunOnce

   D. HKEY_LOCAL_MACHINE\Software\Microsoft\Windows\CurrentVersion\Run

   ☑ **A, B, C, and D.** Creating malware and infecting a machine with it is only accomplishing the basics. Getting it to hang around by having it restart when the user reboots the machine? Now we're talking. The Run, RunOnce, RunServices, and RunServicesOnce registry keys within the HKEY_Local_ Machine hive are great places to stick all sorts of executables. Because of this, it's helpful to run registry monitoring on occasion to check for anything suspicious. Sys Analyzer, Regshot, and TinyWatcher are all options for this.

16. Which of the following best describes a sheepdip computer?

    A. A system used to confuse malware developers, attracting them away from real network systems.

    B. A system that has multiple malware infections.

    C. A system used to screen physical media for malware.

    D. A system infected with botnet malware.

    ☑ C. So it's admittedly rare that animal husbandry and IT Security cross paths, but this is one of those rare moments. In sheep farming, the lovable little creatures are sometimes given a chemical bath to rid them of parasites, to clean their wool before shearing, or to prevent something I didn't really want to learn about (and refuse to elaborate on here) known as "sheep scab." A sheepdip computer is the same thought process, only virtual—with less bleating and scabs. Sheepdip computers are set up to check physical media, device drivers, and other files for malware before they are introduced to the network. Typically, these computers are used for nothing else and are isolated from the other computers. Sheepdip computers are usually configured with a couple of different AV programs, port monitors, registry monitors, and file integrity verifiers.

    ☒ A, B, and D are all incorrect definitions of a sheepdip computer and are included as distractors.

17. Which denial of service attack involves sending SYN packets to a target machine, but never responding to any of the SYN/ACK replies?

    A. SYN flood

    B. SYN attack

    C. Smurf

    D. LOIC

    ☑ A. In a SYN flood attack, the attacker sends thousands of SYN packets to the target, but never responds to any of the return SYN/ACK packets. Because there is a certain amount of time the target must wait to receive an answer to the SYN/ACK (network congestion may be slowing things down, in a legitimate example), it will eventually bog down and run out of available connections.

    ☒ B is incorrect because EC Council defines a SYN attack and a SYN flood differently. Whereas a SYN flood takes advantage of tons of half-open connections, the SYN attack goes one step further—by spoofing the sending IP address in the first place. The target will attempt to respond with a SYN/ACK but will be unsuccessful because the sending address is false. Eventually, all the machine's resources are engaged and the DoS is successful.

☒ **C** is incorrect because a Smurf attack is a DoS attack making use of ICMP packets and broadcast addresses. The idea is simple: Spoof the target's IP address and send multiple ping requests to the broadcast address of the subnet. The entire subnet will then begin sending ping responses to the target, exhausting the target's resources and rendering it a giant paperweight.

☒ **D** is incorrect because Low Orbit Ion Cannon (LOIC) is a simple-to-use DDoS tool that floods a target with TCP, UDP, or HTTP requests. It was originally written open source to attack various Scientology websites, but has since had many people voluntarily joining a botnet to support all sorts of attacks. Recently, LOIC was used in a coordinated attack against Sony's PlayStation network, and the tool has a track record of other successful hits: the Recording Industry Association of America, PayPal, MasterCard, and several other companies have all fallen victim to LOIC.

18. A user sees the following pop-up window appear:

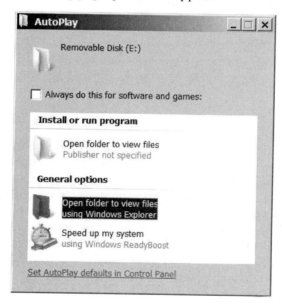

Which of the following best describes the pop-up?

A. A hardware corrupted USB drive is inserted into the machine.

B. The pop-up is purely informational.

C. The pop-up indicates a Conficker worm propagation attempt.

D. None of the above.

☑ **C.** When it comes to worms on the exam, you'll definitely be asked about Conficker, and I'd bet a cold adult beverage you'll probably see this pop-up somewhere. It's *the* classic indication Conficker is attempting to run wild on your machine. Clicking the first option under Install or Run Program will execute the worm: The authentic Windows option is the "Open folder to view files using Windows Explorer" under General Options. Conficker spreads as soon as it is opened (by clicking the first option) to open shares, unpatched systems on the network, and systems with weak passwords. The Conficker worm disables services, denies access to administrator shared drives, locks users out of directories, and restricts access to security-related sites.

🗵 **A** is an incorrect description of this pop-up. A hardware problem would create a pop-up noting the drive was unreadable—or there would be no indication at all.

🗵 **B** is incorrect because the pop-up definitely indicates a potential problem with the removable drive and is not harmless. The legitimate Windows option may be mistakenly ignored in favor of Conficker's addition.

🗵 **D** is incorrect because there is an appropriate answer to the question.

19. IPSec is an effective preventative measure against session hijacking. Which IPSec mode encrypts only the data payload?

  A. Transport

  B. Tunnel

  C. Protected

  D. Spoofed

☑ **A.** IPSec is a wonderful encryption mechanism that can rather easily be set up between two endpoints, or even across your entire subnet if you configure the hosts appropriately. You won't need to know all the bells and whistles with IPSec (and thank goodness, because there's a lot to write about), but you do need the basics. Transport mode does not affect the header of the packet at all, and only encrypts the payload. It's typically used as a secured connection between two endpoints, whereas Tunnel mode creates a VPN-like connection protecting the entire session. Additionally, Transport mode is compatible with conventional NAT (Network Address Translation).

🗵 **B** is incorrect because Tunnel mode encapsulates the entire packet, including the header. This is typically used to form a VPN connection, where the tunnel is used across an untrusted network (such as the Internet). For pretty obvious reasons, it's not compatible with conventional NAT; when the packet goes through the router (or whatever is performing NAT for you), the source address in the packet changes due to Tunnel mode and, therefore, invalidates the packet for the receiving end. There are workarounds for this, generally lumped together as NAT-t (NAT Traversal). Many home routers take advantage of something referred to as IPSec Passthrough to allow just this.

🗵 **C** and **D** are invalid terms involving IPSEC.

20. Which of the following are MITM session hijacking tools? (Choose all that apply.)

   A. Netcat

   B. LOIC

   C. Hunt

   D. Paros

   E. T-sight

   F. Nmap

   ☑ **C, D,** and **E.** There are tons and tons of man-in-the-middle (MITM) session hijacking tools available. Hunt and T-sight are probably the two best known of the group, and the two you'll probably see referenced on the exam, but they're by no means your only options. Hunt can sniff, hijack, and reset connections at will, whereas T-sight (commercially available) can easily hijack sessions as well as monitor additional network connections. Paros is a well-known proxy MITM session hijacking tool, and includes such goodies as vulnerability scanning and spidering.

   ☒ **A, B,** and **F** are incorrect because these are not MITM tools. Netcat is a remote access Trojan (even though it doesn't necessarily *have* to be a Trojan, EC Council defines it as one), among other things. LOIC is a DoS application. Nmap is, of course, a well-known scanning tool.

21. Which of the following best describes the comparison between spoofing and session hijacking?

   A. Spoofing and session hijacking are the same thing.

   B. Spoofing interrupts a client's communication whereas hijacking does not.

   C. Hijacking interrupts a client's communication whereas spoofing does not.

   D. Hijacking emulates a foreign IP address whereas spoofing refers to MAC addresses.

   ☑ **C.** Hijacking and spoofing can sometimes be confused with each other, although they really shouldn't be. *Spoofing* refers to a process where the attacking machine pretends to be something it is not. Whether by faking a MAC address or an IP address, the idea is that other systems on the network will communicate with your machine (that is, set up and tear down sessions) as if it's the target system: Generally this is used to benefit sniffing efforts. Hijacking is a totally different animal. In hijacking, the attacker jumps into an already-existing session, knocking the client out of it and fooling the server into continuing the exchange. In many cases, the client will simply reconnect to the server over a different session, with no one the wiser: The server isn't even aware of what happened and the client simply connects again in a different session. As an aside, EC Council describes the session hijack in these steps:

1. Sniff the traffic between the client and the server.
2. Monitor the traffic and predict the sequence numbering.
3. Desynchronize the session with the client.
4. Predict the session token and take over the session.
5. Inject packets to the target server.

☒ A is incorrect because spoofing and hijacking are different. An argument can be made that hijacking makes use of some spoofing, but the two attacks are separate entities: Spoofing pretends to be another machine, eliciting (or setting up) sessions for sniffing purposes, whereas hijacking takes advantage of existing communications sessions.

☒ B is incorrect because spoofing doesn't interrupt a client's existing session at all—it's designed to sniff traffic and/or set up its own sessions.

☒ D is incorrect because spoofing isn't relegated to MAC addresses only. You can spoof almost anything, from MAC and IP addresses to system names and services.

22. Which of the following is an effective deterrent against session hijacking?

   A. Install and use an HIDS on the system.

   B. Install and use Tripwire on the system.

   C. Enforce good password policy.

   D. Use unpredictable sequence numbers.

   ☑ D. As noted already, session hijacking requires the attacker to guess the proper upcoming sequence number(s) to pull off the attack, pushing the original client out of the session. Using unpredictable session IDs in the first place protects against this. Other countermeasures for session hijacking are fairly common sense: Use encryption to protect the channel, limit incoming connections, minimize remote access, and regenerate the session key after authentication is complete. And, lastly, don't forget user education: If the users don't know any better, they might not think twice about clicking past the security certificate warning or reconnecting after being suddenly shut down.

   ☒ A is incorrect because a host-based intrusion detection system may not deter session hijacking at all.

   ☒ B is incorrect because Tripwire is a file integrity application and won't do a thing for session hijacking prevention.

   ☒ C is incorrect because system passwords have nothing to do with session hijacking.

23. A pen test team member types the following command:

```
ettercap –T –q –M ARP /200.70.55.12
```

Which of the following are true regarding this command? (Choose all that apply.)

A. Ettercap is being configured for a GUI interface.

B. Ettercap is being configured as a sniffer.

C. Ettercap is being configured for text mode.

D. Ettercap is being configured for manual mode.

E. Ettercap is being configured for a man-in-the-middle attack.

☑ **C and E.** Ettercap is defined as a "comprehensive suite for man-in-the-middle attacks" by nearly every website devoted to it (do a search for Ettercap and you'll see what I mean), and it's almost universally recognized as one of—if not the—best man-in-the-middle attack suites on the planet. Because of this, you'll need to know some basics about it: not much, but some. Ettercap can run in one of four user interfaces: text only (-T), something called "curses" (-C), a GUI (known as GTK, and using the –G flag), and daemon mode (-D). In this example, text mode is enabled, the –q flag sets things "quiet," and the –M flag sets up man-in-the-middle ARP poisoning.

☒ **A** is incorrect because the –T flag is used to put Ettercap in text mode: -G would put Ettercap in GTK mode.

☒ **B** is incorrect because Ettercap isn't being configured as a sniffer here: It's being set up to perform a MITM attack, not to log packets.

☒ **D** is incorrect because there is no "manual" mode in Ettercap. This is included as a distractor.

24. Within a TCP packet dump, a packet is noted with the SYN flag set and a sequence number set at A13F. What should the acknowledgement number in the return SYN/ACK packet be?

A. A131

B. A130

C. A140

D. A14F

☑ **C.** We've been over the need for predicting sequence numbers before, so I won't bore you with it again other than to restate the salient point here: The ISN is incremented by 1 in the SYN/ACK return packet. Because these values were given in hex instead of decimal, all you need to know is what the next hex value after A13F is. You could split it out into binary (each hex digit is four bits, so this would equate to 1010000100111111) and then pick the next available number (1010000101000000) and split it back into hex (1010 = A, 0001 = 1, 0100 = 4, and 0000 = 0). Alternatively, you could convert directly to decimal (41279) add 1 and then convert back to hex. And, yes, you do need to know number conversion from decimal to binary to hex—so stop complaining.

☒ **A, B,** and **D** are incorrect hex equivalents for decimal 41280 (then next number acknowledgement for the ISN).

25. When is session hijacking performed?

    A. Before the three-step handshake

    B. During the three-step handshake

    C. After the three-step handshake

    D. After a FIN packet

☑ **C.** This question should be an easy one for you, but it's included here to reinforce the point that you need to understand session hijacking steps well for the exam. Of course session hijacking should occur after the three-step handshake. As a matter of fact, you'll probably need to wait quite a bit after the three-step handshake, so that everything on the session can be set up—authentication and all that nonsense should be taken care of before you jump in and take over.

☒ **A** and **B** are incorrect because session hijacking occurs after a session is already established, and the three-step handshake must obviously occur first for this to be true.

☒ **D** is incorrect because the FIN packet brings an orderly close to the TCP session. Why on earth would you wait until it's over to start trying to hijack it?

The Pen Test: Putting It All Together

This chapter includes questions from the following topics:

- Describe penetration testing, security assessments, and risk management
- Define automatic and manual testing
- List pen test methodology and deliverables

I've been exceedingly blessed in my life, in a great many ways I don't have the time or print space here to cover. I have had opportunities to travel the world and experience things many people just flat out don't get to. In one of my travels I wound up in Florence, Italy, and decided to go see the statue of David. Even if you're not familiar with the background of this sculpture, I'll bet you've seen a replica of it somewhere—from garden art re-creations and store displays to one very cool episode of *SpongeBob SquarePants*, where he had to *"BE the marble!"* David was carved by Michelangelo sometime between 1501 and 1504 and is universally acclaimed as one of the greatest sculptures of all time. The statue now sits in a domed atrium within the Galleria dell'Accademia in Florence. It is truly an unbelievable experience to see this work of art, displayed in all its glory in a perfect setting within a beautiful gallery, and is definitely a highlight of any visit to Florence.

What made as big an impression on me, though, was the other, *unfinished* works of art from Michelangelo you had to pass by in order to get to the statue of David. There's a giant hallway leading to the atrium that is literally packed, on the right and left, with sculptures he started but, for whatever reason, never finished. Walking down the hallway (at least in your imagination with me anyway) you're surrounded by stonework that is simply amazing. Here, on the right, is a giant marble stone with half a man sticking out of the left side and chisel marks leading downward to something as yet unfinished. On the left we see the front half of a horse exploding out of a rough-hewn block of granite; the rest of the beautiful animal still buried in the story he never got to finish telling with the sculpture. Traveling down this long hallway, we see other works—a battle raging in one boulder, a face clearly defined and nearly expressionless looking out of a little, almost leftover piece of rock—displayed left and right for us to gape at.

These unfinished works weren't crude by any means; quite the opposite. I stood there among the crowds racing to get a glimpse of monumental talent, marveling at how a man could take a big chunk of rock and shape and smooth it into something that looked so *real*. But these pieces weren't finished, and it showed. There were giant scratch marks over areas that should have been smoothed on some of them, and a few sculptures that simply broke off because the rock itself cracked in two.

What has this got to do with this book, you may be asking? The answer, dear reader, is because we've all put a lot of work into this. We've chipped away at giant boulders of knowledge and are on the verge of finishing. No, I'm not making some crazed corollary to this book being some work of art (anyone who really knows me can attest that's not my bag, baby), but I am saying we, you and I, are on the verge of something good here. Keep hacking away at that stone. Keep sanding and polishing. Sooner or later you'll finish and have your statue to display—just don't forget all the work you put into it, and don't throw any of it away. I promise, you'll want to go back, sometime later, and walk through your own hallway of work to see how far you've come.

This chapter is, admittedly, short and sweet. The questions and answers are easier (if memorizing terms is easy for you, that is), and the write ups on what's correct and what's false will reflect that as well. Sure, I might sneak in a question from earlier in the book—just to see if you're paying attention, and to wrap up terms EC Council throws into this section—but these are all supposed to be about the pen test itself. We've already covered the nuts and bolts, so now we're going to spend some time on the finished product. And, yes, you will see this stuff on your exam. I just hope that you'll be so ready for it by then it'll be like Michelangelo wiping the dust off his last polishing of the statue of David.

 STUDY TIPS   Information covered in this chapter, that you'll find on the exam, generally boils down to basic memorization. While that may sound easy enough to you, I think you'll find that some of these terms are so closely related that questions on the exam referencing them will be confusing in the least—and most likely rage-inducing by the time the exam ends. Pay very close attention to the details and key words for definitions (in particular the insiders, outsiders, and affiliates definitions), and take the time to memorize the phases involved with a pen test and an actual attack itself. Lastly, and I think I've said this before, it's sometimes easier to eliminate wrong answers than it is to choose the correct one. When you're looking at one of these questions that seems totally out of left field, spend your time eliminating the answers you know aren't correct. Eventually all that's left must be the correct choice(s). After all, the mechanism scoring the test doesn't care *how* you got to the answer, only that the right one is chosen.

1. What would you expect to find in a final report from a full penetration test? (Choose all that apply.)

   A. Names of all the participants

   B. A list of findings from the assessment(s)

   C. An executive summary of the assessment(s)

   D. A list of vulnerabilities that were patched by the team

2. A team is starting a security assessment. The target organization has provided a system on an internal subnet, but no other previous knowledge of any pertinent information has been given. Which type of test will the team be performing?

   A. Internal, white box

   B. Internal, black box

   C. External, white box

   D. External, black box

3. Which of the following provide automated pen test–like results for an organization? (Choose all that apply.)

   A. Metasploit

   B. Nessus

   C. Core Impact

   D. CANVAS

   E. SAINT

   F. GFI Languard

4. An assessment against a network segment tests for existing vulnerabilities, but does not attempt to exploit any of them. What is this called?

   A. Penetration test

   B. Partial penetration test

   C. Vulnerability assessment

   D. Security scan

5. You are reviewing recent security breaches against an organization. In one case, a spouse of an employee illegally used the employee's credentials to gain access and then carried out an attack. Which of the following best defines the attacker?

   A. Outside affiliate

   B. Outside associate

   C. Insider affiliate

   D. Insider associate

6. In which phase of a pen test is scanning performed?

   A. Pre-attack

   B. Attack

   C. Post-attack

   D. Reconnaissance

7. An organization wants a security test but is concerned about time and cost. Which of the following tests is generally faster and costs less than a manual pen test?

   A. Automatic

   B. Internal

   C. Black box

   D. External

8. The most dangerous threat to an organization is a disgruntled insider. Which of the following best defines a disgruntled employee's (a normal user inside the network) attack against the organization?

   A. External black box

   B. Internal gray box

   C. Internal announced

   D. External white box

9. Joe is part of an environmental group protesting AnyBiz, Inc., for the company's stance on a variety of issues. Frustrated by the failure of multiple attempts to raise awareness of his cause, Joe launches sophisticated web defacement and denial of service attacks against the company, without attempting to hide the attack source and with no regard to being caught. Which of the following best defines Joe?

   A. Hactivism

   B. Ethical hacker

   C. Script kiddie

   D. Suicide hacker

10. A security team has been hired by upper management to assess the organization's security. The assessment is designed to emulate an Internet hacker and to test the behavior of the security devices and policies in place as well as the IT Security staff. Which of the following best describes this test? (Choose all that apply.)

    A. Internal

    B. External

    C. Announced

    D. Unannounced

11. In which phase of a pen test will the team penetrate the perimeter and acquire targets?

   A. Pre-attack

   B. Attack

   C. Post-attack

   D. None of the above

12. Which of the following test types presents a higher probability of encountering problems and takes the most amount of time?

   A. Black box

   B. Grey box

   C. White box

   D. Internal

13. Which of the following best describes the difference between a professional pen test team member and a hacker?

   A. Ethical hackers are paid for their time.

   B. Ethical hackers never exploit vulnerabilities; they only point out their existence.

   C. Ethical hackers do not use the same tools and actions as hackers.

   D. Ethical hackers hold a predefined scope and agreement from the system owner.

14. Sally is part of a penetration test team and is starting a test. The client has provided a network drop on one of their subnets for Sally to launch her attacks from. However, they did not provide any authentication information, network diagrams, or other notable data concerning the system(s). Which type of test is Sally performing?

   A. External, white box

   B. External, black box

   C. Internal, white box

   D. Internal, black box

15. Joe is part of a pen test team that has been hired by AnyBiz to perform testing under a contract. As part of the defined scope and activities, no IT employees within AnyBiz know about the test. After some initial information gathering, Joe strikes up a conversation with an employee in the cafeteria and steals the employee's access badge. Joe then uses this badge to gain entry to secured areas of AnyBiz's office space. Which of the following best defines Joe in this scenario?

   A. Outside affiliate

   B. Outside associate

   C. Insider affiliate

   D. Insider associate

16. In which phase of a penetration test would you compile a list of vulnerabilities found?

    A. Pre-attack

    B. Attack

    C. Post-attack

    D. Reconciliation

17. Which of the following has a database containing thousands of signatures used to detect vulnerabilities in multiple operating systems?

    A. Nessus

    B. Hping

    C. LOIC

    D. SNMPUtil

18. Cleaning registry entries and removing uploaded files and tools are part of which phase of a pen test?

    A. Covering tracks

    B. Pre-attack

    C. Attack

    D. Post-attack

19. Jake, an employee of AnyBiz, Inc., parks his vehicle outside the corporate offices of SomeBiz, Inc. He turns on a laptop and connects to an open wireless access point internal to SomeBiz's network. Which of the following best defines Jake?

    A. Outside affiliate

    B. Outside associate

    C. Insider affiliate

    D. Insider associate

20. Which of the following are true regarding a pen test? (Choose all that apply.)

    A. Pen tests do not include social engineering.

    B. Pen tests may include unannounced attacks against the network.

    C. During a pen test, the security professionals can carry out any attack they choose.

    D. Pen tests always have a scope.

    E. The client is not notified of the vulnerabilities the team chooses to exploit.

21. Which of the following is a potential cause of a security breach?

    A. Vulnerability

    B. Threat

    C. Exploit

    D. Zero day

22. Which Metasploit payload type operates via DLL injection and is very difficult for AV software to pick up?

    A. Inline

    B. Meterpreter

    C. Staged

    D. Remote

23. Metasploit is a framework allowing for the development and execution of exploit code against a remote host, and is designed for use in pen testing. The framework is made of several libraries, each performing a specific task and set of functions. Which library is considered the most fundamental component of the Metasploit framework?

    A. MSF Core

    B. MSF Base

    C. MSF Interfaces

    D. Rex

24. EC Council defines six stages of scanning methodology. Which of the following correctly lists the six steps?

    A. Scan for vulnerabilities, check for live systems, check for open ports, banner grabbing, draw network diagrams, prepare proxies.

    B. Banner grabbing, check for live systems, check for open ports, scan for vulnerabilities, draw network diagrams, prepare proxies.

    C. Check for live systems, check for open ports, banner grabbing, scan for vulnerabilities, draw network diagrams, prepare proxies.

    D. Prepare proxies, check for live systems, check for open ports, banner grabbing, scan for vulnerabilities, draw network diagrams.

25. Which of the following may be effective countermeasures against an inside attacker? (Choose all that apply.)

    A. Enforce elevated privilege control.

    B. Secure all dumpsters and shred collection boxes.

    C. Enforce good physical security practice and policy.

    D. Perform background checks on all employees.

1. A, B, C
2. B
3. A, C, D
4. C
5. C
6. A
7. A
8. B
9. D
10. B, D
11. B
12. A
13. D
14. D
15. C
16. C
17. A
18. D
19. A
20. B, D
21. B
22. B
23. D
24. C
25. A, B, C, D

1. What would you expect to find in a final report from a full penetration test? (Choose all that apply.)

    A. Names of all the participants

    B. A list of findings from the assessment(s)

    C. An executive summary of the assessment(s)

    D. A list of vulnerabilities that were patched by the team

    ☑ **A, B, and C.** It seems fairly obvious that if you hire someone to perform a security audit of your organization that you would expect a report at the end of it. Pen tests vary from company to company, and test to test, but some basics are part of every pen test final report to the customer. The basics that are part of every report are listed here:

    - An executive summary of the organization's overall security posture (if testing under the auspices of FISMA, DIACAP, HIPAA, or other standard, this will be tailored to the standard)

    - Names of all participants as well as dates of all tests

    - A list of findings, usually presented in order of highest risk

    - An analysis of each finding as well as recommended mitigation steps (if available)

    - Log files and other evidence from your toolset

    ☒ **D** is incorrect because a pen test is not designed to repair or mitigate security problems as they are discovered. The point of a pen test is to identify these potential security shortcomings so the organization can make a determination on repair or mitigation: There may be an acceptable level of risk versus the cost to fix for certain findings that the customer is perfectly comfortable with. Something that may seem to you, the pen tester, as a glaring security hole dooming the organization to certain virtual death simply may not matter to the client—no matter how clearly and forcefully you try to stress that point.

2. A team is starting a security assessment. The target organization has provided a system on an internal subnet, but no other previous knowledge of any pertinent information has been given. Which type of test will the team be performing?

    A. Internal, white box

    B. Internal, black box

    C. External, white box

    D. External, black box

☑ **B.** EC Council defines two types of penetration tests: external and internal. An external assessment analyzes publicly available information and conducts network scanning, enumeration, and testing from the network perimeter—usually from the Internet. An internal assessment, as you might imagine, is performed from within the organization, from various network access points. On your exam, just as it is here, this pure definition term may be combined with the white, gray, and black box testing terms you're already familiar with.

☒ **A** is incorrect because although the test is indeed internal, it is not a white box test—where the team would be provided with all knowledge of the inner workings of the system.

☒ **C** and **D** are incorrect because this is not an external test.

3. Which of the following provide automated pen test–like results for an organization? (Choose all that apply.)

   A. Metasploit

   B. Nessus

   C. Core Impact

   D. CANVAS

   E. SAINT

   F. GFI Languard

☑ **A, C,** and **D.** Automated tool suites for pen testing can be viewed as a means to save time and money by the client's management, but (in my opinion, at least) these do not provide the same quality results as a test performed by security professionals. Automated tools can provide a lot of genuinely good information, but are also susceptible to false positives and false negatives, and don't necessarily care what your agreed-upon scope says is your stopping point. Metasploit has a free, open source version and an insanely expensive "Pro" version for developing and executing exploit code against a remote target machine. Metasploit offers a module called "autopwn," which can automate the exploitation phase of a penetration test.

Core Impact is probably the best-known, all-inclusive automated testing framework. From their website (www.coresecurity.com/content/core-impact-overview), Core Impact "takes security testing to the next level by safely replicating a broad range of threats to the organization's sensitive data and mission-critical infrastructure—providing extensive visibility into the cause, effect and prevention of data breaches." Core Impact tests everything from web applications and individual systems to network devices and wireless.

Per the Immunity Security website (www.immunitysec.com), CANVAS "makes available hundreds of exploits, an automated exploitation system, and a comprehensive, reliable exploit development framework to penetration testers and security professionals." Additionally, the company claims CANVAS's Reference Implementation (CRI) is "the industry's first open platform for IDS and IPS testing."

For you real-world purists out there, of the three, only Core Impact provides an actual, true, one-step automated pen-test result feature. Metasploit offers "autopwn," and CANVAS has a similar "run everything" mode; however, both lack the true, solid result and report features of IMPACT. In the true sense of "automated pen test," only IMPACT does this, but for your exam stick with all of them.

☒ **B, E, and F** are incorrect for the same reason: These are all vulnerability assessment tool suites, not automated pen test frameworks. Nessus is probably the most recognizable of the three, but SAINT and GFI Languard are both still listed as top vulnerability assessment applications.

4. An assessment against a network segment tests for existing vulnerabilities, but does not attempt to exploit any of them. What is this called?

   A. Penetration test

   B. Partial penetration test

   C. Vulnerability assessment

   D. Security scan

   ☑ **C.** A vulnerability assessment is exactly what it sounds like: the search for, and identification of, potentially exploitable vulnerabilities on a system or network. These vulnerabilities can be poor security configurations, missing patches, or any number of other weaknesses a bad guy might exploit. The two keys to a vulnerability assessment are that the vulnerabilities are identified, not exploited, and the report is simply a snapshot in time. The organization will need to make the determination how often they want to run a vulnerability assessment.

   ☒ **A** is incorrect because team members on a pen test not only discover vulnerabilities, they actively exploit them (within the scope of their prearranged agreement, of course).

   ☒ **B and D** are incorrect because they are not valid terms associated with assessment types, and are included as distractors.

5. You are reviewing recent security breaches against an organization. In one case, a spouse of an employee illegally used the employee's credentials to gain access and then carried out an attack. Which of the following best defines the attacker?

   A. Outside affiliate

   B. Outside associate

   C. Insider affiliate

   D. Insider associate

☑ **C.** There are few truisms in life, but this is one of them: You will need to memorize certain terms that are very important for the exam you are taking, but probably don't amount to a hill of skittles in the real world (and this memorization will infuriate and frustrate you to no end). This is a prime example. In the CEH world, you can define attackers by a lot of different criteria (for example, white hat versus black hat). When it comes to these terms, you differentiate attackers by who they are in relation to the company, and how they gain access.

Defining inside versus outside may seem simple, but you've got to be careful. It has nothing to do with where the attack is coming from, but everything to do with the person's relationship to the company. *All company employees (including contractors)* are considered "inside." Anyone who is not an employee is considered "outside," with one notable exception: an inside affiliate is a spouse, friend, or acquaintance of an employee that makes use of the employee's credentials to gain access and cause havoc. It's a tricky little differentiation that you'll definitely see on your test somewhere. For memorization purposes:

- Insiders are employees and contractors of the organization.

- Outsiders are everyone else attempting to get in (hackers and so on).

- *Affiliate* deals with the credentials used in the attack: insider affiliate is the employee's credentials (most often used by a spouse, friend, or client) and outsider affiliate is the use of open access (such as open wireless).

- *Insider associates* are contractors, janitors, and so on, who may have limited access to resources. This authorized access isn't necessarily to IT resources, but it does allow the attacker to roam freely into and out of organization offices and buildings—which makes things such as social engineering attacks easier.

☒ **A** is incorrect because an outside affiliate is someone who is not employed with the company in any way (a hacker or maybe a corporate spy) and makes use of open access to the organization's network. For example, a corporate spy may park his car close to a building and tie in to an unsecured WAP to look for information on the network.

☒ **B** is incorrect because "outside associate" isn't a term EC Council defines.

☒ **D** is incorrect because an *insider associate* is someone who has limited access to resources, such as a guard or a contractor.

6. In which phase of a pen test is scanning performed?

   A. Pre-attack

   B. Attack

   C. Post-attack

   D. Reconnaissance

☑ **A.** I know you're sick of CEH definitions, terms, and phases of attacks, but this is another one you'll just need to commit to memory. Per EC Council, there are three phases of a pen test: pre-attack, attack, and post-attack. The pre-attack phase is where you'd find scanning and other reconnaissance (competitive intelligence, website crawling, and so on).

☒ **B** is incorrect because scanning is completed in the pre-attack phase. The attack phase holds four areas of work: penetrate the perimeter, acquire targets, execute attack, and escalate privileges.

☒ **C** is incorrect because scanning is completed long before the post-attack phase. Actions accomplished in post-attack include removal of all uploaded files and tools, restoration (if needed) to original state, analyzing results, and preparing reports for the customer.

☒ **D** is incorrect because reconnaissance is not a phase of pen testing.

7. An organization wants a security test but is concerned about time and cost. Which of the following tests is generally faster and costs less than a manual pen test?

   A. Automatic

   B. Internal

   C. Black box

   D. External

☑ **A.** Automated tests—using tools such as CANVAS and Core Impact—are generally faster and cheaper than manual pen testing, which involve a professional team and a predefined scope/agreement. These automated tests are more susceptible to false positives and false negatives. Perhaps more importantly, though, they also don't necessarily care about any scope or test boundary. With a manual pen test, you have a predetermined scope and agreement in place. With an automated tool, you run a risk of it running past the boundary of your test. It's difficult to negotiate with a piece of software. Additionally, automated pen tests suffer the same flaw as most virus scanners: They rarely find anything a real hacker would use. Automated tools are dependent on the same signature-based mindset of most of the AVs out there, so if you really want to know whether your custom application, your complex architecture, your websites, and your users are vulnerable, you should hire a professional.

☒ **B** is incorrect because this definition doesn't match an internal test. Internal testing is performed from inside the organization's network boundary. Internal testing can be announced (IT staff know it's going on) or unannounced (IT staff is kept in the dark and only management knows the test is being performed).

⊠ C is incorrect because black box doesn't necessarily have anything to do with cost. It generally takes longer than, say, white box testing, but it doesn't fit this question.

⊠ D is incorrect because this definition doesn't match external testing. External testing is all about publicly available information, and attempts to enumerate targets and other goodies from outside the network boundary.

8. The most dangerous threat to an organization is a disgruntled insider. Which of the following best defines a disgruntled employee's (a normal user inside the network) attack against the organization?

   A. External black box

   B. Internal gray box

   C. Internal announced

   D. External white box

   ☑ B. I understand some of you are going to try arguing semantics with me on this one, but trust me, the "best" designator in this question covers me here. *Most* employees are going to have at least some idea of internal networks or operations within the company—even if it's just the domain to log into, password policy, or lockout policy. The internal gray box test best describes this: an attack inside the network by someone who has some information or knowledge about the network and resources being attacked.

   ⊠ A is incorrect because a disgruntled employee would not need to perform an external test—much less a black box (no knowledge) one. Is it possible a disgruntled employee wouldn't take advantage of his internal knowledge? Is it possible he would ignore the built-in advantage of already being on the network and having login credentials there? Sure it is—it's just not likely.

   ⊠ C is incorrect because the attack most certainly will not be announced (that is, the IT Security staff notified it is being conducted). It's highly unlikely the disgruntled employee will want to assist the IT Security team in noting and patching security problems within the network.

   ⊠ D is incorrect, but just barely so. It is possible that this particular employee has all knowledge of the network segment he's attacking. And it's plausible he may even decide to run an attack externally. However, ignoring the advantage of being inside the network to launch an attack—even if it's simply to set up a listening port to be used from a remote location—is highly unlikely. This choice simply isn't the best description of the disgruntled employee attack.

9. Joe is part of an environmental group protesting AnyBiz, Inc., for the company's stance on a variety of issues. Frustrated by the failure of multiple attempts to raise awareness of his cause, Joe launches sophisticated web defacement and denial of service attacks against the company, without attempting to hide the attack source and with no regard to being caught. Which of the following best defines Joe?

A. Hactivism

B. Ethical hacker

C. Script kiddie

D. Suicide hacker

☑ **D.** This is another definition term from EC Council you'll see on your exam. And, much like in this question, you'll almost always see it paired with "hactivism" as an answer. A *suicide hacker* is an attacker who is so wrapped up in promoting their cause they do not care about the consequences of their actions. If defacing a website or blowing up a company server results in 30 years of prison time, so be it: as long as the cause has been promoted. In some instances (I've seen this in practice test exams before) the suicide hacker even *wants* to be caught—to serve as a martyr for the cause.

☒ **A** is incorrect because *hactivism* refers to the act, not the attacker. Hactivism is the act of hacking for a cause, but those participating may very well want to avoid jail time. Suicide hackers don't care.

☒ **B** is incorrect for obvious reasons. As a matter of fact, if you chose this answer, stop right now and go back to page one—you need to start the whole thing over again. An ethical hacker is employed as part of a team of security professionals, and works under strict guidelines and agreed-upon scope.

☒ **C** is incorrect because a *script kiddie* is a point-and-shoot type of "hacker" who simply pulls information off the Internet and fires away.

10. A security team has been hired by upper management to assess the organization's security. The assessment is designed to emulate an Internet hacker and to test the behavior of the security devices and policies in place as well as the IT Security staff. Which of the following best describes this test? (Choose all that apply.)

A. Internal

B. External

C. Announced

D. Unannounced

☑ **B and D.** An external test is designed to mirror steps a hacker might take from outside the company perimeter. The team will start, of course, with publicly available information and ratchet up attempts from there. Because the question states it's testing security devices, policies, and the IT staff, the indication is this is an unannounced test. After all, if the IT staff knew the attack was going to occur in advance, it wouldn't be a true test of their ability to detect and react to an actual, real attack.

☒ **A and C** are incorrect because this attack is not internal to the organization's network perimeter, nor has it been announced to the IT staff.

11. In which phase of a pen test will the team penetrate the perimeter and acquire targets?

   A. Pre-attack

   B. Attack

   C. Post-attack

   D. None of the above

   ☑ **B.** EC Council splits a pen test into three different phases: pre-attack, attack, and post-attack. In the attack phase, the team will attempt to penetrate the network perimeter, acquire targets, execute attacks, and elevate privileges. Getting past the perimeter might take into account things such as verifying ACLs by crafting packets as well as checking the use of any covert tunnels inside the organization. Attacks such as XSS, buffer overflows, and SQL injections will be used on web-facing applications and sites. After acquiring specific targets, password cracking, privilege escalation, and a host of other attacks will be carried out.

   ☒ **A** is incorrect because these actions do not occur in the pre-attack phase. Per EC Council, pre-attack includes planning, reconnaissance, scanning, and gathering competitive intelligence.

   ☒ **C** is incorrect because these actions do not occur in the post-attack phase. Per EC Council, post-attack includes removing all files, uploaded tools, registry entries, and other items installed during testing from the target(s). Additionally, your analysis of findings and creation of the pen test report will occur here.

   ☒ **D** is incorrect because there is an answer for the question listed.

12. Which of the following test types presents a higher probability of encountering problems and takes the most amount of time?

   A. Black box

   B. Grey box

   C. White box

   D. Internal

   ☑ **A.** Tests can be internal or external, announced or unannounced, and can be classified by the knowledge the team has before the test occurs. A black box test, whether internal or external, is designed to simulate a hacker's attempts at gaining entry into the organization. Obviously this usually starts as an external test, but can become internal as time progresses (depending on the pen test team's scope and agreement). Because it's a test with no prior knowledge to simulate that true outsider threat, black box testing provides more opportunity for problems along the way and takes the most amount of time. External, black box testing takes the longest because the tester has to plan higher-risk activities.

☒ **B** and **C** are incorrect for the same reason: In both cases, the information provided to the team greatly reduces the amount of time and effort needed to gain entry.

☒ **D** is incorrect because there is no reference in the question to where this attack is actually taking place. As an aside, an internal test, where the team is given a network access point inside the network to start with, should obviously provide a leg up in both time and effort compared to an external one.

13. Which of the following best describes the difference between a professional pen test team member and a hacker?

   A. Ethical hackers are paid for their time.

   B. Ethical hackers never exploit vulnerabilities; they only point out their existence.

   C. Ethical hackers do not use the same tools and actions as hackers.

   D. Ethical hackers hold a predefined scope and agreement from the system owner.

☑ **D.** This one is a blast from the book's past, and will pop up a couple of times on your exam. The only true difference between a professional pen test team member (an ethical hacker) and the hackers of the world is the existence of the formally approved, agreed-upon scope and contract before any attacks begin.

☒ **A** is incorrect because although professional ethical hackers are paid for their efforts during the pen test, it's not necessarily a delineation between the two (ethical and non-ethical). Some hackers may be paid for a variety of illicit activities. For one example, maybe a company wants to cause harm to a competitor, so they hire a hacker to perform attacks.

☒ **B** and **C** are incorrect for the same reason. If a pen test team member did not ever exploit an opportunity and refused to use the same tools and techniques that the hackers of the world have at their collective fingertips, what would be the point of an assessment? A pen test is designed to show true security weaknesses and flaws, and the only way to do that is to attack it just as a hacker would.

14. Sally is part of a penetration test team and is starting a test. The client has provided a network drop on one of their subnets for Sally to launch her attacks from. However, they did not provide any authentication information, network diagrams, or other notable data concerning the system(s). Which type of test is Sally performing?

   A. External, white box

   B. External, black box

C. Internal, white box

D. Internal, black box

☑ **D.** Sally was provided a network drop inside the organization's network, so we know it's an internal test. Additionally, no information of any sort was provided—from what we can gather she knows nothing of the inner workings, logins, network design, and so on. Therefore, this is a black box test—an internal, black box test.

☒ **A** and **B** are incorrect because this is an internal test, not an external one.

☒ **C** is incorrect because a white box test would have included all the information Sally wanted about the network—designed to simulate a disgruntled internal network or system administrator.

15. Joe is part of a pen test team that has been hired by AnyBiz to perform testing under a contract. As part of the defined scope and activities, no IT employees within AnyBiz know about the test. After some initial information gathering, Joe strikes up a conversation with an employee in the cafeteria and steals the employee's access badge. Joe then uses this badge to gain entry to secured areas of AnyBiz's office space. Which of the following best defines Joe in this scenario?

A. Outside affiliate

B. Outside associate

C. Insider affiliate

D. Insider associate

☑ **C.** You had to know I would check to see if you're paying attention, right? Otherwise there would be no explanation for asking nearly the same question twice within one chapter. Unless, of course, I was trying to make a point about how important these definitions are. Remember, an insider affiliate is someone—a spouse, friend, or acquaintance—that uses the employee's access credentials to further their attack.

☒ **A** is incorrect because an outside affiliate is someone who is not employed with the company that makes use of open access (such as unsecured wireless) to the organization's network.

☒ **B** is incorrect because "outside associate" isn't a term within CEH study.

☒ **D** is incorrect because an insider associate is a member of the organization—such as a guard or a subcontractor—that has limited access to resources.

16. In which phase of a penetration test would you compile a list of vulnerabilities found?

A. Pre-attack

B. Attack

C. Post-attack

D. Reconciliation

☑ **C.** Another simple definition question you're sure to see covered on the exam. You compile the results of all testing in the post-attack phase of a pen test, so you can create and deliver the final report to the customer.

☒ **A** and **B** are incorrect because this action does not occur in the pre-attack or attack phase.

☒ **D** is incorrect because "reconciliation" is not a phase of a pen test, as defined by EC Council.

17. Which of the following has a database containing thousands of signatures used to detect vulnerabilities in multiple operating systems?

A. Nessus

B. Hping

C. LOIC

D. SNMPUtil

☑ **A.** Nessus is probably the best-known, most-utilized vulnerability assessment tool on the planet—even though it's not necessarily free anymore. Nessus works on a server/client basis and provides "plug-ins" to test everything from Cisco devices, Mac OS, and Windows machines to SCADA devices, SNMP, and VMWare ESX (you can find a list of plug-in families here: www.tenable.com/plugins/index.php?view=all). It's a part of virtually every security team's portfolio, and you should definitely spend some time learning how to use it.

As an aside—not necessarily because it has anything to do with your test, but because I am all about informing you to become a good pen tester—Openvas (www.openvas.org) is the open source community's attempt to have a free vulnerability scanner. Nessus was a free scanner for the longest time. However, once purchased by Tenable Network Security, it, for lack of a better term, angered a lot of people in the security community because it became a for-profit entity instead of a for-security one. Don't get me wrong, Nessus is outstanding in what it does—it just costs you money. Openvas is attempting to do the same thing for free, because the community wants security over profit.

☒ **B** is incorrect because Hping is not a vulnerability assessment tool. Per Hping's website (www.hping.org), it is "a command-line-oriented TCP/IP packet assembler/analyzer" used to test firewalls, fingerprint operating systems, and even to perform MITM (man-in-the-middle) attacks.

☒ **C** is incorrect because LOIC (Low Orbit Ion Cannon) is a distributed interface denial of service tool. It's open source and can be used, supposedly legitimately, to test "network stress levels."

☒ **D** is incorrect because SNMPUtil is an SNMP security verification and assessment tool.

18. Cleaning registry entries and removing uploaded files and tools are part of which phase of a pen test?

A. Covering tracks

B. Pre-attack

C. Attack

D. Post-attack

☑ **D.** Cleanup of all your efforts occurs in the post-attack phase, alongside analysis of findings and generation of the final report. The goal is to put things back exactly how they were before the assessment.

☒ **A** is incorrect because covering tracks is part of the phases defining a hacking attack, not a phase of a pen test.

☒ **B and C** are incorrect because these steps do not occur in the pre-attack or attack phase.

19. Jake, an employee of AnyBiz, Inc., parks his vehicle outside the corporate offices of SomeBiz, Inc. He turns on a laptop and connects to an open wireless access point internal to SomeBiz's network. Which of the following best defines Jake?

A. Outside affiliate

B. Outside associate

C. Insider affiliate

D. Insider associate

☑ **A.** Here we are again, back at a pure memorization question you're sure to see on your exam. EC Council defines four different types of attackers in this scenario: a pure insider (easy enough to figure out), an insider associate, an insider affiliate, and an outside affiliate. In this example, Jake best fits outside affiliate. He is a nontrusted outsider: He's not an employee or employed contractor, and he's not using credentials stolen from one. His access is from an unsecured, open access point (usually wireless, but doesn't have to be).

☒ **B** is incorrect because EC Council does not define an "outside associate."

☒ **C** is incorrect because an insider affiliate is someone who does not have actual, authorized, direct access to the company's network, but they use credentials they've stolen from a pure insider to gain entry and launch attacks.

☒ **D** is incorrect because an insider associate is defined as someone that has limited access (to the network or to the facility itself) and uses that access to elevate privileges and launch attacks. The most common examples of this you'll see are subcontractors, janitors, and guards.

20. Which of the following are true regarding a pen test? (Choose all that apply.)

    A. Pen tests do not include social engineering.

    B. Pen tests may include unannounced attacks against the network.

    C. During a pen test, the security professionals can carry out any attack they choose.

    D. Pen tests always have a scope.

    E. A list of all personnel involved in the test is not included in the final report.

    ☑ **B and D.** Pen tests are carried out by security professionals who are bound by a specific scope and rules of engagement, which must be carefully crafted, reviewed, and agreed on before the assessment begins. This agreement can allow for unannounced testing, should upper management of the organization decide to test their IT Security staff's reaction times and methods.

    ☒ **A, C, and E** are incorrect because these are false statements concerning a pen test. Unless expressly forbidden in the scope agreement, social engineering is a big part of any true pen test. The scope agreement usually defines how far a pen tester can go—for example, no intentional denial of service attacks and so on. Clients are provided a list of discovered vulnerabilities after the test, even if the team did not exploit them: There's not always time to crack into every security flaw during an assessment, but that's no reason to hide it from the customer. Lastly, the final report does include a list of all personnel taking part in the test.

21. Which of the following is a potential cause of a security breach?

    A. Vulnerability

    B. Threat

    C. Exploit

    D. Zero day

    ☑ **B.** A *threat* is something that could potentially take advantage of an existing vulnerability. Threats can be intentional, accidental, human, or even an "act of God." A hacker is a threat to take advantage of an open port on a system and/or poor password policy. A thunderstorm is a threat to exploit a tear in the roof, leaking down to your systems. Heck, a rhinoceros is a threat to bust down the door and destroy all the equipment in the room. Whether those threats have intent, are viable, and are willing/able to take up the vulnerability is a matter for risk assessment to decide; they'll probably beef up password policy and fix the roof, but I doubt much will be done on the rhino front.

☒ **A** is incorrect because a vulnerability is a weakness in security. A vulnerability may or may not necessarily be a problem. For example, your system may have horribly weak password policy, or even a missing security patch, but if it's never on the network and is locked in a guarded room accessible by only three people who must navigate a biometric system to even open the door, the existence of those vulnerabilities is moot.

☒ **C** is incorrect because an exploit is what is or actually can be done by a threat agent to utilize the vulnerability. Exploits can be local or remote, a piece of software, a series of commands, or anything that actually uses the vulnerability to gain access to, or otherwise affect, the target.

☒ **D** is incorrect because a zero-day exploit is simply an exploit that most of us don't really know much about at the time of its use. For instance, a couple years back some bad guys discovered a flaw in Adobe Reader and developed an exploit for it. From the time the exploit was created to the time Adobe finally recognized its existence and built a fix action to mitigate against it, the exploit was referred to as *zero day*.

22. Which Metasploit payload type operates via DLL injection and is very difficult for AV software to pick up?

   A. Inline

   B. Meterpreter

   C. Staged

   D. Remote

   ☑ **B.** For those of you panicking over this question, relax—it's not that bad. You do not have to know all the inner workings of Metasploit, but it does appear—from the variety of study materials available for the version 7 exam—that EC Council does want you to know some basics, and this question falls in that category. There are a bunch of different payload types within Metasploit, and *meterpreter* (short for Meta-Interpreter) is one of them. The following is from Metasploit's website: "Meterpreter is an advanced payload that is included in the Metasploit Framework. Its purpose is to provide complex and advanced features that would otherwise be tedious to implement purely in assembly. The way that it accomplishes this is by allowing developers to write their own extensions in the form of shared object (DLL) files that can be uploaded and injected into a running process on a target computer after exploitation has occurred. Meterpreter and all of the extensions that it loads are executed entirely from memory and never touch the disk, thus allowing them to execute under the radar of standard anti-virus detection."

☒ **A** is incorrect because *inline payloads* are single payloads that contain the full exploit and shell code for the designed task. They may be more stable than other payloads, but they're easier to detect and, because of their size, may not be viable for many attacks.

☒ **C** is incorrect because *staged payloads* establish a connection between the attacking machine and the victim. They then will read in a payload to execute on the remote machine.

☒ **D** is incorrect because "remote" isn't a recognized payload type.

23. Metasploit is a framework allowing for the development and execution of exploit code against a remote host, and is designed for use in pen testing. The framework is made of several libraries, each performing a specific task and set of functions. Which library is considered the most fundamental component of the Metasploit framework?

    A. MSF Core

    B. MSF Base

    C. MSF interfaces

    D. Rex

☑ **D.** Once again, this is another one of those weird questions you may see (involving any of the framework components) on your exam. It's included here so you're not caught off guard in the actual exam room and freak out over not hearing it before. Don't worry about learning all the nuances of Metasploit and its architecture before the exam—just concentrate on memorizing the basics of the framework (key words for each area will assist with this) and you'll be fine.

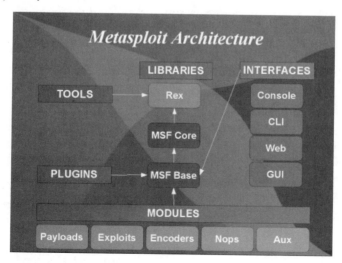

Metasploit, as you know, is an open source framework allowing all sorts of automated (point-and-shoot) pen test methods. The framework is designed in a modular fashion, with each library and component responsible for its own function. The following is from the Metasploit's development guide (http://dev.metasploit.com/redmine/projects/framework/wiki/DeveloperGuide#12-Design-and-Architecture): "The most fundamental piece of the architecture is the *Rex* library, which is short for the Ruby Extension Library. Some of the components provided by Rex include a wrapper socket subsystem, implementations of protocol clients and servers, a logging subsystem, exploitation utility classes, and a number of other useful classes." Rex provides critical services to the entire framework.

☒ A is incorrect because the MSF Core "is responsible for implementing all of the required interfaces that allow for interacting with exploit modules, sessions, and plugins." It interfaces directly with Rex.

☒ B is incorrect because the MSF Base "is designed to provide simpler wrapper routines for dealing with the framework core as well as providing utility classes for dealing with different aspects of the framework, such as serializing module state to different output formats." The Base is an extension of the Core.

☒ C is incorrect because the MSF interfaces are the means by which you (the user) interact with the framework. Interfaces for Metasploit include Console, CLI, Web, and GUI.

24. EC Council defines six stages of scanning methodology. Which of the following correctly lists the six steps?

   A. Scan for vulnerabilities, check for live systems, check for open ports, banner grabbing, draw network diagrams, prepare proxies.

   B. Banner grabbing, check for live systems, check for open ports, scan for vulnerabilities, draw network diagrams, prepare proxies.

   C. Check for live systems, check for open ports, banner grabbing, scan for vulnerabilities, draw network diagrams, prepare proxies.

   D. Prepare proxies, check for live systems, check for open ports, banner grabbing, scan for vulnerabilities, draw network diagrams.

   ☑ C. I can hear the complaints now: "You mean to tell me I have yet another list of steps to remember? Another methodology I've got to commit to memory?" Unfortunately, the answer to that question is yes, dear reader. I would apologize, but you're probably used to at least a little bit of CEH madness by now.

   EC Council defines the process of scanning by splitting it into six steps. First, you determine which hosts are alive on the network, followed by a check to see which ports they may have open. Next, a little banner grabbing will help in identifying operating systems and such. In step four, you'll turn your attention to vulnerabilities which may be present on these systems.

Next (and the step I, personally, find very humorous to be involved in this particular methodology), you'll put all this together in a neat little network drawing, for future reference. Lastly (in another step I find, personally, to be a weird addition), you'll start preparing proxies from which you will launch attacks later.

These six steps are outlined in EC Council's official study preparation for the exam. Get to know them, because you'll see a question like this somewhere on your exam.

☒ **A, B,** and **D** are all incorrect because they do not list the correct steps in order.

25. Which of the following may be effective countermeasures against an inside attacker? (Choose all that apply.)

A. Enforce elevated privilege control.

B. Secure all dumpsters and shred collection boxes.

C. Enforce good physical security practice and policy.

D. Perform background checks on all employees.

☑ **A, B, C,** and **D.** All of the answers are correct. Admittedly there's nothing you can really do to completely prevent an inside attack. There's simply no way to ensure every single employee is going to remain happy and satisfied, just as there's no way to tell when somebody might just up and decide to turn to crime. It happens all the time, in and out of Corporate America, so the best you can do is, of course, the best you can do.

Enforcing elevated privilege control (that is, ensuring users have only the amount of access, rights, and privileges to get their job done, and no more) seems like a common-sense thing, but it's amazing how many enterprise networks simply ignore this, and a disgruntled employee with administrator rights on his machine can certainly do more damage than one with just plain user rights. Securing dumpsters and practicing good physical security should help protect against an insider who wants to come back after hours and snoop around. And background checks on employees, although by no means a silver bullet in this situation, can certainly help to ensure you're hiring the right people in the first place (in many companies a background check is a requirement of *law*). Other steps include, but are not limited to, the following:

- Monitor user network behavior.
- Monitor user computer behavior.
- Disable remote access.
- Disable removable drive use on all systems (USB drives and so on).
- Shred all discarded paperwork.
- Conduct user education and training programs.

About the CD-ROM

The CD-ROM included with this book comes complete with MasterExam and an electronic copy of the book in PDF format (the electronic book). The software is easy to install on any Windows XP/Vista/7 computer and must be installed to access the MasterExam feature. To register for the bonus MasterExam, simply click the Bonus MasterExam link on the main launch page and follow the directions to the free online registration.

System Requirements

Software requires Windows XP or higher and Internet Explorer 8.0 or above and 200 MB of hard disk space for full installation. The electronic book requires Adobe Acrobat Reader.

Installing and Running MasterExam

If your computer CD-ROM drive is configured to auto run, the CD-ROM will automatically start up upon inserting the disk. From the opening screen you may install Master-Exam by clicking the MasterExam link. This will begin the installation process and create a program group named LearnKey. To run MasterExam, use Start | All Programs | LearnKey | MasterExam. If the auto run feature did not launch your CD, browse to the CD and click the LaunchTraining.exe icon.

MasterExam

MasterExam provides you with a simulation of the actual exam. The number of questions, the type of questions, and the time allowed are intended to be an accurate representation of the exam environment. You have the option to take an open book exam, including hints, references, and answers; a closed book exam; or the timed MasterExam simulation.

When you launch MasterExam, a digital clock display will appear in the bottom right-hand corner of your screen. The clock will continue to count down to zero unless you choose to end the exam before the time expires.

Help

A help file is provided through the Help button on the main page in the bottom left-hand corner. An individual help feature is also available through MasterExam.

Removing Installation(s)

MasterExam is installed to your hard drive. For best results removing programs, use the Start | All Programs | LearnKey | Uninstall option to remove MasterExam.

Electronic Book

The entire contents of the book are provided in PDF format on the CD. These files are viewable on your computer and many portable devices. Adobe's Acrobat Reader is required to view the files on your PC and has been included on the CD. You may also use Adobe Digital Editions to access your PDF files.

For more information on Adobe Reader and to check for the most recent version of the software, visit Adobe's web site at www.adobe.com and search for the free Adobe Reader or look for Adobe Reader on the product page. Adobe Digital Editions can also be downloaded from the Adobe web site.

To view the electronic book on a portable device, copy the PDF files to your computer from the CD and then copy the files to your portable device using a USB or other connection. Adobe offers a mobile version of Adobe Reader, the Adobe Reader mobile app, which currently supports iOS and Android. For customers using Adobe Digital Editions and the iPad, you may have to download and install a separate reader program on your device. The Adobe web site has a list of recommended applications, and McGraw-Hill Education recommends the Bluefire Reader.

Technical Support

Technical support information is provided below by feature.

LearnKey Technical Support

For technical problems with the software (installation, operation, removing installations), please visit www.learnkey.com, e-mail techsupport@learnkey.com, or call toll free (800) 482-8244.

McGraw-Hill Technical Support and Customer Service

For questions regarding the PDF files, e-mail techsolutions@mhedu.com or visit http://mhp.softwareassist.com. For questions regarding book content, please e-mail customer.service@mcgraw-hill.com. For customers outside the United States, e-mail international_cs@mcgraw-hill.com.

INDEX

Numbers

3DES (Triple Data Encryption Standard), 49
802.11 standards for wireless networks,
    227–228, 237–238
802.16 standards for wireless networks, 237–238

A

A (Address) record, zone file, 82
access, gaining/maintaining, 20
access points. *See* APs (access points)
ACK flag, TCP, 95, 97, 130
ACK scans
    features of, 97
    nmap switch indicating, 105–106
    stateful firewall against, 131
    using hping3, 96
acknowledgement number prediction, 248
active footprinting, 12–13, 22–23, 24
active sniffing, 126–127
Address (A) record, zone file, 82
ADMmutate, for IDS evasion, 135
ADS (Alternate Data Streams)
    syntax for, 148
    tools for detecting, 159
ADS Spy tool, 159
AES (Advanced Encryption Standard)
    bulk encryption with, 40
    WPA2 utilizing, 223, 224
AfriNIC (African Network Information Center)
    registry, 79
air locks, for physical security, 169
Aircrack tool, cracking WEP with, 229–230
airsnarf tool, username/password theft and, 233
algorithms
    AES, 40, 223, 224
    asymmetric. *See* asymmetric algorithms
    hash. *See* hash algorithms
    RSA, 40, 48
    symmetric. *See* symmetric algorithms
Alternate Data Streams (ADS), 148, 159
AngryIP footprinting tool, 77
announced testing, 279
anomaly-based IDS, 130–131
anonymous footprinting, 73

antenna placement for wireless networks, 226
antennas
    MIMO technology for, 237–238
    omnidirectional, 235
    placement for wireless networks, 234
APNIC (Asia Pacific Network Information
    Centre) registry, 68, 79
Apocalypse Trojan, 255
application-level attacks, 25
application-level rootkits, 157
APs (access points)
    airsnarf tool utilizing, 233
    enabling MAC filtering on, 236
    of omnidirectional antenna, 235
    rogue, 225, 230, 232
    in wireless network architecture, 233–234
Archive.org, for passive footprinting, 71–72
ARIN (American Registry for Internet Numbers),
    68, 79
ARP poisoning, 78, 119–120
Asia Pacific Network Information Centre
    (APNIC) registry, 68, 97
assessment phase
    of attacks, 24
    of pen tests, 21–22, 28
asymmetric algorithms
    benefits of, 51
    for encrypted communication, 43–44
    features of, 39–40
    Kerberos utilizing, 151
    RC5, 48–49
    RSA, 40, 48
attack phase, of pen tests, 277, 280
attacks
    on Bluetooth device, 228–229, 237
    brute force. *See* brute-force attacks
    chosen plaintext, 42–43
    dictionary, 147
    DNS spoofing, 74
    DoS. *See* DoS (denial of service) attacks
    evil twin wireless, 225, 232
    external, 21
    hybrid, 151–152
    inside vs. outside, 26
    integrity, 15–16

chosen ciphertext, 45
chosen plaintext, 42–43
CIA (confidentiality, integrity, availability) triad, 2
ciphertext
    attack methods, 42–45
    converting plaintext to, 39
ciphertext-only attacks, for decoding encrypted
        files, 44
Class C fire extinguishers, 184
classification of information,
        as countermeasure, 182
cleaning registry entries, in post-attack phase, 284
CNAME record
    information contained in, 82
    providing alias entries, 73, 79
collection function, in LEA investigation, 121
command injection, web application attack, 205
Common Gateway Interface (CGI)
        manipulation, 198, 204
community strings, for SNMP tools, 105
competitive intelligence
    defined, 71
    defining network range, 81
    EDGAR database for, 79–80
complexity, of passwords, 153–154
computer-based social engineering attacks,
        173–174, 180
conclusion phase
    of pen tests, 21–22
    reports done during, 28
Conficker worm
    propagation attempt, 259–260
    Windows targeted by, 251
confidentiality
    in CIA triad, 2
    features of, 14, 18
    passwords for, 28
contract and scope agreement, 28, 281, 285
cookie(s)
    defined, 198
    manipulation, 198, 199–200
Core Impact automated pen test, 274–275
costs
    of pen tests, 277
    of vulnerability scanners, 283
covering tracks phase
    delete files command and, 155
    features of, 20, 30
    of hacking attack, 284
covert channels, 255
crackers. See black hats
"Crimes and Criminal procedure", Title 18, 27

cross-site scripting (XXS) attack, 194,
        195–196, 209
crossover error rate (CER), 171
cryptography
    algorithms for. See asymmetric algorithms;
        symmetric algorithms
    bulk encryption, 40
    evading IDS with, 125–126
    known plaintext attack, 44–45
    LAN Manager utilization of, 160
    methodology/purpose of, 39
    within PKI system, 41–42, 46
    transposition method for, 45–46
    wireless networks and, 223–224
    XOR operation, 53

D

data protection
    cryptography and, 39
    hash algorithms for, 28, 39–40
deauthentication packets, for cracking
        WEP ACs, 227
deep web searches, 80
denial of service attacks. See DoS (denial of
        service) attacks
dictionary attacks
    features of, 147
    hybrid attacks vs., 151
dig (domain information groper) command
        syntax, 84
digital certificates
    with 160-bit hash output, 52–53
    fields contained in, 47
    for PKI system, 41
    standard format for, 43
digital signatures, 41
directional antennas, 225–226, 235
directory climbing, 194
directory traversal
    using Unicode, 204–205
    web server attack, 194
disgruntled employees, internal threats and,
        177, 278
DLL injection, meterpreter payload utilizing, 286
DNS (Domain Name System)
    CNAME record type, 73
    dig command syntax, 84
    zone transfers and, 67–68, 74–75, 102
DNS poisoning
    example of, 77–78
    features of, 74
    mitigating against, 78

DNS spoofing, 74
DoS (denial of service) attacks
    availability and, 16, 18
    on Bluetooth devices, 229, 237
    features of, 16
    Fraggle, 252
    ICMP flood, 251
    LOIC attack, 259
    Ping of Death, 251–252
    in reverse social engineering, 171
    Smurf attack, 259
    Smurf attack as, 251
    SYN attack, 258
    SYN flood, 252, 258
dot-dot-slash attack, 194
dumpster diving
    countermeasures for, 289
    as passive footprinting, 22, 71
    social engineering by, 175
dumpster security, 289
-e flag, launching programs and, 248–249

E

e-mail
    phishing indicators in, 178
    sign-in seal protection, 181
ease of use, in SFE triangle, 19
eavesdropping, 172
ECC (Elliptic Curve Cryptosystem), 40
EDGAR (Electronic Data-Gathering, Analysis,
        and Retrieval) database, 79–80
elevated privilege control, as countermeasure, 289
eMailTrackerPro tool, 84
encryption
    algorithms for. See asymmetric algorithms;
        symmetric algorithms
    bulk, with AES, 40
    evading IDS with, 125–126
    known plaintext attack, 44–45
    LAN Manager utilization of, 160
    within PKI system, 41–42, 46
    transposition method for, 45–46
    for wireless networks, 223–224
    XOR operation, 53
enum tool, null sessions and, 95–96
enumeration. See scanning and enumeration
ESS (Extended Service Set), 233–234
ESSID (Extended Service Set Identification), 234
ethical hacking
    features of, 11–12, 29
    locating available targets, 20
    methodology of, 10
    predefined scope in, 29, 281

Ettercap tool
    for MITM attacks, 263
    passive sniffing with, 126
    for session hijacking, 253
evil twin hacking attacks
    features of, 225
    tools against, 232
executive summary, in pen test final report, 273
exploits, vulnerabilities utilized by, 25–26, 286
Extended Service Set (ESS), 233–234
Extended Service Set Identification (ESSID), 234
external attacks
    black box tests for, 23
    exploiting vulnerabilities, 25–26
    simulating, 21
external testing, 23, 278, 279

F

false negatives, IDS shortcomings and, 129
false rejection rate (FRR), 171
FAR (false acceptance rate), 129, 171
Federal Information Security Management Act
        (FISMA), 17
fgets(), buffer overflow vulnerability and, 198
file injection, 205, 210
filtering
    of ports, 119
    Wireshark, 122
FIN flag
    TCP, 94, 95
    for XMAS scan, 97
financial sites, competitive intelligence from, 71
fingerprinting
    banner grabbing for, 103–104
    tools for, 24, 100, 201
fire extinguishers for electrical fires, 184
firewalls
    code 3 indicating, 97–98
    HTTP tunneling for, 132
    types of, 131
flags
    FIN, 94, 95, 97
    netcat, 248–249
    SYN, 95, 106, 263
    URG, 95, 97, 107
flooding, evading IDS with, 126
footprinting
    APNIC for, 68
    in CEH methodology, 10
    EDGAR database for, 79–80
    job boards for, 70
    passive vs. active, 12–13, 22–23
    in pen testing, 21–22

pseudonymous, 72–73
tools for, 69
traceroute tool for, 76
tracking e-mail messages, 84
Fraggle attack, 252
Fragroute, IDS evasion with, 135
Freedom of Information Act, 17, 27
frequency analysis, of encrypted files, 50
FRR (false rejection rate), 171
full-connect scans, 104, 108
functionality, in SFE triangle, 19
fuzzy logic error code scanning, 206

G

gaining access, 20, 30
Gecos field, in passwd file, 150
gets(), buffer overflow vulnerability and, 198
GID field, in passwd file, 150
GifShuffle tool, 45
Google Cache, for archival material, 72
Google hacking
    creating search string for, 83
    utilizing, 69–70, 72
Googlebot crawler, 210–211
government-sponsored hackers, 177
gray box test
    by black hat, 14–15
    features of, 10–11
    for internal threats, 23, 278
GUI Trojan, BioDox as, 255

H

"h", indicating hidden attributes, 158–159
hackers
    black hats, 14–15, 18, 24
    ethical. See ethical hacking
    ethical hackers vs., 29, 281
    government-sponsored, 177
    suicide, 279
hacking
    Bluetooth, 228–229, 237
    Google, 69–70, 72, 83
    wireless networks, 225–227, 229–233, 234–335
hactivism, 17, 279
half-open scan, of ports, 108
halo effect, 170
hardening methods for web servers, 208
hardware keyloggers
    offline password attacks, 154–155
    for password theft, 147–148
hash algorithms
    collision of, 42
    MD5, 41

for secure storage of passwords, 55, 146
SHA-1, 47–49, 52–53
SHA-2, 49
verifying data integrity, 28, 39–40
hash values
    discovering, 42
    rainbow tables capturing, 55, 147
    signature for, 41
hashing, Kerberos and, 151
heap-based buffer overflow, 203, 210
HH (Honeypot Hunter), Send-Safe, 133
hidden fields
    altering price values in, 197
    "h" indicating, 158–159
HIDS (host-based intrusion detection
        system), 252
Hierarchical Trust system, 52
highly directional parabolic antenna, 226
Home Directory field, in passwd file, 150
honeypots, tools for identifying, 132–133
hping tool, 283
hping3 tool, 96
HTTP GET method, 207
HTTP POST method, 207
HTTP RAT (remote access tool), 253–254, 255
HTTP tunneling, for firewalls, 132
HttpRecon web server fingerprinting tool, 201
human-based social engineering attacks,
        173–174, 180
Hunt tool, for session hijacking, 253, 261
hybrid attacks, 151–152
hybrid box test, 11

I

IAP (intercept access point), sniffing traffic
        and, 121
ICMP (Internet Control Message Protocol)
    filtering, 99
    flood, 251
    traceroute utilizing, 76–77, 80–81
    types/codes with, 97–98
idempotent, 207
identity theft, 176
IDLE scans, 98–99
IDS (Intrusion Detection System)
    shortcomings of, 129
    Snort operating mode, 124
    tools for evading, 125–126, 134–135
    types of, 130–131
impersonation, 172, 173
incrementing fragment identifiers (IPIDs),
        98–99

restarting executables for, 257–258
sheepdip computers against, 258
types of, 250–251
man-in-the-middle attacks. *See* MITM (man-in-the-middle) attacks
man traps, physical security and, 169–170
management process changes, for security, 182
manual pen tests. *See* penetration (pen) tests
marketing step, in reverse social engineering, 179–180
MBSA (Microsoft Baseline Security Advisor), 100
MD5 algorithms, 41, 49
Mean Time Between Failure (MTBF), 183–184
Mean Time To Repair (MTTR), 183–184
mediation device, for traffic sniffing, 120–121
metamorphic viruses, rewriting ability of, 249
Metasploit automated pen test
features of, 274–275
framework of, 287–288
meterpreter payload and, 286
meterpreter payloads, 286
Microsoft Baseline Security Advisor (MBSA), 100
Microsoft Office, macro viruses attacks on, 249
Microsoft Windows
Conficker infection of, 251
installing winPcap, 125
nbtstat command output, 156
registry keys for executables in, 257–258
SAM file on, 150–151
setting hidden attribute, 158–159
SID in, 152
Wikto web security scanner, 206
MIMO (multiple in, multiple out) antenna technology, 237–238
misconfiguration attacks, 25
MITM (man-in-the-middle) attacks
configuring Ettercap for, 263
features of, 54
for session hijacking, 261
tools for, 253
MSF Base, in Metasploit framework, 287–288
MSF Core, in Metasploit framework, 287–288
MTBF (Mean Time Between Failure), 183–184
MTTR (Mean Time To Repair), 183–184
multicast MAC messages, 119
multipartite viruses, 249
multiple in, multiple out (MIMO) antenna technology, 237–238
MX (Mail Exchange) records, 73, 82

N

Name Server (NS), 74
National Institute of Standards and Technology (NIST) FIPS 140-2 compliant encryption, 223

nbtstat tool, command output, 156
Nessus
identifying honeypots with, 133
strengths of, 283
for vulnerability scanning, 69, 100, 201–202
NetBIOS name resolution issues, 156
netcat tool
features of, 202
flags used with, 248–249
remote listening port with, 255–256
Netcraft
anti-phishing toolbar, 179, 200–201
features of, 69
netstat command-line tool, 256–257
NetStumbler tool
for active network discovery, 229
discovering rogue APs, 232
features of, 230
NetSurveyor tool, detecting rogue APs, 232
NetWitness, sniffing tool, 123
network diagrams, in scanning methodology, 288–289
network IDS (Intrusion Detection System). *See* IDS (Intrusion Detection System)
NIC (network interface controller)
in listening mode, 134
in promiscuous mode, 125, 126
Nikto, vulnerability-scanning program, 201–202, 205
NIST (National Institute of Standards and Technology) FIPS 140-2 compliant encryption, 223
nmap tool
banner grabbing with, 104
network discovery/security auditing with, 202
ping sweeping with, 94
pros and cons of, 99–100
scanning and enumeration with, 77, 84
stack fingerprinting with, 100
switches for, 105–106
nonrepudiation
defined, 42
symmetric algorithms and, 44, 51
NOP (No Operation) sled attacks, 209–210
NS (Name Server), information contained in, 74, 82
NSAuditor, SNMP enumeration tool, 103
nslookup
features of, 69
interactive/noninteractive modes of, 77
zone transfers and, 67–68, 74
NTFS file streaming
syntax for, 148
tools for detecting, 159

NTLMv1 (NT LAN Manager v1), 160
NTLMv2 (NT LAN Manager v2), 160
null sessions
    ports required for, 105
    reliability and, 104, 108
    syntax for, 95–96

O

omnidirectional antennas, 226, 235
open ports check, in scanning methodology,
    288–289
Openvas vulnerability scanner, 283
operational security measures, 175, 177, 178
OpUtils, SNMP enumeration tool, 103
'OR 1=1, indicating SQL injection, 195
OS (operating system)
    attacks, features of, 25
    prediction, tools for, 100, 104
outside affiliates, 276, 282, 284
outside attacks, 26
overt channels, for legitimate communication, 254
-P0 switch, within nmap, 95

P

packet capture dumps, 135–136
packet capture logs, Snort, 130
packet-filtering firewalls, 131
Packet Logger mode, Snort, 124, 135
parameter tampering (manipulation)
    features of, 196
    web server attack, 194, 195
partial knowledge attack, 11
participant list, in pen test final report, 273, 281
passive footprinting
    activities considered, 71
    features of, 12–13, 22–23
    job boards for, 70
passive sniffing, 126, 229
passwd file fields, Linux, 149–150
password hash, plaintext password from, 152–153
passwords
    airsnarf tool and, 233
    authentication and, 14, 28, 160
    brute-force attacks on, 146–147
    complexity of, 153–154
    dictionary/hybrid attacks on, 151–152
    hash algorithms for secure storing, 55, 146
    Kerberos secure transmission of, 151
    L0phtCrack for recovering, 42
    LM hashed, 146
    offline attacks, 154–155

remote cracking of, 205
theft methods, 147–148
PATRIOT Act, 17, 27
penetration (pen) tests
    automated tools for, 274–275
    conclusion phase, 28
    final report contents in, 273
    manual vs. automated, 277
    phases of, 21–22, 276–277, 280
    types of, 10–11, 273–274
permission, written, for ethical hacking, 11–12,
    29. See also scope agreement, for pen testing
personal information protection, 16–17
phishing attacks
    features of, 172, 173
    indicators of, 178
    tools against, 179, 181, 200–201
Phishtank tool, 179
physical security measures
    categories of, 175
    equipment maintenance for, 183–184
    man traps, 169–170
    securing dumpsters, 289
piggybacking, 170, 172, 176
PII (personally identifiable information), 16–17
Ping of Death attack, 251–252
ping sweeping
    lack of response to, 99
    nmap tool for, 94
    during scanning phase, 22
    tools for, 102
pipl.com, for people search, 80
PKI (public-key infrastructure) systems
    digital certificate for, 41
    encryption/decryption within, 46
    private key for encryption in, 54
    Single Authority trust model for, 52
plaintext
    attack methods, 42–43, 44–45
    converting password hash to, 152–153
    converting to ciphertext, 39
Pointer Record (PTR), 74
polymorphic viruses, 251
port 80, HTTP tunneling and, 132
port security, 123
port(s)
    checking for open, 288–289
    for DNS zone transfer, 102
    filtering/flooding of, 119
    for null session connection, 105
    responses indicating state of, 107
    scanning methods of, 108

snow, steganography tool, 45, 84
SOA (Start of Authority) records
  contents of, 73
  information contained in, 82
  limiting DNS poisoning, 78
  TTL for, 75–76
  updating, 75
social engineering attacks
  computer based, 173–174
  countermeasures for, 177–178, 180–182
  dumpster diving, 175–176
  by ethical hackers, 29
  features of, 16
  in pen testing, 285
  phishing, 173
  piggybacking, 176
  reverse social engineering, 171–172
  shoulder surfing, 172
  types of, 170
software keyloggers, for password theft, 148
Solar Winds, SNMP enumeration tool, 103
-sP switch, within nmap, 94
span port configuration, 123
speed, of MIMO antenna technology, 237–238
SpiderFoot tool, 80
spoofing
  features of, 16, 27, 261
  MAC addresses, 122
Spy Act (2007), 27
SQL injection
  blind, 208
  features of, 194, 195
  indications of vulnerability to, 201, 203
SRV (Service) record, 82
SSH (Secure Shell)
  deterrent to sniffing, 121–122
  substitution for, 121–122
SSIDs (Service Set Identifiers)
  cloaking, 227, 236
  identifying wireless networks, 210–211, 231
SSIs (Server Side Includes), 204
SSL (Secure Sockets Layer) steps, in session key
  creation, 48
-sT switch, within nmap, 94
stack-based buffer overflow, 203
stack fingerprinting tools, 100
StackGuard tool, preventing buffer overflow,
  197–198
staged payloads, 287
Start of Authority (SOA) record, 73
Startup Program field, 150
stateful firewalls, 131

steganography
  defined, 44
  tools for, 45, 84
stream ciphers, 40
substitution method of encryption, 45–46
suicide hacker, 279
switches
  filtering/flooding by, 119
  nmap, 105–106
  sniffing traffic on, 123
symmetric algorithms
  3DES/AES, 49
  AES, 40
  drawback of, 44
  features of, 39–40
  Kerberos utilizing, 151
  scalability of, 50–51
SYN-ACK step, in three-way handshake, 94,
  106–107
SYN attack, 258
SYN flag, TCP, 95, 106, 263
SYN flood, 252
SYN scans, 104, 107
Syskey encryption
  bits required for, 159
  features of, 146
system binaries folder, Linux, 157–158

T

T-sight session hijacking tool, 261
tailgating, 172, 176
TCP (Transmission Control Protocol)
  flags, 95
  port 53, zone transfers and, 102
  sequence/acknowledgment number prediction
    in, 248, 263–264
  three-way handshake, 94, 106–107
tcpdump packet capture tool
  for sniffing, 127–128
  syntax for, 134
technical security measures, 175, 182–183
technical support attack
  features of, 170
  in reverse social engineering, 179–180
telnet, SSH substitution for, 47
Temporal Key Integrity Protocol (TKIP),
  224, 230
TGT (Ticket Granting Ticket), Kerberos
  utilizing, 151
THC-Hydra, remote password cracker, 205
THC-Scan, war-dialing application, 102

threats
   defined, 25–26, 285–286
   external. *See* external attacks
   internal. *See* internal threats
three-way handshake
   session hijacking after, 264
   steps in, 94, 106–107
time
   with automated/manual pen tests, 277
   with test types, 280–281
time to live (TTL) mechanism. *See* TTL (time to
      live) mechanism
Tini, default port number for, 254
Title 18, "Crimes and Criminal procedure", 27
TKIP (Temporal Key Integrity Protocol)
   forcing key change, 230
   WPA2 utilizing, 224
ToneLoc tool
   locating open modems, 100
   war-dialing application, 102
traceroute command-line tool
   features of, 69
   route mapping with, 80, 104
   utilizing ICMP, 76
traffic sniffing. *See* sniffing
Transport mode of IPsec, 260
transposition method of encryption, 45–46
Trinoo, default port number for, 254
Triple Data Encryption Standard (3DES), 49
Tripwire
   for IT security, 45
   protection against Trojans, 252
Trojans
   activity of, 251
   default port number for, 253–254
   Tripwire protection from, 252
   types of, 255
   utilizing wrappers, 253
TTL (time to live) mechanism
   on ECHO packets, 76
   limiting DNS poisoning, 78
   for SOA records, 75–76
   in tracking packet routes, 80
Tunnel mode of IPsec, 260
two-factor authentication, 182–183

U

UDP (User Datagram Protocol)
   port 53, zone transfers and, 102
   port scans, 101
UID field, in passwd file, 150
unannounced testing, 279, 285

unicast MAC addresses, 119
Unicode, directory traversal utilizing, 204–205
United States Code Title 18, 27
unsigned drivers, Sigverif listing, 154
URG flag
   TCP, 95
   for urgency, 107
   for XMAS scan, 97
URI (Uniform Resource Identifier), encoding
      input into, 207
URL tampering, 194, 195, 196
USA PATRIOT Act, 17, 27
User Datagram Protocol (UDP), port scans,
      101, 102
user education, 177, 180–181, 182
user intervention, malware requiring, 251
User Name field, in passwd file, 150
username theft, 233

V

var RULE_Path entry, in Snort configuration,
      128–129
viruses
   types of, 249
   user intervention and, 251
vulnerabilities
   banner grabbing indicating, 100–101
   defined, 286
   exposure of, 11–12
   pen test report on, 273, 282–283
   scanning for, 288–289
   to SQL injection, 201, 203
   threats exploiting, 25–26
   tools for identifying, 99–100, 201–202
vulnerability assessments
   features of, 12–13, 275
   pen test phase, 28
vulnerability mapping, 24
-w flag, 134

W

war chalk, indicating wireless network features,
      222–223, 234
war dialing tools, 102
war driving
   defined, 102
   features of, 234
war walking, 234
WarVox, war-dialing application, 102
Web of Trust model, 52
web server/application attacks

BlackWidow, 72, 84, 200
blind SQL injection, 207–208
buffer overflow, 195, 197–198, 203
CGI manipulation, 204
cookie manipulation, 198, 199–200
cross-site scripting, 195–196, 209
directory traversal, 194, 204–205
Googlebot crawler, 210–211
hardening against, 208
HTTP GET and, 207
NOP sled, 209–210
parameter tampering, 196
password cracking, 205
shell injection, 205–206
SQL injection, 195, 201, 203
vulnerability scanners for, 201–202, 206
WEP (Wired Equivalent Privacy)
    Aircrack tool cracking, 229–230
    code cracking attempt on, 227
    weak security of, 223–224, 231, 235–236
Wget tool, 72
Whisker, IDS evasion with, 134
white box tests
    features of, 11
    for internal threats, 23, 273–274
    by white hat, 14–15
white hats
    black/white box test by, 14–15
    features of, 23
whois search tool
    features of, 67–68, 72, 76
    for registrar information, 100
Wi-Fi Protected Access (WPA), 224
Wikto web security scanner, 206
WiMax (Worldwide Interoperability for
        Microwave Access), 238
Windows. *See* Microsoft Windows
winPcap, for NIC in promiscuous mode, 125
Wired Equivalent Privacy. *See* WEP (Wired
        Equivalent Privacy)
wireless encryption
    methods used by WEP/WPA2, 224
    NIST FIPS 140-2 compliant, 223
    utilizing 48-bit IV, 224
wireless networks
    802.11 standard series, 227–228, 237–238
    antenna type/placement for, 226
    architecture of, 233–234
    deauthentication packet attack, 227
    detectors/sniffers of, 229
    enabling MAC filtering on, 236
    encryption for. *See* wireless encryption

evil twin hacking attack, 225
    security choices for, 235–236
    SSIDs identifying, 222
    war chalks indicating, 222–223, 234
    war driving attack on, 234
Wireshark
    filter syntax for, 122, 133–134
    NIC in promiscuous mode and, 125
    passive sniffing with, 126
wiretap, traffic sniffing and, 121
worms, 250–251
WPA (Wi-Fi Protected Access), 224
WPA2
    NIST FIPS 140-2 compliant encryption
        with, 223
    as superior encryption choice, 235–236
    utilizing 48-bit IV, 224
    utilizing TKIP and AES encryption, 224
WPA2 Enterprise, 223
wrappers, Trojans utilizing, 253
written permission, for ethical hacking, 11–12,
        29. *See also* scope agreement, for pen testing

X

"x", indicating shadowed passwords, 149–150
X.509 digital certificates
    fields contained in, 47
    standard format, 43
XMAS scans, 97, 108
XOR operation, 53
XXS (cross-site scripting) attack, 194,
        195–196, 209

Y

yagi antennas, for wireless networks, 226

Z

zero-day exploits, 286
Zeus, Trojan horse, 255
zombie cookies, 200
zombie machines
    IDLE scans and, 98–99
    for maintaining access, 29–30
zone files
    refresh interval for, 82
    resource records contained in, 81–82
zone transfers, 74
    from primary server, 67–68
    using port 53, 102